THE GENIUS MYTH

THE GENIUS MYTH

MICHAEL MEADE

GreenFire Press
An Imprint of Mosaic Multicultural Foundation

GreenFire Press
An Imprint of Mosaic Multicultural Foundation

Contents

I

THE GENIUS MYTH

CHAPTER 1

GENIUS TRANSFORMS THE WORLD

Adversity reveals genius, prosperity conceals it.

- Horace

We live in critical times, amidst a worldwide shaking up and breaking down, surrounded by radical changes that severely affect both nature and culture. The world is churning all around us, overheating with climate change and rising seas, but also awash with profound problems and intensifying conflicts. Given the size, scope, and complexity of the problems that currently threaten the world, there can be no single idea, specific political movement, or patented belief system that can save us. Rather, all kinds of ingenious solutions are needed; all types of inspiration, invention, and originality are now required. The idea of a genius self already present and trying to awaken within each of us may serve us better than more common notions of a heroic solution. Awakening genius is a necessary step on the way to becoming a genuine individual and an active agent in the reimagining of the world. Consciously seeking to awaken inner genius may provide a refuge from chaos and an antidote to the spread of nihilism and the increasing levels of despair that characterize a world gone wrong. Each person born, in some unique way, participates in the genius of life and the world at this time is in great need of an awakening of the genius qualities hidden in each of us.

Rather than a heroic journey undertaken by a select few, the genius myth imagines that everyone, by virtue of bearing some genius qualities, is subject to a genuine calling in life. The question becomes not whether or not you are a genius, but in what way does genius appear in you and how might it contribute to both your own well-being and that of the world around you.

The future of this world is so much in question that each person needs to be considered a potential subject of a genuine "calling" to serve in some meaningful way. Not the sense that "many are called, but few are chosen." Rather, the sense that the genius nature in each person is subject to a calling and needed at this time. For, it is the genius within us that our calling is calling to. Everyone has some gift to give if they learn to give from their essential nature.

Genius is the source of purpose and the seed of destiny in each of us. Despite modern confusions about individual purpose and meaning in life, the genius has destinations and destinies in mind for us. A true calling is aimed at the genius qualities already set within each person. In this old way of seeing, each person has some form of genius, each also has a calling or vocation and a purpose in life. On the outside it is felt as a calling and on the inside it is felt as the awakening of one's own way of seeing and of truly being in the world.

AN ACCELERATION OF CALLING

In times of change, just as in periods of personal crisis, there can be intensification and an acceleration of calling. Whether it comes as a daunting challenge or a crushing blunder, a big dream or a cutting loss, each major life event has within it an opportunity to awaken to the call of the deeper self and the resident genius of the soul.

What calls us calls for the giving of the inherent gifts and natural talents we brought to life to begin with. What calls to us calls to the dream set within our soul before we were born. Because each soul is unique, calling comes differently to each person. There is no pattern into which we must fit, because it is the unique pattern at the core of each soul that is the aim of the calling. Because what calls to us is timeless, the calling can come at any time. At each turn in the road our life's work awaits us; thus, our calling keeps calling no matter our age, position, or condition in life. In answering the call, we must depart from the common maps and follow where spirit would have us go; for the aim of spirit in each life involves something uncommon and exceptional. Answering the call opens pathways of genius and imagination that can lead to finding one's "dharma" or natural way of being in life and serving in the world. We are each called to become more fully ourselves and our transformation liberates our spirit, but it also serves something beyond ourselves. In transforming each of us, genius also transforms the world.

The problem isn't a lack of calling, for each of us is called to bring something meaningful to life. Calling and vocation are part of the ancient sense of being born into an adventure of self-discovery aimed at awakening to greater consciousness and life purpose. The problem is that most people now fail to hear the call or else fail to answer to it, so that there can be little evidence of genuine calling to learn from or be encouraged by. The problem is hearing the call amidst increasing levels of distraction and confusion in modern life.

Genius points to something deeply ingrained, markedly original, and ultimately transcendent in human nature. Although widely accepted in traditional cultures, the idea that genius is an original spirit residing in each soul causes problems in modern societies based upon objectivity, rationality, and scientific methods. Modern people tend to talk about things that are useful to them without realizing that the most useful thing in the world is to know who you are at the core of your life and what you are intended to serve in this world. The call to awakening that has been the inherited opportunity of each soul born becomes harder and harder to hear because of all the distractions and misinformation and blatant superficiality of life.

During the statistical era and the age of information, genius becomes reduced to something quantifiable that can be proven, measured, and even developed by will power and hard work. In some cases, genius does appear as high intellect or reason, yet in others it might appear as surpassing imagination, inspired innovation, or even deep compassion. The presence of genius can be awe-inspiring; however, our understanding of genius now suffers from attempts to reduce it to something measurable and controllable.

Genius has its own logic and is a presence of a different order. Genius is a mythological presence that must be intuited in one's own soul. Although it cannot be factually proven to be present, the presence of genius is a fact of life and a defining issue of each person's true identity.

No one can simply prove that human genius exists; yet we know it when we see it and feel it when we hear it. We celebrate its presence in all the awards that must be given out each year as if we must continuously mark its presence, just as its presence continues to mark each person born as unique and worth celebrating in some way. Each time we celebrate the genius qualities or accomplishments of those who succeed, we are unwittingly blessing the genius that each carries within; for everyone has some genius.

As the source of uniqueness and spark of individual life, genius is an indelible, if often overlooked, element of the human soul. Whether it is called a guardian angel or an inner muse, a divine twin or the genius within us, this original resident spirit of the soul gives each person inner purpose and a unique way of perceiving life. The genius of a person refers to a distinct and distinguishing complex of inner gifts, innate talents and native potentials. It is also a unique style or way of being that characterizes each person from within. Genius is the inner spark and spirit that animates each soul, making each person born unique and never to be repeated again. Genius also makes us purposeful and meaningful from within.

When human efforts are reduced to blind production and consumption, life becomes reduced to consuming the world and being consumed with the obvious. People become increasingly available to distractions and obsessions, to trivia and nostalgia. Under the rule of literalism and the dominance of a statistical world view, the children of modern mass cultures can easily find themselves feeling devoid of all purpose and lacking in direction exactly at the time when you would expect them to awaken to a meaningful life. What seems troubling in a new way is that hordes of young people, both educated and less fortunate, enter independent life believing that they are empty inside and lacking any inherent purpose for being in this world.

The myth of the modern world is that this world has no meaning, that it has no center and that we, who find ourselves in the midst of a random universe, are simply accidental beings, both empty of a personal center and lacking in any essential purpose in life. The genius myth offers the sense that each soul enters this world gifted in certain ways and is distinctly shaped from within. In the same way that each infant arrives with a unique set of fingerprints as well as precise brain printing, each soul bears an inner imprint and unique psychic pattern. Human nature includes the hallmark of genius and a stamp of uniqueness provided by great nature. Nature produces life on a massive scale, yet each person born remains singular, never to be repeated. Just as there is no such thing as an average rainfall or an average tree, there is no such thing as an average person. We each stand on the common ground of life with our own way of being present and our own once in a lifetime chance at becoming the person we are intended to be.

Genius stamps each soul as rare and valuable in some way that can both satisfy the individual and serve the world. When seen as an archetypal presence in the soul, human genius marks each person—regardless of age, gender orientation, ethnicity, or social status—as being essentially unique and inherently valuable. More than raw talent or potential ability, genius gives a person their unique way of being in and contributing to the world.

In mythic terms, it is axiomatic that each soul enters the world accompanied by a divine twin, guardian angel, or inner guide of some sort. Traditional cultures around the world have imagined an inner pattern that shapes the soul and provides a guiding force from within. Until modern times, all cultures imagined that each soul arrives with something indelible within that makes each person born a valuable and potentially meaningful individual. Modern attention may focus upon the distinct fingerprints or palm print of each person in order to prove their outer identity. Ancient cultures focused more attention upon the innate qualities and longings that form the true identity of each soul. Amidst the threats and dangers of the modern world there will be ever more refined ways of checking the identity of each person; the question is whether there will be meaningful ways for people to become who and what they are intended to be.

We may have to invent ever more refined ways to prove who we are at the level of common life in order to gain entrance to public places, and to avoid identity theft. Yet a great thievery has already taken place wherein people no longer imagine that they are genius-born, spirit made and intended to contribute something meaningful to the world.

GENIUS AND DIVERSITY

Variation and diversity are part of the magic of creation as well as the wonder of nature. Diversity and uniqueness are also essential ingredients for the survival and meaning of the human species. Thus, no two humans share the same genetic makeup. None of the billions of humans on earth share the same exact configuration of the base pairs of DNA that are strung on the double helix of inherited genes. We are intended to be unique beings and rare souls even from a biological perspective, as there is no single way of being. Neither is there a general form of intelligence; more like billions of intelligent forms seeking more than simple preservation of the species. Just as surely as each of us bears a precise DNA pattern within our cells, we each arrive with a unique and valuable style intended to give more presence to life and greater beauty and imagination to this world.

The genius in us knows from the outset how we are shaped and styled within and how we are aimed at life. Yet, we may rarely feel or fully grasp our greatest natural inheritance: the sense of inner meaning and purpose seeded in our lives. The ancient reverence for the individual, at times so clear and important, becomes easily lost amidst the collectivism of mass culture. For, despite touting themes of individual freedom, modern cultures are permeated with an atmosphere of literalism, materialism, and collectivism. The growing despair under the shining surface of mass culture arises from the sense that collective life increasingly lacks meaning and individual life serves no real purpose.

Despite all the ways of being connected to the modern world, in the depths of ourselves we often feel more isolated and alone. In a world of mass marketing, mass communication, and often massive confusion, it becomes increasingly important to have some idea of who we are at our core and what we each have to give to life.

Amidst the massing of mass cultures and the rise of collectivism, it has become more difficult to feel genuine longing and the natural belonging from which new forms of human community and healthy ways of reconnecting to nature can be imagined and conceived. The notion of each individual having their own resident genius becomes ever more important as the world spins faster and faster around us, for something older and wiser keeps trying to catch up to us. Whereas mass cultures favor duplications and replications, nature only produces originals. There may be no time more pertinent for the rebirth of genius than this age of mass culture and technological dissociation.

THE HALLMARK OF GENIUS

The common notion of genius refers to the exceptional person within the norms and expectations of society. However, the original sense of genius indicated that which is exceptional in each person born. Considering genius in this older, wiser sense shifts the question from whether a particular person might test out to be a genius to how each person might find their genius. Instead of simply elevating people with certain kinds of intelligence or talent, the issue becomes a consideration of how and in what way genius seeks to manifest in each person born. The sense that each of us, regardless of place of origin or social background, has inner gifts and something significant to contribute to the world has practical benefits at both the individual and cultural level.

While each society must define its norms and standards of behavior, genius works outside of norms and sets its own standards. As the exact inner shape and often exacting spirit that is native to each person, genius brings its own expectations for life. The inner genius bears its own exacting standards as well as an inner ethic that is present within us before any considerations of collective morality. Genius sets an inner gold standard, the higher standard that our soul would have us live up to.

Innovation, invention and creativity are trademarks of those who come to know and use their innate genius qualities. Resiliency amidst adversity is another hallmark of genius and an essential capacity to have and develop in a rapidly changing, often disorienting world. Originally, a hallmark was an official stamp that guaranteed purity in articles made of gold. In that sense, genius is the hallmark etched within each person, for each of us bears the official stamp of spirit. Each of us came to this world bearing within certain golden qualities that mark us at our core as the genuine article.

This older, wiser sense of a unique inner genius stands against the collective ideas and designs of modern mass cultures, which are based in mass production and often put us on the verge of mass destruction. Old apocalyptic visions may feature a wrathful god wiping clean the slate of creation, but current dangers increasingly place worldwide destruction in the hands of humankind. Whether it be mankind contributing blindly to global warming or man's continuing inhumanity to man exploding in nuclear disaster, humans seem to have a greater-than-usual hand in the troubles plaguing this world. In that sense, mankind acts like a force of nature and "apocalypse now" involves a sense of self-destruction as well as the potential to annihilate the entire world.

Instead of an angry god punishing his creatures for straying from the rules, something inside humanity becomes the agent of destruction and disaster as reckless technologies and extreme ideologies might conspire to blow everything to kingdom come. On one hand, this points to human grandiosity and a negative inflation as mankind assumes powers typically assigned to the gods. On the other hand, it points to the necessity of recognizing the crucial role of humanity in the delicate balance between nature, culture and the human spirit. Humans are clearly implicated in the disasters of the modern age, yet something hidden within the core of humanity may yet help redeem the precarious condition of the world. Not the simple notion of humans heroically "saving the world", but the idea of people discovering the redeeming nature and capacity for renewal that reside at the core of life itself.

In a rapidly changing world faced with seemingly impossible problems, it becomes important to imagine that each person born might have something to contribute to the solutions. The deepest human resources tend to awaken amidst the greatest human disasters. If everyone has a genius nature, then each naturally has gifts to give and something of value to offer. Rather than being seen as an abstract consumer of goods in a mass culture, each person can be revalued as a unique gift-giver. Genius defines the inner nature of a person and a genuine destiny involves the expression of one's genius nature. By becoming outwardly what is naturally seeded within, the individual becomes an agent of creation and thereby able to add something to life that was not there before.

Accepting the notion that each person has some form of genius will not solve all the problems of life, but it can give more people the courage to develop a life of meaning and find ways to contribute to the world. Everyone already has some talent or vision; what is rare is to find the courage to follow one's vision all the way to the destination to which it aims. An old idea reminds us that we often lie to ourselves about who we truly are and what we can actually do; we hide our true nature from ourselves and obscure what we are meant to serve in this world. One of the few things that can stand against the onslaught of mass culture and the distortions and distractions of mass communication is the sense of an inner uniqueness that distinguishes each individual from all others. As the original agent and source of our talents and gifts, genius stands against blind materialism and the loss of meaning characteristic of mass cultures.

As resident spirit, the genius is the keeper of the inner pattern and root of memory in the soul. Throughout life it remembers that which is most essential to us yet so often forgotten by us. At critical times, the genius in a person draws attention to itself as it seeks to become consciously known by its human host. When the world rattles and everything turns upside down, holding to the inner thread of genius may be the surest way to find a way in life. If we allow the inner thread to pull us, the unique ways in which we are woven and spun will help us find our own way to survive and contribute meaning and beauty to life.

The inner genius is our innate connection to the living, ever-renewing soul of the world; if we allow it to awaken within us, we become both more vital and more purposeful. In allowing the inner genius to transform us, some transformation of the world also occurs. If we follow the genius in ourselves, we recover what we were intended to be from the start and become agents of creation ongoing.

NATURE AND GENIUS

In these times of alternating collapse and discovery, we need to awaken as many inner geniuses as possible in order to meet the multiple threats and complex challenges we face. Rather than the need to heroically save the whole world, the real work of humanity at this time may be to awaken the unique spark and inner resiliency of genius within each person.

Amidst melting ice caps, rising seas, and radical climate change, what remains of the natural world matters more to life than ever before. Yet, as the natural self within us becomes diminished by mass culture, so too does our connection to the great nature all around us. The loss of reverence for nature and the cavalier destruction of the environment reflect the loss of connection to the inner nature and unique core of the human soul. As the world becomes increasingly threatened by extremism, terrorism, and fanaticism, and as nature suffers the storms of climate change as well as the ravages of exploitation, there is a desperate need for the inventiveness, creativity, and resiliency that are the natural hallmarks of human genius. As Ralph Waldo Emerson put it, "When nature has work to be done, she creates a genius to do it."

Could nature, now overburdened and sorely mistreated, be calling on each of us to take up the thread of genius that is closest to our own nature and set to the work of helping to reimagine and reweave the whole divine thing? Not simply the sense of heroic efforts trying desperately to save the world, but rather the sense of a diversity of genius natures awakening to assist the world in renewing itself. As resident spirit of the soul, the genius in each of us is both our natural connection to nature and our secret connection to the divine. The sense of inner genius can offer a thread of revelation that allows us to find what has been missing all along.

The re-imagination of genius may offer a deeper initiation of the creative self within each person. When everything outside tends to fall apart the hidden message inside life may be closer to the surface and calling for attention. In the midst of radical changes in nature and the rattling of culture, revelations of the genius self within may be closer than ever.

THE GREATER SELF WITHIN

Nature loves a mystery and each soul born is a mystery waiting to be revealed, a meaningful story waiting to unfold. No one can prove it, nor can it be simply disproven. But all the old stories depict it and our dreams hint at it and life at critical times requires that we act as if it were true. The awakened individual has always been an agent of change and an assistant to creation ongoing. Human beings are both a genius production of nature and the genius producers of culture. The awakening of our genius self allows us to deliver the gifts we have been given and contribute meaning as well as beauty to the world. An old idea found in many traditions holds that each person comes to this world of change at a time when they have something meaningful to offer. Meaningful solutions to the overwhelming problems of the world would be closer at hand if it was better understood that each person born bears within them a gift that the world might need.

Great crises and impossible tasks can uncover hidden resources and reveal veins of genius that can alter the course of history. The threat of collapse and utter loss can also serve to awaken genius qualities and radical solutions. Each soul desires to be part of something greater, something "larger than life," for we each harbor within ourselves a larger life and a greater self waiting to become known. Everyone intuits the possibility of a greater life; yet this greatness now tends to be imagined as something outside ourselves. Most campaigns that promise liberation—be they political or spiritual, base advertising, or high-energy motivational programs—direct us toward outer goals. Meanwhile, there is a greater self within that tries to surface at each critical turning point in our lives.

The genius of human nature involves innate capacities for creation and invention that are important in the life of each individual and essential to the balance of the world. The true individual, by virtue of being himself or herself, enters a state of partnership with the ongoing acts of creation and thereby adds something to life that was not there before. When the troubles are all around us, everyone can find some place where they are needed, where they can help heal all that is wounded and help protect all that is currently threatened by radical changes and global disturbances.

To borrow from the genius of Emerson again: "This time, like all times, is a very good one, if we but know what to do with it." Yet, knowing what to do with the conditions of the world may depend more than ever on knowing that the soul in each of us is naturally seeded with genius and secretly threaded to the Soul of the World.

CHAPTER 2

A MYTHOLOGICAL TRANSFUSION

The purpose of myth is to make the world meaningful.

Finding the purpose and meaning in life has always been a challenge; but to be modern means to doubt that human life has any meaning or purpose at all. To be modern means to be surrounded by devices intended to move all of life faster while increasingly doubting that there is anywhere meaningful to go. To be modern means to always be on the edge of the next technological revolution, but also to be on the verge of annihilation. To be modern can mean to be lost; to be post-modern can mean to feel forsaken.

As the modern genius Albert Einstein expressed it: "It has become appallingly obvious that our technology has exceeded our humanity." In the upward, onward, and forward at all costs rush of the modern world, the soul of humanity can become lost. Yet, the intensification of cultural and environmental issues can serve as a reminder that something meaningful has gone missing and must be sought for again. It is only when the whole thing seems to be falling apart that people begin to remember that there was something left behind in the great rush to the future.

The human soul is an ancient and knowing thing that cares little for the latest technological devices. It longs to give birth to the innate values, essential ideas, and core images that brought each of us to life to begin with. We are each involved in a unique experiment in life, the clues for which are hidden where most people prefer not to look: inside ourselves, in the surprising inner life of the soul. The inner genius is our inherent and indelible connection to the otherworld of great imagination, original thought and endless renewal. Genius reaches all the way back to the origins of being and ties each of us to the pulse of creation. Human genius is both ancient and immediate at the same time. It brings together past and present and when made conscious can make a meaningful future more possible.

Part of what has become lost in the rush of modern life is the intuitive sense that what becomes wounded or worn out in the daily world must be healed and made whole again by a connection to the 'otherworld.' The otherworld includes the inner world of feeling and deep thought, but also the realm of inspiration and mythic imagination. Humans are mythic by nature, and when we forget that, we become both distant to our true nature and alienated from the realm of living nature all around us.

In the modern world, myth seems a thing of the past with no practical application in the present, or something that can be proven false and patently untrue. Yet, what seems false on the surface can turn out to be quite true when known in depth. Although the word myth now suggests a sense of unreality bordering on fraud, the purpose of myth is to reveal the deeper truths of life. When it comes to knowing the heart of a person or the soul of the world, depth is not an option, but a requirement. It is in the depths of the human soul that mystery resides and history is continually made.

For, history does not simply come from a past behind us; history is shaped in the depths of the human soul where the facts of life continue to be made. Myth involves the stories underlying life and the secret histories of the soul. Those who take the world at face value fail to learn the deeper truths that make meaning of all that happens at the fleeting, rapidly changing surface of life. When we lose our connection to the otherworld of myth and deep understanding we lose our capacity for vertical imagination and the world becomes flat again.

When the daily world becomes a state of chaos and constant turmoil, it is time to turn back to the mythic imagination that resides deep in the soul. For, there is a myth at the heart of things and a core imagination residing in the heart of each person. Part of the secret of life is that each soul carries a primary imagination and a reservoir of essential ideas that can help us make sense of the fleeting world. Imagination is the deepest power of the human soul and mythic imagination helps make meaning of all that happens in the world, even as it helps reveal inner meanings and genuine purpose in the heart of each person.

There are two great stories in this world, the eternal drama that keeps unfolding at the center of life and the personal myth that tries to unfold and become known at the center of each human life. What we learn through myth is the nature of the story trying to live through each of us amidst the ongoing drama of the world around us. The territory of myth includes all the unseen things that affect us most deeply and all the missing parts and hidden dreams that might make us whole. When something essential or meaningful goes missing, it does not simply disappear; rather, it falls back into the realm of myth and imagination from which all things come. When it comes to living in hard times and dealing with radical change, it is important to know that there are hidden truths and secret unities set within the human soul.

HANGING BY THE THREAD OF GENIUS

Myth may be out of fashion, but it remains a timeless presence that leaves meaningful clues of its existence all over the place. When someone has lost their way or lacks understanding of their situation, we say they are "clueless." They haven't a clue which way to turn and no sense of how to proceed. If we follow the word clue back a ways, it leads to the old Anglo-Saxon clew, meaning "a ball of wound thread." If we begin to unwind that old thread, it leads to Greek myths, specifically the mythic image of Ariadne's Clew, and secrets to surviving the labyrinth of life.

Ariadne's clew, or thread, became tied to the story of the hero Theseus, who battled the fearful Minotaur at the center of the labyrinth where many maidens and youth had perished. Yet, the old story holds other clues about the intricacies of life in this world that remains both a mystery and a maze. The name Ariadne can mean "exceedingly bright" or "daughter of the sun," with yet another variant meaning "the most holy." The old Greek word for life is zoe, from which we get zoology. Before her limited role in the tale of Theseus, Ariadne held the holy thread of Zoe, the eternal cord that goes between all things. In older myths, she was depicted as both queen of the underworld and queen of the sky, as if to say that she knew how to hold the darkness and the light together. An old word for wisdom translates as "dark knowledge," leading us to the sense that genuine wisdom combines understanding of the darker side of life with knowledge of the light.

Rather than simply being a maidenly helper to a forceful hero, Ariadne holds the clews for surviving the underworld, which can be experienced as encounters with the unconscious parts of oneself, as a dark period in one's life or as the dark times that can fall upon the world. As daughter of the sun, Ariadne helps reveal "the light hidden in the darkness," an old description for the radiance of the human soul, for each soul brings a hidden light and a thread of meaning to this labyrinth of a world.

The soul has often been imaged as feminine, in contrast to the mind, which can have a masculine dedication to analyzing things and laying out a clear string of ideas. When it comes to solving the deeper puzzles of life, a straightforward or rational approach tends to lead to dead ends. After setting off heroically, we may become lost and clueless and need to discover the subtle and unique thread of our own soul.

An even older word for this mythical ball of thread was mitos, which meant the lifeline that is spun out and rolled into a ball by the at the birth of each human soul. The first sister of fate is Lachesis, who gives each person their lot in life, their specific allotment of the thread of life with the particular clues and qualities that shape that specific soul adventure. The middle sister, Clotho, from whose name we derive cloth and clothing, gives each soul its twist of fate that ties it uniquely into the tapestry of time and eternity. Once our lot has been cast and given its unique twist, a plotline has been set within us and certain things have been set in motion. The story of our lives tries to follow the inner plot until the third sister, Atropos, brings the tale to an end by cutting off the thread of life.

Throughout our life, the unique plotline tries to unfold and lead us through the maze of life. If we accept its presence, it can serve as a gradient for the soul and a guideline through life's inevitable puzzles and perplexities. The soul seeks the unfolding of the unique plot and storyline and the genius of the soul would have us learn its inner meaning and follow it all the way to its intended destiny. Here on earth each life must be limited in fateful ways, yet each soul has a meaningful destination and a purpose to fulfill. If we follow the inner plotline all the way our fate turns out to be our purpose seen from the other end of life. After the story has unfolded enough and hints of our destiny become revealed, we can see why life must be lived forward but can only be understood by looking backward.

For the ancients, a labyrinth offered a metaphor for life on earth, with its complexity of twists and turns, false starts and deceptive dead ends, and all the meandering confusions and compulsive diversions through which each person must find their way. Even today, people will walk the lines of a labyrinth as a moving meditation that might provide a sense of centering or a clue for how to face a dilemma or find a way out of some entanglement.

Mythologically speaking, Ariadne is nearby whenever we find ourselves in a maze or a muddle with no clue of what to do. As a mythical figure, she continues to offer us a ball of thread and many clues for how to survive a world that seems to be coming apart at the seams. The key is to find the inner clew and gradient line of the soul and learn how to follow where it would lead. For the notion that we can be anything we want to be is unwise as well as untrue. In this world we are fortunate if we turn out to be something close to what our soul intends us to be.

THREADED TO THE CENTER

Life is the living labyrinth into which we are born. The story is well underway when we appear on the scene and we seem to arrive without a clue. Lacking a sense of mythic imagination leaves us clueless when it comes to how we best fit into the world and what our inner life is all about. Yet, we are threaded and woven to the skein of life from the beginning and we are wired for a destiny that somehow fits the nature of our individual soul.

Throughout our lives, an invisible cord and inner thread of destiny that was there before the umbilical of our birth first formed, tries to pull us along. In ancient India, the inner thread was known as the upavita—"the thread of life," or golden filament of living imagination that makes each life valuable and each soul noble from the beginning.

This archetypal thread serves as a symbol of the principle that connects us to the origins of life while also providing us with an inner gradient or life line to follow throughout our lives. The life-thread of the soul must take us on a winding path of self-discovery, for the soul finds its way by wandering. The soul feels its way along, by trusting in things that can be felt to be true even if they cannot easily be proven so. Not realizing that a gradient thread connects each of us to the center of life can mean to be lost in the maze of existence with no existential reason for being. The thread of life is one of the "there not there" elements of human existence. It is there from the beginning, yet it cannot be measured, even by the finest instruments; it cannot be found through simple examination or be proven to exist in scientific ways. Yet, it is there, woven within us and offering essential clues at each critical moment and turning point in life. This narrative intelligence of the soul tends to be indirect, but it is story-wise and secretly threaded to the center where life continuously renews itself and would help us awaken and renew as well.

Unbeknownst to most, the inner gradient tries to pull us through all the obstacles and puzzling events of life, all the while keeping us threaded to the hidden center of the whole thing. The loss of a sense of mythic imagination at the core of things has left people adrift in a world that seems to mean less and less. For, myth makes meaning and without this deeper sense the world can seem increasingly random, a chaotic place that makes less and less sense. In times of trouble, we sense again how everything, including ourselves, hangs but by a thread on life's trembling web. In order that it might become known again, I am calling this unique inner filament the thread of genius, which secretly ties us to invisible but necessary things: to our inherent gifts and talents, to our dreams and inspirations, to the styles and inclinations that whisper to us our purpose in a world that needs us to awaken.

A MYTHOLOGICAL ANTIDOTE

In the midst of the fragmentation that now characterizes our world, each person winds up feeling marginal or pushed to the extreme in some way. Since the "center cannot hold," it must be relocated at another level of being. Each person must find a thread of relevance to their own soul. That "soul thread" connects to the eternal thread of life. If enough people follow their essential thread, a new center can be woven of the diverse skein of threads carried by individual souls.

The antidote for the isolation and dissociation so characteristic of modern life lies in finding again the ancient wellsprings of human imagination and the personal thread to the underlying continuity of life. For there is a myth at the heart of things and a hidden wholeness underlies the world. An endless story unfolds from the core of creation and a living thread of imagination woven within the heart connects each of us to it. Secretly, we are tied by a delicate, yet indelible thread to the very heart of things.

Apocalyptic myths often include a stage of apocatastasis or renewal of the cosmos after a period of chaos and dissolution. Apocalypse does not mean the end of everything; rather it means "lifting of the veil," a time of both collapse and renewal as the underlying energies of life become intensely activated and revealed. In mythic terms it is not simply that that collapse is followed by renewal; rather that the two go on simultaneously. As things fall apart on one level, the next world seeks to arise from another level. This can be considered as a "new world" or the same old world renewing itself from its eternal origins. In mythic sense the new world is also the ancient world that has renewed itself time and time again. The problem is not that soon it will all come to an end, rather the issue is how to act when it seems that way.

In contemporary life, the outer world rarely reflects the inner realm of the human soul. When the world rattles and everything turns upside down, holding to the inner thread may be the surest way to find meaning and gain a sense of purpose. While holding to the inner pattern and innate rhythms of our souls, all the moments of our lives can make sense; without those guides all can seem accidental and pointless.

The antidote for the isolation and dissociation so characteristic of modern life lies in finding again the ancient wellsprings of human imagination and the personal thread to the underlying continuity of the Soul of the World. A hidden wholeness underlies the wild dance of creation, although most people no longer know that. Yet, at critical times in life we must take hold of the inner thread and follow where it leads in order to find how we best fit and where our life is threaded to the pulse of existence. If we follow its gradient line, we become agents of creation, rather than victims of chaos. The inner genius is our natural connection to the soul of life; when we allow it to awaken within us, we become more vital and purposeful. If we allow this destiny thread to pull us along, the unique ways in which we are woven and spun and aimed from within will help us not only to survive, but also to find our own way to contribute meaning, vitality and beauty to this increasingly troubled world.

CHAPTER 3

THE DESERTED CHILDREN

The most broken people in a society reveal
where a society is most broken.

Where some might research the greatest minds in history or the most talented inventors of modernity to find the seeds of genius, I came to the study of human giftedness from two unusual places at once. First of all, I kept encountering the image of a unique personal spirit in the myths and stories of cultures from around the world. Secondly, I found myself searching for hints of hidden genius in the troubled lives of young people caught in the margins of culture and in the 'crazy life' of the streets. I found the idea of individual genius invaluable while working with school dropouts, gang members, hard-core street kids, and social outcasts.

In order to learn what is hidden and sorely needed, in order to find an answer that might have value even for those who are undervalued, exiled or outcast, I have gone to juvenile halls and prisons, to refugee organizations and psychiatric hospitals, to veterans meetings and suicide prevention groups. In each place where people feel forsaken, I have found that naming the elusive something that entered the world unseen at the birth of each child can have a healing, wholing effect. I found the most useful name for the inborn quality that makes each of us unique to be the genius of the soul.

In myths and folktales genius refers to an inborn spirit "that which is already there" at the birth of each person. As the inner resident of the soul, the genius gives each person, regardless of circumstances, their unique way of being in the world and their own way of perceiving life. The point is not that each person is a genius, but that each one born has some innate genius. Not simply that some are gifted with genius; but that genius names the giftedness in each and every one. For, each of us enters the world bearing an inner arrangement of talents and gifts intended to be revealed and be given in the course of our lives. Seen this way, genius is not just the exceptional person amongst us, but also an exceptional presence within each of us. If the inner genius is rejected or denied a chance to come to life, it can turn against its human host and become a danger to others as well. Genius that remains unrecognized can become the cause of either depression or violence.

If you work with young people living on the margins of modern societies, you cannot avoid absorbing both the hollowness many feel on the inside as well as the increasing pressures they feel from the outside world. It is the nature of young people to reflect the problems and dilemmas of their society, and modern youth grow into an extreme time of nature rattling and culture seemingly unraveling. Regardless of economic status or social background, young people now grow up in a disturbing atmosphere of seemingly impossible tasks and increasingly unresolvable conflicts. As the margins and gaps in modern societies grow, so does the sense of loss and isolation amongst young people who are considered to have "everything to live for."

The idea of inner genius as a vital key for both surviving in life and finding meaning and purpose became crystalized for me while working closely with severely at-risk young people. In trying to help wounded and endangered girls and boys, I found that most lacked a felt sense that they were valuable in themselves. I am not referring to the modern sense of "self-esteem," which can be more of a social construct, but to a genuine, heart-felt sense of self-worth based upon distinct inner values and natural qualities. Young people tend to get in trouble, not because they are 'bad' or simply anti-social. The inevitable troubles of youth are intended to be the ordeals through which they find both their innate sense of value as well as hidden resources they did not know they possessed.

It has become clear to me that misunderstanding the nature of human genius has contributed to the diminishing importance of individual human life as well as leading to a growing void in the center of education. If each person has natural gifts and innate talents, then the true nature of education must involve the awakening, inviting, and blessing of the inner genius and unique life spirit of each young person. When youth fail to receive enough socialization, they may act against the common interests and sensibilities of their communities. But when young people are not recognized for the spirit and potential qualities that are part of their true nature, they may become self-destructive or seek to destroy their own culture.

It was while working with alienated, violent, and suicidal youth that I realized that genius in its original sense—as a sign of the indelible inner worth of each person—was also an outcast in modern culture. By now, all young people are exposed to extremes of uncertainty and worldwide problems as both nature and culture have become severely at risk in many ways. In the modern world all young people are at risk; yet, some are more at risk than others and more in harm's way far too early in life. By the time they come of age, many young people in the hoods and barrios and other areas of poverty and neglect have suffered extremes of deprivation and violence typically found in times of war or famine.

Early in the process of learning to work with severely at-risk youth, I found myself literally in the middle of an attempt at forging a truce between warring gangs. I walked into a room in an inner-city recreation center and was given a seat in the middle of what turned out to be a dispute between aggrieved young members of opposing local gangs. The truth is that choosing to work with those who are severely at risk also means placing oneself at risk. In fact, the man who was kind enough to drive me to the center simply dropped me off at the curb, saying that it was very unsafe for him to even be there. In one sense, we were right in the midst of the "inner city," while at the same time we were out on a reckless margin of modern culture, where everyone lives on the edge and anything can happen. As soon as I grabbed my gear, he drove off and I began to feel quite alone, a little lost and afraid.

The meeting involved an experiment in truce making, an attempt to stop a local gang war and find ways to reduce the ever-increasing gun violence amongst kids in neighborhood gangs. There were a few courageous adults who were trying anything to halt the violence and I agreed to help them in the experiment. They had managed to bring key members of both gangs together based upon mutual respect for an 'OG' or original gangster from the neighborhood. We had worked together once before and he was the only person present that I knew. Once inside, there was no way to renegotiate the agreement to work with troubled youth, nor was there any time to explain how a seeming "white guy" was going to help defuse the situation by telling them a story. There was no easy way out and no effective way to protect myself except by being myself. I felt somewhat relieved that a story quickly came to mind, even though I had never told it before and was not at all sure if it would make sense given the palpable levels of tension in the room. The only thing I could do was embrace the story and hope it could get all of us out of danger.

The tale focused upon two children who were completely abandoned by their tribe, left behind when everyone went off looking for greener pastures. "Once upon a time," I told them, "not in this place, but in another place— not in this time, but in another time—there was a village in the middle of an open plain. The people of that village had decided that the grass must be greener somewhere else. So, they gathered up all their belongings and headed out for greener pastures, believing they would find a better life."

"Like all the white folks who left the city for the suburbs and took all the good stuff with them?" a young voice asked. "Just like that," I said, further relieved that the story that had appeared might make some sense of the situation we all found ourselves in. The truth is that everyone loves a story and often a genuine story can hold people together long enough to make some sense of an otherwise discouraging and even dangerous situation.

It was an old Native American tale in which a young sister and her little brother, upon returning to their village, found it completely deserted. The children were in great danger because they happened to be out picking berries when the tribe took down their teepees, packed up and left. All they could see was the dust rising from many moccasins as the big people trudged off on the road that crossed a river far ahead. The sister ran after the people, yelling for the tribe to wait for them. The little brother ran as well, but his legs were short and he was soon left behind in the dust. Since the sister did not wish to abandon her little brother, she turned back and the two of them began to make a life in the hollowness of the deserted village.

In the quiet magic of stories, we each sat with our own feelings as the orphan children were left alone with nothing but some bare teepee poles and the wisps of smoke rising from abandoned family fires. It became clear that everyone present could relate to the sad fate of the deserted children. No one had to draw lines to connect the dots between the old abandoned village and the hollowed-out feeling of the inner city buildings all around us. We knew without saying that we were in both places at once and could consider the parallel situations of cultural abandonment.

When the story went on to describe how the little brother grew up but was often silent and moody, everyone could also relate to that. When it turned out that he spent more and more time sitting with his head down, caught either in a mood of anger or resentment, we were moving even closer to the core issues at hand. When it developed that each time the brother lifted his head and stared at something living, it died, we were right where we needed to be. So, I stopped the story and asked what everyone thought about the abandoned children and the young brother with the killing stare. You can only meet a story with your life and everyone present could relate to the moods of the little brother. When his head was down he was caught in the pull of sorrow and the pain of loss. When he lifted his head, he felt the rise of anger, rage, and resentment as the emotions came together and boiled over into the outer world. Painfully but thankfully, we entered a deep conversation about the roots of rage and resentment that to this day continue to grow wherever young people feel rejected early in life and abandoned for no good reason.

At this point, the sense of bitter abandonment that comes from generations of social injustice and cultural rejection had to be expressed in the room or we would be abandoning ourselves. Many of the young people spoke up and some found words that spoke for everyone present and for many others as well. The truth was that it became difficult to simply glare at the brothers in the opposing gang because we were closer to the causes behind all the anger, resentment and violence. Strangely enough, having the burning feelings of abandonment and injustice residing clearly in the brother in the story allowed everyone to be more at ease with each other. When someone summarized that abandoned children have to live with a deep sense of being wrong in themselves, not simply the feeling of being wronged by others, we were close to the sense of despair that drives much of the violence in modern life.

In the sad silence where each of us thought our own thoughts, it seemed time to return to the children in the story. Despite being left in the deserted village, the sister kept finding things that were surprising or life-supporting in the world around them. She would repeatedly call her brother to look up and see some wonder that the world brought to their solitary village. Mostly he refused, keeping his head down, preferring his inner emotions and moods. One day, a whole herd of buffalo came thundering by. The sister called her brother to look up and see the wonder. He refused, but the sister insisted that he had to see the marvelous sight. What could he do? It was his sister, the only one who cared for him, the only one who had not abandoned him. He raised his head, looked at the wondrous animals and no sooner did he glance upon them than they all fell down dead at the edge of the village.

Surprisingly and as if by magic, the sister began to skin the hides and strip the meat from the buffalo. Soon, she had fashioned great robes to keep them warm at night. She also built racks and set the strips of meat to dry in the sun. Later on the same thing happened when a herd of elk came grazing across the nearby plain. The brother slew them with the killing stare and the sister used their skins to cover a teepee frame that had been left standing. She dried the elk meat on the racks and after that the children had plenty of food to live on.

"How could she do it?" someone asked when I paused the tale again. Everyone began to puzzle over the power of the sister to make things and save their lives when there was no one there to instruct or help them. They were abandoned very young, left behind with no adults or elders to guide or educate them. So, where did her knowledge and abilities come from? How could there be such magic amidst the devastation and abandonment? The truth was that it was far easier to recognize the killing stare of the little brother than to understand the creative power and inner strength of the sister. He was caught in his moods and the violence that erupted from them; but she was able to create things on her own. Everyone got the sense that one side of the abandonment created death and the other side seemed to generate life; but how did that work and was it possible?

Clearly, it was a teaching story; but what was it trying to teach us? We were in the crux of the story, at the point where one side of the abandonment led to killing and death, while the other side offered magical capacities for generating and sustaining life. Since I had brought the story, it was assumed that I had the answers to the questions it posed.

It seems strange to people now, but everyone used to know that young people eventually reach a place where they realize that they have innate power, often the power of life and death. Children can be persuaded, even forced to behave in certain ways; but with the coming of age comes the power to destroy or to enhance life and each culture must eventually deal with the powers and the wounds of the next generation. Traditional cultures typically fashioned rites of passage to help socialize young people, while also offering them wisdom and healing from childhood neglect or other wounds. Modern societies often abandon their youth exactly at the time when they find themselves facing the core human issues of life and death.

We were now deep into a story that would have been used to teach young people about life and death, about gifts and wounds and about the greater responsibilities of the elders to the youth. We were in suspended animation in an uncared for rec center; yet we were also in what people used to call "hedge school" or "bush school." I had learned from study that the ancient Irish storytellers used to wander from village to village using old stories to bring life lessons to light for both the young and the old. After the colonization of Ireland, there were severe punishments for even using the native language. The old tellers had to pull the young people out of sight, often behind the hedges in order to share the wisdom of stories.

Thus, "hedge school" named a moveable place of sudden education being offered amidst the dangers of life. While working with African tribespeople, I learned that they also had the tradition of "bush school" as a place where everyone heard stories and learned lessons about life and death. Something similar was true for Native American tribes, who often called the deeper paths of learning the "Road of Life and Death."

The truth is that everyone gets wounded on the road of life and death and the justice of it must be that each is also gifted in some way. Everyone in this world must be gifted in some way and the old term for gifts hidden in the soul of each person was their genius. If that is not true, then there would be seeming justification for the continuing tragedies that occur when certain children and groups of people become rejected and abandoned simply because of the color of their skin or the ethnicity of their ancestors. In this situation, everyone understood that the wounds of life were more evident and immediate than the gifts. Sitting with the weight of generations of abandonment, I recalled the old idea that a person's true genius resides near their deepest wounds. There is a psychic alignment between a person's natural gifts and the inevitable wounds of life.

The abandoned sister and brother represent an essential pairing and complex relationship between life's gifts and wounds. When the genius nature of someone becomes conscious and can be used creatively, they begin to see and feel the wonder of the world and can realize how to best contribute to life. On the other hand, life is not neutral and when young people are mistreated or denied the opportunity to become themselves, the wound grows deeper and the inner brilliance can turn against life and even toward serving death.

The sister in the story represented the talents in everyone. Even if some talents in the room were being underserved or being misused, it had to be that everyone had some giftedness to begin with. That was an important idea and an important place to stop for a while. The talk turned to how each person, regardless of age or background, had some kind of natural gift or talent. If someone could not name it in themselves, they could see it clearly in their younger siblings or in someone else that they loved. Everyone could acknowledge that we each carried some mixture of gifts and wounds regardless of our age, gender, ethnicity, or social origins. By now, there was little tension left in the room as a shared sense of both woundedness and human value served to connect us all. However, the story went on and we had to follow where it led.

One day a raven flew over the abandoned village with its dark wings flashing in the sun. The sister did not bring the appearance of the bird of omens to the attention of her brother. Instead, in her generous fashion she threw a piece of dried buffalo meat up to the bird. The raven caught the meat and carried it in its beak until it arrived at the site of the new village where the tribe had settled. As it turned out, the people who set off in search of grass that was greener found themselves in a place where famine had developed. Instead of living off the fat of the land, they inhabited a wasteland with no game to hunt and little to eat but the roots they could gather.

As the raven flew over, the young people were distracting themselves from the hunger they felt by playing games. When the bird dropped the buffalo meat in their midst, the young ones began to fight angrily over the scrap of food. They barely heard when the raven announced that back in the place of the old village there was plenty to eat. Eventually, someone stopped the fight and the scrap of food was brought to the elders for consideration. They decided to send scouts to verify if what the raven said was true. The scouts returned with tales of racks full of buffalo and elk meat drying in the sun and piles of buffalo robes as well.

Soon, the whole village packed up again and returned along the path they had taken when they had high hopes of finding abundance. They arrived at the old village and stood in awe of all the dried meat, elk skins, and buffalo robes. They hesitated to enter the altered village but began shouting greetings to the children as if they had not earlier deserted them. The sister asked why they had not stopped when she cried out to them with all her breath. They all became silent and sat on the ground. Then the sister asked her brother to look up and see the wonder that had come to the deserted village on that day.

Understanding what would happen, the brother refused to look. Now, as if their roles had switched, she insisted that the killing stare be employed, while he argued for the side of life against death. As in any dilemma, something had to give. She was his only sister, who had refused to abandon him when all the others left him behind. How could he refuse her now? He had no choice but to raise his head and gaze upon those who had turned their backs upon them in their hour of greatest need. And, no sooner did he gaze upon them, than they all fell dead, right there on the ground.

People listening groaned out loud at the notion that the whole thing could end in a slaughter that left the deserted children all alone again. Talk about a tragedy and a disaster. But, in true mythic fashion, the story went on further. The sister began to walk amongst the fallen bodies of all those who had deserted them when they were young and helpless. She began to speak to them saying: "I wish that all those who have love in their hearts might rise up again. I wish that those who can seek forgiveness and can forgive others might come back into life and live here with us and help make the village over again."

As the people with good hearts began to rise into life again the sister continued to speak. "May those who live remember what happens when they desert their children for something they cannot even see and may never actually find. May those who hear this story never forget what happens when people abandon their children and leave them behind."

Now, we were all in a different place. Technically, we were still in the recreation center, where the paint was peeling from the walls and the atmosphere of abandonment seemed to overwhelm any sense of recreation. Yet, we were also in the place where our hearts were open to each other regardless of differences, perceived or actual. For a time, we were all in the same village. For a moment, we were in the village of forgiveness and acceptance and we could forgive ourselves and each other for all the acts of desertion and abandonment that brought us to that point. I am serious; we were in that place long enough to be at peace with each other and have a temporary truce.

We were a mixed group, mostly Latino Americans, some African

Americans, and one Anglo American. Most were young men and women facing both life and death on the nearby streets. We were being held together by an old Native American story, as if the roots of story were still alive in the ground below us and might still be drawn upon to hold us in a village of acceptance and understanding.

When telling stories to people you can see their faces clearly, as each must open up to allow the story to enter their psyche. The faces change as they listen and most people become younger when attending to a story. It's as if stories can make us young again and being young means being near both the gifts and the wounds of life. Meanwhile, the wisdom hidden in the storehouse of stories can help restore the sense of meaning and even renew the sense of unity in life.

In working with severely at-risk young people, it was often reward enough to see them lose their perpetual scowls and killing stares. There was something satisfying in seeing hardcore "bangers" become young again, for most of those raised in the hoods and barrios miss out on having a genuine childhood. Like the children in the story many suffer the harsh realities of abandonment too early and have to live with it too long. It was encouraging to watch them forget their sadness and resentments as they brightened with wonder and an ancient story made them young again.

The point, however, was not simply reclaiming some nostalgia for childhood. The point always became how to find a way to alter the dangerous courses their young lives had taken. And the possibility of a life changing direction became more real whenever the sense of genius trying to awaken in lost souls could be brought to awareness. For, the genius in each person knows what gifts they bring to the world and how their lives should be oriented.

At the same time, the return of the village of healing and wholeness requires that people face the anger and resentments of all the abandoned parts of the community. When people abandon the natural genius of their children, they leave both their past and their future behind. Finding a way to a genuine sense of community means turning back to find what has been left behind, that which has been trying to catch up to us all along. In facing the wounds of anger and resentment, we also awaken the possibilities of rediscovering the boldness and magic of human genius. All of that can be seen and be found in the midst of the most abandoned places in modern culture, for it exists in the heart of each person.

I wish I could say that the truce continued and everyone found a path to fulfillment; but that would not be the truth. The truth is that some of those who were present in that momentary village of healing went to prison and some died way too young and unfulfilled. The story could not stop the pressure of the outside world and the patterns of abandonment for long. Yet, after a lot of hand shaking and brief hugs, we each left with a greater sense of how the angry brother and the magical sister live inside us. And, for me it began a serious study of the idea that each person, no matter how mistreated, no matter how falsely judged and abandoned, still carries within them a unique spark of genius that might contribute in some way to the recreation of a living village of healing and inclusion.

That was many years ago and by now the margins of abandonment have grown much greater as the sense of desertion in the inner cities and the barrios continues to deepen. At the same time, the suburbs that seemed to offer a haven of greener grass have their own kinds of emptiness and abandonment. Now, the wasteland appears in urban neighborhoods that have been abandoned; but also in the hollowness in more affluent suburbs. The collapsed condition of the abandoned children in the old story has become much more common amongst more privileged girls and boys. As the global village becomes the deserted village in more and more ways, increasingly they too feel the shadow side of mass cultures that blindly seeks fulfillment in the latest technology or fashions.

It may seem a strange thing, but a culture cannot effectively exile its own youth. Those who don't find a way to fit into respectable life come to live a shadow life on the edges of the village. The less the human village does to help young people find a rightful place in life, the more prisons it will have to build on its own periphery. The lost youth of any society represent something important lost at the heart of the culture. For, young people cannot help but feel and sometimes express the symptoms of the society in which they grow.

Increasingly, the symptoms of mass societies appear in both the violent acts and suicidal tendencies of young people who feel abandoned and not truly invited into the village of life. Those in danger of becoming lost can now be found at all levels of society. Not only are young people abandoned to their own increasingly technological devices, but older people commonly fail to become elders despite living longer and longer. In the global village, we often find ourselves alone together; each of us connected day and night through the internet, while also left alone in the new village of desertion.

The bright sister who represents the creative genius in each of us and the little brother who bears the burdens of anger and resentment wait for us to return. In acknowledging both their suffering and their natural gifts, we act in service of life over death. Humans are the makeweights in the scales of time and in the issues of life and death. As has become increasingly evident, we cannot dominate nature or simply build culture on the basis of greed. Yet, humanity has always had the ability to tip the scales towards life over death and forgiveness over revenge. There is something present in each human heart from the beginning that longs to become part of the living community of the soul. The issue is never simply what we might receive from this world, but also what gifts we might offer to it.

What is common now is a loss of soul that leaves everyone more isolated, more exposed to the extremes of raw emotions, and more at the mercy of human folly. With the loss of soul we lose the understanding that each person is wounded by life and therefore naturally deserving of sympathy and respect. Each person brings something valuable and meaningful to the life of the human village simply by virtue of being born. At the level of the soul, each person born has a genius nature that carries innate gifts and talents intended to be delivered to the world. If education was aimed at bringing the genius out of each student, there would be much greater knowledge at hand and many more ways to enhance both the dignity and the quality of life for everyone.

Amidst the loss of soul and increasing alienation and marginalization of youth, there needs to be a sense that something in the human heart remains resilient, creative, and capable of renewal. The old story serves as a mythic reminder that even when we feel most lost and abandoned, the inner genius does not desert us. We may have to face inner wounds that we would rather avoid and learn to express our inner pain, but in doing so, we will find ourselves closer to the vision and vitality of our natural genius. Genius is the resident spirit of the soul, the source of unending imagination in each person and the deepest resource as well. In times of abandonment we may be closer to our natural genius and able to express it, if only we do not abandon ourselves.

As an old saying found in the gnostic gospels proposes: If you bring forth what is within you, what you bring forth will save you. If you do not bring forth what is within you, what you do not bring forth will destroy you. Even if we have been abandoned repeatedly by others, the worst thing is to abandon the spirit within ourselves. Even when we feel most deserted in this world, there is something within us that cannot desert us. What waits to be found within each of us and be brought forth through us is the innate genius and guiding spirit that enters the world along with us at the moment of birth. On one level, we are each but a speck of life in an uncertain world; on another level, we are each a unique torchbearer, capable of bringing a bit of magic and the possibility of creation to a world in dire need of renewal.

CHAPTER 4

THE WASTELAND WE ARE IN

The point isn't the future of humanity but the presence of eternity.

The phrase "genius myth" unites two essential words that tend to be both misunderstood and diminished in the modern world. Genius tends to be reserved for those who demonstrate high levels of intelligence or display astonishing talent. Yet, original meanings of genius include "the entirety of traits united in a begotten being" and "that which is just born." Genius is the entirety of traits and talents that are already there in the soul of each person born. Some are born with prodigious gifts and talents; but each of us brings to life some inner gifts and our own genius way of being. Human genius functions as the "free radical" that refuses to be simply categorized and transcends all attempts to quantify it. In that sense, it can also seem abnormal and irrational and can be patently unpredictable.

We are each genius born and mythic by nature as genius is the mythic imprint within us. The sense of myth has been reduced to "just myth," meaning a falsehood. Yet, myth means "emergent truth," the truth trying to emerge from just under the skin of so-called "reality." Through contact with myth we become more imaginative and find again the subtle, symbolic ground hidden in our lives. Myth is the inside story of the world we live in, and we are each and all mythic by nature. Each of us has some genius to bring to life and each life is a meaningful story trying to unfold from within. Each person can be a genius at being themselves, and the genius of each of us is needed in these times when trouble takes on mythic proportions. For, these are mythical times with seemingly impossible tasks and intractable problems needing genius solutions.

Another old pairing of terms might serve to underscore the need for being more open-minded about the nature of human genius and its place in our world view. Throughout the ages, humans have proven to be both "tough-minded" and "tender-minded." Tough-minded attitudes have supported all the skills of survival as well as tendencies toward rational approaches and practical solutions. In the tough state of mind, people become deeply determined and narrowly focused, often wanting just the facts and the figures. By contrast, the tender-minded attitude tends to be more imaginative and intuitive, more tuned to feeling than thought. The tender-minded perspective is mythic, poetic, and connected to timeless things and places of mystery.

The tough-minded attitude appears in the conservative, deterministic, and often reactionary type of person. It also manifests as the orthodox supporter and true believer of whatever might be the local way, the political belief or the dominant system. The tender-minded tends to feel the timeless impulse, the subtle sense of immanent change as well as the possibility of transcendence. The tender-minded intuits the immediacy of spirit rather than the doctrinal ideas of religion. The tender style inclines more to nature's endless flow of change and the imagination that exists right under the surface of life. The tough-minded prefers objectivity and rationalism, while the tender-minded seeks the hidden unity behind all the divisions and entrenched oppositions.

As a word, tough can mean "strong and firm," "tenacious and steadfast." The tough-minded can become overly determined, hard-headed, and even hard-hearted. In excess, they can become fundamentalists, survivalists, or extremists of many kinds. Tender comes from roots meaning, "soft, delicate or young," implying weaknesses associated with being "fresh, green or new." Tender are the new shoots just trying to break through the hardened ground and enter the world. Tender-hearted are those who are "kind, affectionate and loving," and thus able to tend to those things that are young and fragile or just beginning to be. In the extreme the tender-minded can become too soft-hearted, too lenient, too forgiving and too humane for their own good.

The two sides can manifest as the hard thinkers as opposed to the deep feelers. Yet, the question is not so much which one is better as much as which qualities are most needed at this time. Like our ancestors, each of us must bear a mixture of the two attitudes; both the tough and the tender ways of being are necessary for human survival and for sustaining human cultures. Currently, we live in hard times when the tendency to be hard-minded and hard-hearted can intensify as a reaction to the pressures of great uncertainty and radical change. It becomes easier to grab hold of something that offers to simplify or rationalize everything and just hold on for dear life. There is a growing tendency to commit to a fundamentalist belief system, a fixed ideology, or a "strong man" type of leader. Soon enough, any issue becomes a trigger for everyone to simply pick a side, dig in hard, and double-down on everything. Holding hardline attitudes or fixed beliefs makes it easier to justify actions that punish or reject those who happen to see things differently. As people become increasingly afraid of what might happen, they become more willing to believe that the other side is dead wrong, ill-intentioned, and possibly evil.

Since we also live in a time when rationalism dominates over imagination, each side of any issue can rationalize its position, leaving neither side open-minded or tender enough to allow the new shoots of imagination to arise and alter the grounds of the debate. We live in reactionary times when economics, politics, or religion can become the hardline basis for increasing social disparity and widening separations of all kinds. There is an increasing disparity in the gap between the haves and the have nots and a growing imbalance between the hard-headed and tender-minded views. This leads to greater and greater gaps of understanding and intensifying conflicts as more and more issues seem to have no solution.

In order to understand the conditions we are in, we must place ourselves not in the mainstream of life but in the timeless stream of myth. As the fabric of life loosens, the veil between this world of hard facts and the otherworld of great imagination also becomes thinner and more permeable.

Just as time seems to be running out, timeless things try to slip back into human awareness. Things become both impossible and more possible at the same time. Amidst a hardening sense that it all might end at any time, new ideas and surprising designs appear if we allow room for them. Mythic stories and wisdom tales indicate how hidden threads continue to pull life in surprising and innovative ways and the world renews itself and goes on.

If we meet a myth with our lives and deepest concerns, the mythic oracles speak directly to us. Myths are oracular in the sense that each person can receive a message or an insight that relates to their life circumstances. The point has never been to "believe" in myths or to simply accept what others have said they mean. The key issue with mythic images is to let them speak to us, wherever and whenever we find ourselves seeking guidance, permission, or understanding.

RETURN OF THE WASTELAND

Mythic stories depict the universal themes and challenging dilemmas that keep recurring in life. The theme of the wasteland appears in myths and legends throughout the world because the abundance of nature can always be exploited and misused; but also because the wonder of human imagination keeps being wasted. The wasteland stands as a symbol for any time when force far exceeds the presence of love, when the narrowing of ideas and diminishing of imagination leaves both the beauty of the earth and the meaning of culture in danger of wasting away. In mythic terms, we are in a modern wasteland, where human life can easily go to waste while nature becomes more exploited and devastated all the time.

The modern wasteland includes the rise of literalism and materialism, both of which drain the world of beauty and wonder. Mass culture not only diminishes the importance of the individual soul, it also spreads across the planet, laying waste to the land and draining all the resources just to keep itself in place. The hard-hearted scourge of modern terrorism is an outgrowth of the growing wasteland, where hard dogmas override human sympathy and blind beliefs obliterate the compassion natural to the human soul. Fixed ideologies intensify the presence of the wasteland in the sense that an ideology allows a person to do and allow inhuman things while avoiding personal responsibility for their actions. In the wasteland, everyone goes a little blind and cold as fundamentalism grows and ideologies substitute for genuine vision and creative thought. The decline of culture follows as failures of thought and loss of imagination lead to hardening attitudes and dogmatic rules, which increasingly rigidify as if foreshadowing the death of the world.

Although it represents a time of devastation to both nature and culture, the wasteland also points to the fact that the two are eternally entwined and mutually involved. In mythic stories the wasteland develops when there is a profound lack of inspired and noble leadership. The old idea was that the king, queen, or ruler of society was secretly at one with the land, thus able to balance culture with nature as well as bring together the tough-minded with the tender-hearted. If a leader or group should rule with an iron fist or allow injustice to spread over the land, the subtle connections with nature and its abundance become frayed and nothing much will grow. All efforts become fruitless while all oppositions intensify until a living balance can once again be restored.

The old phrase, "the king is dead, long live the king" referenced the mythic sense that someone needed to quickly take up the crown before a gap could develop between the ruler and the land. The wasting condition would begin to develop if a rightful ruler died and no one could be found to embody the state of union required for genuine leadership. That seems to be what happened once upon a time in a town in Phrygia in old Asia Minor. At that time, which now seems a much simpler era, each area and sizeable town had a king. In the case of Phrygia, the king had died and no suitable replacement could be found. The result was an extended period of turmoil, civil unrest and ever-decreasing harvests as life seemed about to waste away. Having reached the end of their collective rope, the townspeople decided to consult an oracle in the hopes of finding a way out of their mounting troubles. The oracle announced that the period of oppressive troubles would only come to an end when a new king appeared. Fortunately, this announcement also provided a way to identify the next king. The new leader would appear as a stranger who would arrive at the gates of the town while riding on an oxcart. One day, it happened just as the oracle had predicted. A stranger appeared at the gates of the town riding, along with his wife and young son, in an oxcart. The people of the city, desperate for change and having placed their trust in the oracle, wasted no time in proclaiming the stranger to be the new king.

In an act of gratitude to the unseen forces of life, Gordius, for that was the name of the new king, thanked the gods for this fortunate turn of events. As it turned out, Gordius had also received an oracle of his own. One day a magnificent eagle landed on the pole of his oxcart and Gordius interpreted the sudden presence of this noble bird as a sign that he would one day become a king. In order to honor the gods and specifically thank Zeus, the ruler of the gods in Olympus, Gordius tied the lucky cart with an intricate knot and stationed it near the entrance to the town. The image of the ox and cart tied together came to represent the power of the occasion and the knot that tied it all together became known as the Gordian Knot.

In the strange way of this world of unfolding mysteries where one thing can be secretly tied to another, a new oracle pronounced that if any person could undo the knot made by Gordius, they would come to rule across the entire continent of Asia. Because of that oracle with its promise of great power, and as a result of the intrigue of the Gordian Knot, the town became famous the world over and was renamed Gordium.

For many years, would-be heroes came to the town in hopes of undoing the Gordian Knot, but none were successful. One day, while wintering near Gordium, Alexander the Great entered the town in order to fulfill his prophesied destiny of coming to rule over Asia and beyond. Some say that when Alexander could not find the end of the knot in order to unbind it, he simply sliced it in half with his sword, seemingly solving the great dilemma with a single heroic stroke. To this day, people refer to the Gordian Knot when a person has made a quick, decisive move or if, when faced with a dilemma, they have taken forceful action to cut through the impasse. This idea of cutting through the obstacle has been used to justify decisiveness as well as the use of heroic force in the face of any dilemma.

Yet, there exists another more nuanced and intriguing version of the tale, an alternative legend that shows Alexander in a different light. Rather than the tough-minded decisiveness that the use of a sword might signify, it is said that the great leader became compelled by a sudden insight that revealed something others had not noticed. Rather than focus narrowly only upon the knot as all others had, Alexander observed the entire situation and soon struck upon the true nature of the entanglement. Then, he simply removed the pin around which the famous knot had been tied and the ox and cart became separated from the pole.

The solution involved more of a genius insight than a heroic act, more of a tender-minded way of seeing the big picture and finding a subtle resolution. Right next to the image of heroic forcefulness can be seen the more discerning move of a genius insight that sees into and beyond issues that tie other people in knots. It may have been the destiny of old Gordius to suddenly become king of a town; it certainly was the destiny of Alexander to become one of the most famous conquerors and rulers of all time. One of the old meanings of famous was the sense of being seen standing with one's genius revealed and having become visible to others. Genius has its ways and genius can open the way for one person where others only become stymied and stuck. One of the great puzzles of human life involves the revelation of the inner genius that knows our inner destiny, yet can remain hidden until a moment of revelation occurs.

POSSIBLE AND IMPOSSIBLE

To this day, scholars still argue over the exact nature and shape of the Gordian Knot and there are many interpretations of what the old story might mean. I am interested in the difference between the two solutions that seem to contrast the hard-minded use of the sword with the more subtle or tender insight that revealed what was truly at the center of the knot and the dilemma it represents. For we live in complicated times when the entire world becomes a global village with interconnected threads of all kinds and intricate problems that affect both nature and culture. The Gordian Knot can stand as a mythological symbol for any complex problem or intricate dilemma that cannot be solved by simple force or common logic. We live in a time when either natural disasters influenced by human behavior or cultural collisions based in man's inhumanity to fellow man can bring overwhelming disaster down upon everyone. Sometimes the facts are all that matters; at other times, there are things that matter much more than the simple facts. The ability to be tough-minded remains useful; but by now, the fact that we are all in trouble in terms of both nature and culture can only be denied by those who become overly conservative and blindly reactionary. The more tender-hearted imagination that suggests we are all in this together and that there must be an underlying unity in life may be the only way to survive.

Under the reign of reason and the statistical view of the world, the value and presence of mythic imagination becomes quite limited. One of the few mythic themes widely known in modern culture is the myth of the hero. In fact, the hero's journey has often been seen as a "monomyth," a single story from which all other tales can be derived. Yet, myth is multiple in its nature and diverse in its manifestations. Only myth with its inexhaustible variations and multiple interpretations can compare to nature with its endless diversities and boundless iterations of life. Myth and nature are the two great garments of the world, with nature being the living green garment that covers the planet and myth being the multidimensional, many-colored fabric that continually weaves human culture.

The hero myth has much to offer in terms of helping people imagine life as a great adventure in which to participate. The idea of a hero's journey gives meaning to the stages of life and offers the promise that something heroic might be called out of us. As a popular myth, the hero's journey reinforces the sense of seeking greater purpose in life. Yet, the focus upon winning heroic victories and acquiring an outer boon may in fact lead people away from the natural gifts and talents they already carry within.

Popular culture now abounds with seemingly endless sequels of superheroes that keep defeating evil and saving the day in blockbuster movies. Darker versions of the forceful hero appear in increasingly violent video games. Meanwhile, the problems we face on a global basis become increasingly complex, more intricate and more puzzling and less likely to be solved by heroic attitudes.

Maybe the hero's journey has taken us far enough, and the time has come for a different mythic imagination to rise and offer multiple approaches to the many dilemmas and complicated problems. Whereas the hero's journey tends to be conceived as a courageous search in distant lands, the genius myth involves a turn within that leads to a deeper sense of self, and a return to the origins of our lives. As the inner resident of the soul, the genius gives each of us our unique way of being and perceiving the world. When allowed to manifest, it reveals our best ways of contributing to the beauty and meaning of life.

Whereas the popular sense of the hero myth tends to have a masculine shape and depends upon the use of strength and power, the genius myth can appear in any form and be based in subtle feelings as well as intricate imaginings. Where the hero tends to be called to seek for boons in the outer world of action, the genius resides within a person from the beginning and only waits to become awakened and confirmed within us. As the outer world becomes more polarized, more beset with interconnected dilemmas and deepening threats, there may be a greater need for the endless diversity of genius qualities waiting to be discovered within each of us.

INNER NOBILITY

If we accept that the issues facing the planet cannot be solved by heroics alone, it becomes wiser to seek solutions that are more diverse in nature and more inclusive by design. The old idea of genius points to innate qualities that define a person from within but also indicate how each of us might best serve the living community of the spirit. The real solution for the recurring problem of the wasteland has always depended upon the authenticity of those who seek to solve it. When the wasteland begins to spread again, you can be sure that the core of culture has once again become inauthentic.

What is most lacking in the modern world of duplications and facsimiles, of endless information and intentional misinformation, is the authenticity that makes life truly meaningful and spiritually rewarding.

The proper response to the presence of the wasteland has always been the awakening of the inner nobility in the hearts and minds of people and the stirring of authentic genius qualities within us. Authentic comes from Greek roots meaning, "original, genuine, principal," as when a person acts upon their own authority. Although old stories refer to royal rulers like kings and queens, the deeper reference is to the innate nobility of each of our souls. For each person bears from birth an inner nobility and original purpose that tries to surface and become known throughout life. When we act from that which is original and genuine in ourselves, we bring a deeper authority than any position can confer upon us. We also move from the typical plot of the hero to a wider range of mythic possibilities and a greater inclusion of all types of people.

Nature only produces originals, and when we act from our authentic selves, we bring something unique and original to the world. What each of us genuinely has to offer to the world in these times of mass media, mass culture, and massive problems is our unique and authentic self. The growing split between nature and culture can only be healed when enough of us awaken to the unique nature of our own genius selves and begin to follow where the genius paths might lead us. For, the split between nature and culture truly begins where people become divided from the true nature and noble qualities of their own inner being.

Rather than a heroic journey undertaken by a select few, the genius myth imagines that everyone by virtue of bearing some genius qualities is subject to a genuine calling in life. On the outside, it is felt as a calling; on the inside, it is felt as the awakening of one's own way of seeing and being in the world. The point of the call involves an awakening of the deep self within and the opportunity to begin to live the life the soul was aimed at all along. Following the call of spirit leads not simply to character development, but to becoming the main character in a life-long story of self-revelation. The inner eyes of genius have always been able to see surprising ways to shape paths of meaning, purpose, and healing where others see only darkness and confusion. On one level we are only frail beings trying to survive in a rapidly changing, often fearful world; on another level we are nascent geniuses trying to contribute meaning, intelligence and beauty to the world around us. The genius of our lives was there before we entered this world and it would lead us further into the world than most of us would choose on our own. Genius precedes us and would lead us and happens to know which direction we would best go in life. As such, genius is the original guide to our life's path and our life's work. Yet, the inner genius is part of the mystery and wonder of life, something that must be intuited and repeatedly sought for even though it has been with us from birth.

In the long run the point of invention and innovation is not simply progress; the point of all great imagination and innovation is the continuation of creation. For creation is not something that once happened in the distant past. Creation is the core activity of this world that makes itself over and over again. Genius is the source of all innovation and invention, but also the driving spirit of human participation in the ongoing creation of the world. The human soul with its resident genius is intended to be an agent of creation, a knowing participant in the constant re-creation of the world. The genius myth ties each of us to the ongoing story of creation and calls upon us to awaken to the precise ways that we might help heal the wounds of history and contribute to the reweaving of nature and culture.

ONE KNOT AFTER ANOTHER

The Arabic word for belief derives from a root that can mean "to tie together, to knot" or more gently, "to join together, to make an agreement." There is a subtle difference found at the roots of belief where one stem can tie a person in knots and overly restrict their innate imagination, obscuring their original way of being. The more tender-minded and open-hearted side of belief can inspire a genuine sense of being woven into this world and secretly connected to the underlying union of life.

A sacred knot has been sewn into each heart; it holds within us the elements of our authentic life and also holds a truth about the world. Each of us has come to life to learn to untie the unique knot set within us and unfold the dream that it holds. To be purposeful in life does not simply mean to be goal-oriented; rather, it means to seek to reconnect to the source and meaning of our life. The hardest thing in life may be to learn to truly trust that there is something noble and generative in ourselves. This is a greater sense of the notion of believing in our self; to truly believe in oneself means to uncover the inner core of imagination and authenticity that can also be called the genius within us. When we connect to the inner resident of the soul, we also learn how we are woven to the Soul of the World.

In another subtlety of language, unite and untie are contrasting and complementary words made from the same letters, as if to point to the idea that we must untie certain knots in the heart of the world in time to reweave a greater union between nature and a reimagined human culture.

We are each tied to the eternal web of life at a distinct place and in a particular manner. Understood in this way, the knot in life can be related to Yoga, with its ancient sense of being yoked to something greater than our little selves. To conform to what we each are at the core of our being is one of the meanings of the old idea of dharma, the inner law of each person. Dharma means the natural law woven within each soul, that which gives each person an inner authenticity as well as natural virtues and noble qualities. Our inner dharma, or way of being, also aims us at particular ways of being in service to the world around us and adding something unique to the greater good of humankind.

There will always be the facts of life to contend with, and there are times when the facts can become overwhelming. Yet, there is a poem at the heart of things and a mythic story in the heart of each of us. At certain times it is the poetry of life and the mythic imagination of the soul that become necessary in order to heal the wounds inflicted by an excess of reason or an overuse of force. When we unfold the story wound within our souls and untie the knots within us, we add presence to the world and contribute to the spirit of life in a specific and authentic way. As we transform ourselves from within, we also help in some way to transform the world. Surprisingly, we add to the solutions of worldwide problems by solving the mystery and puzzle of our own lives.

In mythic terms, the earth is a place of mystery and wonder where life always hangs by a thread and all the events of history are loosely stitched upon the endless loom of eternity. Secretly, we are each tied to the divine. It used to be better known that humans were the "makeweights" in the scales between time and eternity. Human awareness was thought to be the extra element in creation, able at times to help tip the scales toward renewal.

At a time when human society faces impossible tasks in all areas of culture as well as most aspects of nature, we may be able to redeem genius as an inherent aspect of soulfulness that connects us both to great nature and to the true nature of our own lives. In the great drama of life, the awakened human soul becomes the extra quantity and uniquely living quality needed to help tip the balance of the world toward ongoing creation.

Considering genius in this older, wiser sense shifts the question from whether a particular person might test out to be a genius, to how each person might find their innate genius. The sense that each person, regardless of place of origin or social background, has inner genius and something significant to contribute to the world has practical benefits at both the individual and cultural levels.

In a time of global problems and impossible tasks, the deepest resources of humanity must be tapped. I am suggesting that genius, in its original sense as the spirit that brought each of us to life, may also be the natural resource that allows us to generate and protect new forms of life and new ways of being together. I am suggesting that there may be no better time to embrace the more tender-minded view that imagines that each of us has some innate value and inner genius that might bring something new and necessary into the world.

What we need to do in these times of alternating collapse and discovery is awaken as many inner geniuses as possible in order to meet the multiple threats and complex challenges we face. Rather than the need to heroically save the whole world, the real work of humanity at this time may be to awaken the unique spark and inner resiliency of genius within each person.

CHAPTER 5

IN DIRE STRAITS

We are all inventors, each sailing out on a voyage of discovery,
guided each by a private chart, of which there is no duplicate.
The world is all gates, all opportunities. – Ralph Waldo Emerson

We live in a time when all the possible conflicts and oppositions come crashing all around us. The world becomes more chaotic and threatening as antagonisms of all kinds intensify and harden into stone. There are ever more radical "clashes of civilization" that seem to threaten the entire course of human events. We live in a time of seemingly impossible problems and we seem to be running out of time. The size and complexity of issues we face as a global community are so extensive and intractable as to be mythic in scope.

Yet, we tend to turn away from myth as being too irrational or unreal to be helpful. However, to be without myth means to lack a containing story in which to place the seemingly random and often disturbing events of daily life. To be without cohering narratives means to be even more exposed to the raw energies and often harsh polarities of this world. From a mythic viewpoint, the present moment, which is so burdened with conflicts and oppositions, can be a crossroads in time that opens to surprising solutions that defy logic and rationality. Myth can make the most sense when all else seems to make no sense. As the poet W.B. Yeats once put it, "Imagination has some way of lighting on the truth that reason has not."

When things become polarized and stuck, it is helpful to know something about mythic imagination, for myths turn dilemmas into adventures and seeming dead ends into thresholds of change. Myth offers a third place to stand or a third way to see when we find ourselves caught between opposing ideas and hardening ideologies. The origin of "being between a rock and a hard place" might be found in the old story of Jason and the Argonauts, who set sail once upon a time determined to recover the famous golden fleece that alone could restore justice, balance and peace to their troubled homeland. The crew of would-be heroes found themselves facing a great dilemma in the form of clashing rocks that formed the dangerous gateway to the Black Sea.

The Symplegades were a pair of enormous stones that appeared as a deadly obstacle to whoever might wish to sail between them. Symplegades means "to strike together," and the great stones rolled perpetually against each other while the sea roiled and boiled up around them. If a ship tried to sail straight between the clashing rocks, it would quickly be crushed and smashed to bits. For Jason and his crew there would be no real adventure and no possibility of returning balance to the land and justice to the realm if they could not find a way between the crushing sides of the dilemma before them. Given the conflicts and polarization throughout the world at this time we may be facing similar dilemmas where brute strength, heroic force and straightforward solutions cannot win the day. Something wiser and more subtle than either raw power or strict logic is required, or we may suffer soul-crushing defeats with regard to both nature and culture.

The story of Jason and the Argonauts seeking the mythical golden fleece is a timeless tale that rides over the oceans of time as an archetypal shape that may have influenced the Odyssey of Ulysses as well as Arthur's quest for the Holy Grail. Originally a nautical reference, argonaut came to mean anyone on a quest, so that we wind up with the astronauts and cosmonauts sailing through the cosmic sea of stars. Ironically, the flood of miners searching for veins of actual gold in California's famous gold rush were also nicknamed the Argonauts. Fact and myth frequently become entangled, and in the modern age mythic images often become literalized. The original golden fleece represents the mythical "treasure hard to obtain," something once known but now lost, a golden symbol that might return some balance to the world and righteousness to the realm of humankind. It can appear to us as a paradise lost, a missing sacred code, or a horde of treasure; but humanity has felt from the beginning that something important is missing and it must be sought under the earth, in a distant land or an otherworld.

In this ancient Greek story, it was a golden fleece that represented the qualities of genuine authority and social justice that were missing in the land. Young Jason plays the role of the eternal seeker searching for justice, meaning, and beauty. He had gathered a kind of "dream team" of the greatest heroes of the area and they had set sail on the winds of high ideals in search of the lost treasure. Of course, the destination can only be a part of any great story, as obstacles and dilemmas encountered along the way become the thresholds through which the seekers can reveal what they are truly made of. The true nature of the treasure being sought must be found in some measure in those who are seeking it. What we most desire to find in the outside world secretly exists within us in some form.

Once underway on the paths to self-awakening and self-discovery, there are bound to be both those who can help us find the way as well as those who must be helped along the way. The great tests in life can reveal the gifts and wisdom hidden in the soul, but they are also tests of character. That is to say, the tests we face are intended to build enough character to be able to carry our own gifts and use any knowledge we may find wisely.

A BLIND SEER

After surviving some initial challenges, the Argonauts caught a favorable wind and landed at the kingdom of Thrace, which sat between the waters of the Aegean Sea and the Black Sea. The ruler of the land was a blind king named Phineus. The notion of a king who cannot see goes against all reason, as kings were supposed to be without blemish. In this case, Phineus was a seer; he was blind in one sense, but could see what others could not discern. Unfortunately, those who have the gift of "second sight" often have trouble seeing how to use their abilities and how to keep things in balance. The king had been blinded by the gods and left in darkness as a punishment for overusing his genius gift of seeing into the future.

The king had once been a renowned prophet; but now was cursed with blindness and troubled with even more consuming problems. The gods had also sent the Harpies to harass him whenever he tried to eat. As soon he would reach for food, the raucous birds with the heads of old women and razor-sharp claws would swoop down with the speed of the West Wind and snatch the food from his hands. After having their fill, they would defecate on all the leftovers. So foul was the odor they left on the food that no normal person would go near it. But poor Phineus was also cursed with an insatiable appetite and the putrid morsels left behind were just enough for him to survive the daily torments of his life.

As they used to say, everyone has their cross to bear and for many, being gifted can seem a double-cross as well. The first problem is that we cannot find what our native gifts might be. The next problem comes when having found our genius, we must learn to live with it. The bigger the gift, the bigger the wound, they used to say when considering the old kings like Midas, who also could not eat because everything he touched turned to gold. Heavy is the head that wears the crown, and often an empty feeling comes with it as well.

In true form, the Argonauts took pity on the old seer and, after a feast was prepared, they waited for the arrival of the tormenting birds. When the Harpies swooped down to feed upon the royal food, the crew attacked them, eventually driving them off to a faraway land where they would never bother the old king again. At the feast of great relief that followed, everyone enjoyed their food more than ever and none more than the king, who ate each bite joyfully. As a reward, the old seer used his gift of prophecy to counsel the Argonauts regarding the dangers they would face in the course of their journey.

After a short stay, the crew set sail and just as the old seer predicted, they soon reached the narrow and winding strait guarded by the clashing of the Symplegades. The massive stones crashed against each other with such force that even a vessel made of iron would be crushed between them. But there was an even greater problem: no discernible pattern to the crashing and clashing could be seen. The irregular movements of the colliding stones made it impossible to devise a logical plan or reason out a passage to safety. Those who tried to apply reason or use force would certainly be crushed by the random nature of the crashing stones.

There might be no further tale to tell, except the old seer had counseled the crew about one thing that could trigger the clashing of the rocks. If something living tried to pass between them, they would immediately and harshly respond. In return for their service to him, the king had given them a gift to use in dealing with the dilemma. It seemed that something had to be offered as a sacrifice to the guardians at the watery gate in order for them to pass through the dangerous threshold. The parting gift was a little bird, a dove to be specific.

Following the instruction from the king, Jason released the dove to fly between the towering rocks. As the stones quickly crashed together, the bird shot forward, only having its tail nipped in the resounding collision. While the great rocks recoiled, the Argonauts, combining all their efforts together, bent their oars like bows and shot through the gap. The seas churned and the waves roiled, but the ship only suffered the loss of the stern ornaments as it pulled free and surged into the open sea upon a gigantic wave.

The king had wisely advised them to send the dove ahead, but to follow the bird into the gap only if it survived the dilemma. Should the dove perish before them, they should turn back and live to strive another day. Many more obstacles and challenges awaited the Argonauts in their pursuit of justice and the recovery of the lost golden fleece. However, the momentous moment of passing through the gates of destruction offers insights for whoever might consider the huge dilemmas and crushing oppositions currently facing the modern world.

GENIUS PATHS VERSUS THE HERO'S JOURNEY

Collectively, we have reached the point where the storms of climate change and the intense clashes of culture have us between the rocks and a hard place. In the midst of many crushing dilemmas, being overly rational, simply willful, or falsely heroic can only make matters worse. Finding ways through the many opposing forces requires some wisdom, some sacrifices, and a willingness to act in surprising and unexpected ways.

Three things come together in the moment of passing through the clashing rocks that represent all the crushing dilemmas of life that polarize entire countries and paralyze even the strongest individual. There needs to be some guidance and good counsel from an unusual source. In a true dilemma, the usual methods and typical ideas contribute to the stalemate, rather than help shape a solution. Those who simply hold positions of power and any who represent either opposing force can rarely provide the insights and vision needed to actually move beyond the impasse. Not only that, but those who have never fallen, misused authority or mishandled power may not understand how to hold the tension long enough to perceive a way through the narrow straits.

It is no accident that the seer who provided the counsel that saved the ship and all the crew was a ruler who had fallen upon hard times himself. Be careful of those who have not fallen, because they will fall when times become hard and seas become heavy. Be careful of those who claim they have not fallen, as many current political and religious leaders tend to do. The old king represents several kinds of power being held in the same hands. As king or ruler, he has the authority and power of position; as a seer, he has found his inner genius and natural power in life. But to be a wise counselor he must learn the proper uses of both kinds of power and the limits of his appetites for the things of this world.

No one knows what is enough until they know what is too much. Until a person has failed significantly or missed the boat, they will not know how to hold the tension until the right moment or how to test the waters before pushing on. Timing can be everything and wisdom requires the patience to wait as well as the courage to leap when the time becomes right. Not only that, but some sacrifice is required if a transformation would be achieved. How often have great projects and people's lives been dashed to bits when a small sacrifice might have eased the way? We live in a time of intensifying polarities and multiplying dilemmas and need to learn how to sacrifice again. Surviving a clash of cultures, religions, or ideologies requires that something becomes consciously sacrificed or else many become unconsciously and unnecessarily sacrificed. The little bird that triggers the great clash of hardened attitudes is a dove, often considered a bird of peace and love. In a true dilemma, both sides become hawkish and each becomes ready to destroy the other. Taking a side in a dilemma can feel righteous as well as powerful and even those who take the side of peace can become quite hawkish about it.

In order for things to truly change, the tension of the opposites must intensify and be tolerated long enough for a third energy to appear. A bird of good omen or some other sign must emerge in the midst of all the tension and opposition in order to reveal the hidden patterns and motivations of the clashing forces. Then, in the moment of revelation everything must be risked at once and everyone must somehow pull together or else the dilemma will return and likely do so at an even deeper level.

THE KAIROS MOMENT

Change, which is the only constant thing in this world, happens in the flash of a moment. People can prepare for a great change and make careful plans; yet in order to make the change, all preparations and expectations must be released in favor of a flash of vision and inspiration. Of course, ancient people had a name for that moment when time stands still, when the usual forces are suspended and almost anything can happen. In Sanskrit, the opportune moment was called ksana, or "the flash in time, the inspired instant." In Greek the moment that becomes momentous was termed kairos. The kairos moment opens before us and we must be as swift as a bird or else miss out on the opportunity to slip past the guardians and ride through the gates of time. Kairos names the moment of sweeping change that arrives "just in the nick of time" and turns everything around. The opportune moment is a crack in time, a breach in the march of time in which the eternal enters and redeems us from certain doom.

The ancient Greeks had two primary words for time: kronos and kairos.

Kronos referred to sequential time, the "chronological" order of time marching on; the arrow of linear time always moving forward. Thus, time waits for no one. Kronos is quantifiable and measurable time; the hourglass emptying out, the end of time coming ever closer and closer. Kairos referred to a different order of time altogether, a timeless stretch that cannot be scheduled ahead of time; an alteration of time in which impossible things become momentarily possible. Whereas kronos stands for quantitative time, kairos time is qualitative in nature. Under the unforgiving rule of kronos we have to be on time, do our time and pay our dues. When we are under the influence of kairos, time stops and opens before us. There is a break in time as something timeless and beyond time enters and alters the world around us. The kairos moment arrives when it will, when the time is just right, when things become more possible and life becomes ripe for change. Kairos is the mythic moment that is end and beginning at once, when the hard pulse of time becomes "once upon a time" and past, present, and future secretly converse with each other.

In many ways we have entered a kairos moment, a time beset with both danger and opportunity as the world tries to change amidst the clashing of entrenched ideas and fixed beliefs and the availability of crushing weapons of all kinds. There is an increasing tendency for issues to polarize and for people to see only one side of each issue. Under the rule of reason and the rise of ideologies of all kinds people simply pick one side and reject the other as being wrong-headed, unreasonable or even insane. As the dependence upon reason has grown, a loss of imagination has developed as well as the deeper understandings traditionally provided by the mythic imagination needed to make sense of a volatile world.

The single eye of reason can become blind to greater visions and deeper insights that might shift pieces in a stalemate or loosen polarized positions and allow an unexpected third way to open. The old idea of the kairos moment brought more than the power of reason to bear on the issue at hand as the ancient world included more than one way of thinking. The current moment in which oppositions throughout the world intensify and so many elements of culture become paralyzed may be the right moment for people to turn to mythic imagination again. Creative imagination is the only outcome of conflict that can satisfy the soul, and myths can provide universal examples of creative solutions.

A UNIVERSE DIVIDED

We live in a universe shaped by dynamic pairs of opposites that contrast and conspire, that oppose each other and at times unite. A single word can tell a whole story and universe tells a lot with two little syllables. Uni stands for the "one," the whole and entire thing rolled up into a unifying oneness. Verse or versus means the opposite, literally "to turn against" and "be opposed." The universe is a great oneness experienced as a play of dynamic opposites like light and dark, night and day, positive and negative, nature and culture, left and right, masculine and feminine, yang and yin. A unity underlies all the oppositions; yet the opposites must first be faced and be embraced in order for the unifying moment to appear.

So, the ancient Greeks, amongst others, developed two primary ways of thinking and gathering knowledge about the world. They called them logos and mythos with both words having the sense of "an accounting," as in "describing" or "giving an account of what has happened." Both logos and mythos can be said to be true, with each presenting a truth of a different order. Like night and day, each offers a different level of seeing and understanding both the universe and our place within it. In the ancient world those who could think in both logical and mythological terms were considered wise. Being double-minded in this way, they could see things on more than one level and perceive ways to proceed where others became caught on one side of a dilemma or the other.

In the modern world, logos translates to being logical and using reason to examine everything empirically and scientifically. Logos seeks to find objective truths, the kind of definitive explanations that can be proven with the use of observable facts and controlled experiments.

Mythos, on the other hand, approaches the world through less direct, more imaginative and intuitive means. The accounts of mythos are more narrative, tending towards subjective aspects of life such as individual feelings and personal experiences. A narrative involves an "accounting and recounting" of what happens; not just the facts, but also the feelings. A narrative method also involves "relating to" others who are involved in the sense of "feeling connected to" or "sympathetic to" others.

The logical report may offer the facts and nothing but the facts, but a genuine narrative will have more subjective qualities and feelings that create a relationship between the teller and the listener. Logos tends to divide and analyze; it dissects and separates objects in order to distinguish one thing from another. Mythos seeks to uncover hidden connections between things and underlying patterns that shape the world from within. Logos seeks out that which is demonstrable and objective, while mythos searches for that which is deeply subjective and even mysterious. Each offers a truth of a different order and quite naturally, we have inherited a treasury of both logical ideas and mythical narratives.

Both ways of thinking help us account for the things we encounter; yet in the modern world, where time and money tend to dominate, accounting tends to refer to bank accounts and financial reporting. The modern world finds it easy to account for the methods of logos, much more difficult to account for the presence and persistence of mythos.

MYTHO-LOGICAL

The term mytho-logical suggests that myth has its own logic, just as logic has its own story. The story of logic tends to take the form of history, whereas myth would take us on the paths of mystery. The light of logos would make everything clear and accounted for, whereas the paths of mythos lead towards the unseen, the unknown, and the unbelievable. Logos tends to be forward-looking, even future oriented. Mythos would remind us that the past is always with us, being hidden within us. Mythos connects, not to the historical past, but to ancient images and primordial events that keep recurring. Logos connects to linear time and measurable space, while mythos favors timelessness and eternal presences. Logos might argue that whatever has a beginning must come to an end; the narrative intelligence of myth suggests that when a story comes to an end, it starts all over again. Where logic arrives at seemingly inevitable conclusions, myth finds hidden threads and multiple ways to spin the story of the world ever onward.

If the power of logos is reason, the power of myth is imagination as myths tends to employ images and symbols, using creative imagination to connect more deeply to life. Myth is about underlying, archetypal patterns that affect life from within; thus it involves the inner lives of people and the living mysteries of the soul. The power of myth lies in the presence of deep imagination that can reconnect the past with the present moment and the depths of the individual soul with the roots of the soul of the world.

Humans are both mythical and logical by nature, therefore potentially double-minded rather than single-eyed. It is in our nature to engage in logical thinking and apply reason in the pursuit of knowledge. It is also in our nature to mythologize and use narrative forms both to communicate and to seek deeper ways to understand events experienced in the objective world. Logos can deliver logical and factual, even provable, knowledge of the world. However, logos cannot assist much when it comes to issues of human grief or love, or the need to find some unifying meaning that can bring diverse people together. Humans have always gathered around fires and told stories in order to bear the darkness of the world and the immensity of its forces, and survive its tensions and inevitable dilemmas.

The truths of logos should correspond with some accuracy to external reality, while the images of mythos should reveal the inner truths of life. One method seeks knowledge in the realm of matter, the other seeks understanding in what matters most to us.

Human genius can take the form of clear reason and fine logic, using surpassing intellect as it does in the work of philosophers, scientists, and inventors. In the modern world genius has become identified with high levels of intellect and the ability to reason accurately and be logical. Yet, genius begins as an element of myth before it ever becomes limited as a measure of reason or level of intellect. Genius is a mythical entity that resides in the depths of the human soul where it sustains the dream of our lives and the very reasons for which we live. The original meaning of the word genius may be "that which is born." For, that which is born has its genius, an inner light of spirit that gives it genuine presence and a distinct way of being. There is a myth at the heart of things and some element of genius in the heart of each person born.

When the world is more balanced than unbalanced mythos and logos can be seen to work together and be less at odds and more complementary to each other. The problem now is that logical thinking and rationalism have assumed such prominence that many no longer realize that another, equally valuable approach to understanding exists. With the rise of reason and the increasing tendency to "believe" in positivistic science, there has been a corresponding loss in the importance of mythic imagination and traditional ways to embrace the deeper values of human life. The loss of an understanding of the role and value of mythic imagination leads to the rise of both literalism and extreme forms of fundamentalism.

The problem is that the subject-object split keeps growing greater and people no longer have the unifying stories that might bring them back together. The subject-object split can make logical sense in the fields of science, yet it can cause dissociation when it comes to the realm of culture and society. It is one thing to develop educational methods to train young people in the practical sciences for the sake of competing in the modern, technological world. It is quite another thing to offer true educational practices that help people make sense of their own lives in a rapidly changing world that requires greater resiliency and more than one way to imagine the future.

In many ways, people now long for the healing presence of myth without even knowing it. When the troubles get deep enough, when the problems become greater than us, when the weight of the world is on our shoulders, mythos can offer more imaginative ways to proceed than the narrow paths of logic and reason. Myth has its own logic and it makes most sense when the underlying sense of the world is being sought and when the enduring values and transcendent meanings of human life must be found again. The deepest truths of life tend to be unifying and healing elements that reconnect us to the very sources of being. Such deep and abiding truths can never be proven through scientific methods, but must be grasped intuitively and found through lived experience.

REIMAGINING THE WORLD AROUND US

Under the rule of reason and the tyranny of facts, people often say with seeming certainty, "the fact of the matter is" one way or another. They forget that the facts can be used to tell different stories, even opposing truths. The fact is that the facts can never tell the whole story; it is the job of myth and narrative intelligence to make meaning of all the facts of life. Logos is essential for human survival and for sustaining social systems; yet it is only logical that logos be found to have limitations. True reasoning must be able to admit the limits of reason. One mistake would be to undervalue the clarity of logos; another would be to dismiss mythos for being irrational. By now, the exaggerated reliance on seeming objectivity and supposed reason tends to disorient people with regards to the importance of having a genuine inner life of the soul.

When logos came to the end of a line of reasoning, people used to instinctively turn to mythos to pick up the thread and continue the story. At critical moments in the life of individuals and of societies, it is not necessarily the facts that are needed as much as a profound narrative that makes sense of life's conflicts and misunderstandings. When all seems to be falling apart and becoming less rational and more chaotic, it is usually a different story that is needed to make things whole again.

Mythic imagination can break the spell of time and open us to a level of life that remains timeless. Myth is not about what happened in past times; myth is about what happens to people all of the time. In the realm of myth, Icarus is always flying too high, going too close to the radiance of the sun and falling from the sky. Icarus does not age but remains eternally young, as he symbolizes anyone who rises too quickly to the heights only to fall just as suddenly back to earth. In the same way, young stars of the stage and screen rise quickly on the wings of fame only to burn up or burn out in the bright lights of worldwide celebrity. They come crashing down to the ground of reality and fall into depression or fall apart through addictions.

The problem is not simply that people should not soar when the opportunity presents itself; rather, the trouble comes when people fly higher than they can manage psychologically. In the modern world it is easy to become over-exposed either to the raw rays of the sun or to the hungry attention of too many people. Icarus soared on wings manufactured from wax and feathers that were never intended for great heights. The presence of the "Icarus factor" can now be seen in the endless number of devices that promise to solve our problems and allow us to fly faster and higher. It becomes easier to be ungrounded in our lives while being superficially interconnected all the time.

Despite all the time-saving devices and supposedly liberating technologies, people still struggle just to make it through another day. Just as old Sisyphus worked hard each day, pushing stones up a hill only to find them at the bottom again the next morning, so too people in modern culture work harder and harder just to keep up. Sisyphus-like, we become more burdened and busier all the time despite and because of all the work-saving, time-saving technological devices that, after all, operate on the basis of a little stone hidden inside them.

At the same time, an "Achilles' heel" keeps being discovered in religious leaders and politicians who claim to work for the benefit of others or swear that they did not take that bribe or sleep with that person. Gifted and celebrated athletes, who began with ideals of honest competition and fair play, are caught cheating or using drugs just to win one more contest. Everyone has an Achilles heel, a fatal flaw that works against the dream of life we each carry in our soul. Like King Midas, those obsessed with wealth keep choosing gold and fortune over love and care. Old Oedipus, who became blind and lost, can now be seen wandering blindly about in the shape of older folks who somehow lose their memory, fail to recognize their own families, and just walk off in some parking lot or back road.

Myths are always with us; they depict those things that are archetypal and enduring, the patterns that keep happening throughout the passage of time. And all the myths are happening at the same time because the domain of myth involves those things that are both timeless and timely. When we place our immediate conflicts in the territory of an archetypal story, we can better see the nature of our problems and find solutions that bring creative imagination to bear upon the realm of hard facts and hardening dilemmas.

The genius within us knows the story we came to live out and live through. If a person can decipher some aspects of their genius nature, they can find ways to express and live more fully the self-defining inner pattern. When we follow our inner thread of mythos we can take up the same tasks day after day; but unlike old Sisyphus, we can relish the effort and contribute something to the ongoing creation of the world. If we learn to fly on the wings of our own spirit we can soar to the heights and still return to the ground of our being. If we find the inner gold of our genius, which is the golden fleece we truly long for, we can find contentment where others can never get enough of what they don't really need.

We may be able to think about anything we wish; but we can only meet a story with our life and when we do that we can see life with a broader vision and a greater scope of imagination. When Jason and the crew find themselves faced with the clashing rocks of life, they do not act in the ways that people expect heroes to act. Nor do they act as scientists developing logical experiments. The method for passing through the impossible conflict turns out to depend more upon inspiration at the right moment than the forceful methods of heroics. Whoever can accept the tension of a given dilemma and then act with the vision and spontaneity of genius will find themselves to be resilient where others become paralyzed and trapped between one thing and another.

NOT TO BE BELIEVED

Myth has its own effectiveness, and it can be especially useful when all else fails and everything seems about to fall apart, again. Myths are forever things that offer endless meanings to those willing to open their hearts and minds to the living mystery of life. A myth can be "debunked" and be proven to be factually false; yet myths are not intended to be believed in, but to be learned from. For the ancients, myth meant a true story, a real story that unveils something psychologically true and essentially meaningful about this world and human life.

Myths are not aimed at clear objectivity, but at deep subjectivity. By their nature, myths are multiple and open to many interpretations. And there are usually different versions of the same story. Mythologically speaking, there can be no 'true version' of a story. The word version carries meanings of "a turning, a translation," so that a myth turns one way or another depending on the translator. We can only meet a myth with our own story; for myths speak to that which is most deeply subjective in each person. Since each person must meet a metaphor on their own terms, myths speak to each person individually. As symbolic vehicles myths speak differently to each person, allowing each to find meaning in terms of their own life experience.

When Ulysses fashions the famous Trojan Horse to finally end the ten-year siege of Troy, we don't have to be of Greek heritage to get the notion that a great problem must often be solved from the inside out. At the same time, the phrase "beware of Greeks bearing gifts" is not so much a critique of the Greek character as a psychological insight and warning that all kinds of people can have ulterior motives. Myths are not intended to be straightforward messages to be opened as much as they are territories that we can visit again and again to gain a deeper view of the world and a better understanding of our place within it. Myths are vehicles of wisdom and genuine stories are pregnant with meaning. Yet, we might have to brood upon a mythic scene in order for the inner sense to be revealed to us. Myths offer archetypal images that can open before us to reveal deeper truths and psychological understandings of the human condition.

Myths are not remembered for centuries because people once "believed" in them. Rather, myths persist and remain pertinent because they help us remember important truths about life on earth. Myths offer metaphors that help us reflect on the great drama of life and gain insights into the dynamic shifts and changes in our own lives. Through contact with real stories, we reconnect to the Unseen realm behind common reality, we re-locate the subtle, symbolic ground hidden in our own lives. For, we are mythic by nature of being human and we are closer to great Nature when in touch with the mythic nature within us. Humans can't help but be mythic and must have mythic narratives through which to view and grasp the mysteries and wonders of the world.

STRAIT IS THE WAY

Many important buildings and public structures have distinct thresholds with potent looking guardians flanking the entrance. Paired lions stand at the gates of some Buddhist shrines, sphinxes at the entrance of temples and museums, and griffins over the doors of old Christian churches. One message from the animal spirits and mythic figures poised at the gates is that the entrance is not open to just anyone. There is even the suggestion that something must be sacrificed in order to pass through. Even at the end when a soul seeks to return to paradise, it encounters a pair of angels with flaming swords guarding the Tree of Life that stands at the center of the eternal garden.

Life is full of thresholds and something as common as passing through a doorway can change our lives forever. We enter a strange place and everything can change or leave a place that has become too familiar and life opens before us again. One side of the threshold becomes the past being left behind and the other becomes the future unfolding. Any passage through the gates of time can symbolically involve a thorough change of state. There is a metaphysical casting off of whatever might hold us back from transforming our lives. Much as a snake sheds its skin to continue to live, we must release that which holds us back from entering a kairos moment in which the tension of life resolves at a new level and we are as if born anew and full of life's endless potentials again.

Each pair of symbolic figures serves as a reminder that life can change at any moment and at each threshold we encounter. Each set of figures also warns that the clashing jambs of the living door can close and that strait is the way that leads to meaningful change. It is important to note that strait has often been confused with "straight," as if the point is to "go straight," to be "direct and honest" or be "uncompromising and on the straight and narrow." However, the true dilemmas of life are not solved by being "straight-laced" and upstanding in the sense of being correct and conventional. The close path that passes between clashing rocks is a precarious strait in the sense of a "narrow passage of water;" more a "dire strait" than a straightforward approach to complex issues.

When it comes to genuine dilemmas that engage the spirit and the soul, the simple moral strictures cannot apply in a meaningful way. The opposites that we encounter at the doors of change are intended to bring forth our deep resources of both vitality and genuine imagination. Awakening happens when all the logical approaches, moral admonitions and belief systems have failed or become stuck. An excess of self-restriction is usually part of the problem and fixed beliefs cannot provide a solution. What must be shed in order to pass are the one-eyed views of the ego and the habitual attitudes that keep a person more narrow and unimaginative than they are intended to be.

The point cannot be that "straight is the way," as in a path direct and proper; but strait as in a narrow crossing place that divides past from future, where the old self must be shed for the greater self within us to be discovered and released. The kairos moment in which transformation occurs happens in an altered state where time seems to slow down even if it is all over in a flash. Such moments not only change us forever, they also live timelessly within us in the same way that the surprising crossing made by Jason and the Argonauts continues to live through the ages.

TAKING MYTHIC STEPS

The point is to allow the immediate powers of myth and imagination to give us a poetic grasp of our own lives and of the events of the world. Without such a mythic sense the world becomes a random place and we become stuck in our fears and paralyzed by conflicts and uncertainties. The point is not so much the making of a "new myth" as much as seeing into old stories in new ways. We are fully alive when open to and in harmony with the eternal symbols; wisdom involves a return to them; healing requires that we enter their enduring waters.

Mythos involves an immersion in the 'living waters' of imagination in order to release the meanings in each life. Myth is not so much the story of when the waters parted and the Israelites were liberated from their captivity in Egypt. Living myth is about the experience of the waters parting again in the here and now. As a critical moment opens before us the spirit of life and genius of the soul speaks to us and through us. What was about to crush us suddenly parts before us and we shoot forward with the sudden vitality of life, fueled by the living imagination needed to survive.

Hearing a story awakens the mythic story living in each of us. It places us in a "mythic condition" that reconnects us to the core imagination and living story at the center of our soul. Being touched by myth carries us to the center where the world is always ending and always beginning again. From there, meaningful changes and transformations can be precipitated in our lives, just as happens to the characters in stories and myths.

Myths are dynamic, archetypal and therefore timeless narratives, being cut from primordial cloth they can be refashioned and altered to suit the times. In that sense, we can consider that we are in a similar mythic condition as the Argonauts who realized that something essential to life had been lost. Whether imagined as a holy grail that removes the wasteland, the water of life that revives the soul or the golden fleece that restores justice and balance between nature and human culture, something quintessential to life has gone missing again.

The tragedies and calamities of life have left us in the lurch and increasingly in the grip of worldwide dilemmas. The remedy for the terrors of history involves an engagement of deep imagination found outside the restrictions of time. In stepping outside historical time we become available to the elemental vitality and deeper meanings sewn within our lives. Thus, we take mythic steps to change historical conditions, working the ground of imagination to open things to the timeless and touch the eternal again.

The logic of myth is primordial and pre-systematic; in forsaking mythic imagination for an excess of reason we have lost things that are our primordial inheritance and that must be found again if we are to survive the time of impossible tasks. Mythic imagination is necessary for re-imagining, re-storying, and thus re-storing the world as a place of wonder, beauty, and truth. When the troubles get deep enough, when the problems become greater than us, when the weight of the world is on our shoulders, mythic imagination can offer more ways to proceed than the more narrow paths of logic and reason. In the heart's way of knowing and thinking, images and ideas go together. For, there is thought in the heart that is connected to the deepest power of humanity: the power of imagination. When we live whole-heartedly we become able to unite logos with mythos and see the world for the wonder that it offers us moment to moment.

CHAPTER 6

THE ANGEL OF CONCEPTION

I saw the angel in the marble and carved until I set him free.

- Michelangelo

The great artist Michelangelo not only sought to free the angel hidden in the stone, but his name means the "angel of god." It is as though the artist liberated the angel within himself as he worked to free the spirit in his art. Describing his creative process, he elaborated: "In every block of marble I see a statue as plain as though it stood before me. I have only to hew away the rough walls that imprison the lovely apparition to reveal it to other eyes as mine see it." Michelangelo was a genius of his time and was also credited with saying that, "the greatest danger for most of us is not that our aim is too high and we miss it, but that it is too low and we reach it."

The genius myth says that each person must bring some talent or vision to the world; what is rare is the courage to follow one's vision or talent all the way to where it would lead. The danger of setting our sights too low becomes greater as the modern world surrenders to the spells of materialism and collectivism. The loss of vertical imagination can leave everyone blind to the angel in the stone and in the soul. Thomas Edison is now considered one of the greatest inventors of all time. His inventions, including the phonograph and the motion picture camera, have influenced life around the world. He, too, was a genius of his time; however, it was a time when the focus of invention had shifted from releasing the angel from the forms of nature to harnessing the forces of nature in service of the newly developed power of the "production line."

Edison may be most famous for inventing a long-lasting version of the electric lightbulb which subsequently became the common symbol for the sudden light of inspiration. Thus, the imagination of an angelic presence waiting to be discovered shifts to the mechanism of a light being switched on and human inspiration becomes diminished to something that can be reached through effort alone. Edison became possessed with ideas of mass production and also became famous for claiming that "Genius is one percent inspiration, ninety-nine percent perspiration."

To be modern can mean to have the lights on for twenty-four hours a day, yet still be in the dark when it comes to grasping the value, the purpose, and the meaning of inspiration in this world. The substitution of invention for creation—of perspiration for divine inspiration—means to become more distant from both nature and the divine. To perspire simply means "to blow or breathe constantly;" whereas inspire means "to breathe life into," as in old stories where a creator breathes life precisely into each creature born to this world. Inspiration brings the breath of spirit into this world just as it brings the touch of genius out of a person. Rather than a production line that constantly pushes out replicas of one thing or another, the surprise of inspiration reminds us that the source of all creation and invention can be traced back to the breath of spirit that continues to animate the world.

Regardless of the dominance of production over creation in modern culture and despite the outpouring of data and statistical information flooding the world day in and day out, the majority of modern people still believe in things like angels and little birds that seem to speak at just the moment when encouragement or guidance is needed. Like the endless production lines of manufacturing, polling must now go on twenty-four hours a day in order to gather data on every possible subject matter—even things that people imagine and believe yet cannot prove exist.

As it turns out, even a century or more after mass production began, most modern people still believe in angels. More than three-quarters of Americans believe in some kind of angelic presence in the world. We may now live primarily by the sweat of our brows, driven by technologies rather than drawn on by unseen presences, yet the presence of unseen messengers persists. Angel essentially means "messenger," or "one who announces," and the ancients imagined each person's innate genius to be a guardian spirit that guided and protected them and, at crucial moments in life, might inspire them. The role of a guardian spirit that protects and guides the soul appears throughout the world and forms a parallel to the idea of a genius companion present in the soul.

Whether we term it a guardian angel or a "little bird that told me," the messengers or guides tend to move with the subtlety of wings. An idea or an image suddenly appears before us; it arises seemingly from nowhere yet provides a sense of connection to another realm and a hint of how to proceed in life. Something in humankind refuses to give up the instinctive connection to things divine and the possibility of messages and guidance from unseen sources. The modern world, with its vast separation between subject and object, keeps losing the intuitive sense of in-between presences that secretly keep everything connected.

The ancient world allowed that intermediaries were always nearby. By insisting on objectivity, we have lost the delicacy of symbols and the deep subjectivity that can bridge our inner natures with the great soul of nature. Like other mythical presences, the issue of angels and spirits is not simply a matter of belief, but more a matter of imagination. If we leave room for the angel, the world itself has more room in it. It has more enlivened space and less dead air and emptiness between things. Allowing the intermediaries to be present to us helps creates more presence in the world around us.

An old English word for an angel was aerendgast, literally "an errand-spirit." Thus, angels appear as intermediaries who carry messages between the worlds and mediate between the seen and the Unseen. Angels help fill the space between the down-to-earth realities of this world and the elusive, intuitive sense that there is a creative otherworld nearby. Angels fill a space between the divine and the human. As elemental go-betweens, they deliver messages between heaven and earth and fill the gap between human sensibilities and divine presence. They are present as betwixt and between elements, hovering at the edges of the halo of human intelligence and in the margins of human imagination.

Angels have accompanied humankind throughout history and appeared in traditions throughout the world. Benevolent celestial beings have been variously depicted in Jewish, Christian, and Islamic traditions, but are also present in Hinduism and Buddhism, as well as in Celtic and Norse folklore and most other mythologies. The Devas in Hinduism and Buddhism are celestial beings referred to as the "shining ones" who visit and advise those open to spirit. Dharma-palas are a type of guardian angel envisioned as "dharma protectors" who help a person find and keep their alignment with spirit and their essential way of being in service to the world.

In the mystical traditions of Islam, the Angel of the Face appears as a divine presence that each soul perceives before being born. Throughout life on earth, the soul longs to find again that angelic presence. We might see this Angel of the Face in the precise expressions of those we love most, for they remind us of the face we saw before we could see. So, we refer to children as "little angels" and send cards with angels bearing bows and arrows to those whose love has penetrated our hearts.

We may be lost in the objectifications and mindless productions of the modern world, but the angels still travel with us. We call upon our "better angels" when we know the time has come to face a challenge or simply to face up to life. Strangely, we become more truly human by connecting to the celestial dimension of the world and to the archetypal angel, which is an inner inheritance of the human soul. The issue has never been bare survival and the dull continuance of life on earth. We have always been tied to the Soul of the World that connects our inner nature to outer nature and sustains the dance of matter with the breath of spirit.

PRE-HISTORY OF THE SOUL

A rich old story from the treasure trove of Jewish traditions combines the ancient ideas of the angel with Rabbinical and Kabbalistic considerations of the intermediaries between heaven and earth. The story begins with a depiction of the origin of human souls in the Garden of

Paradise. Paradise is the archetypal, original garden, the mythic plot and mystical ground from which all gardens and many origin stories grow. And, paradise is the spot where humans first began and the place we all dream of finding again in one form or another. People can't help but imagine the protected garden paradise, even if it is only as "paradise lost."

Rather than the tale of forbidden fruit and the Tree of the Knowledge of Good and Evil, this story begins at the root of the Tree of Life, which stands at the center of creation and secretly connects this world to the otherworld. Rather than a story of original sin, this is a tale of original gifts. It tells the inside story of what we lost when first we were born and had to leave the protected garden where all souls originate.

Typically, the eternal garden grows from a tree around which flows a stream that carries the water of life. The tree at the center is one of the most potent symbols of life, signifying both the living roots of nature as well as the shared heritage of human cultures. To this day, people feel deep and enduring connections to trees. Many myths say that is because human souls first take shape at the roots of the Tree of Life.

In the old folk tale, the angels dwelt near the roots of the Tree of Life, where they took a particular interest in each individual soul whose original shape first appeared in the roots of the central tree. Besides being the divine messengers moving between heaven and earth, angels were also considered the "second movers" of creation. As interlocutors in the chain of being, angels handled and embraced each soul born as it made its transition between the eternal garden of origins and life on earth.

After taking shape from the roots, the individual souls would move up to the branches of the great tree. There, they would blossom and begin to ripen as the time drew near for them to begin their descent toward life on earth. But before a soul could enter the bodily womb from which they would appear on earth, the ripening soul would fall into a place called the Treasury of Souls. Once there, the angel Gabriel would offer a transitional helping hand to begin the process that moved each soul from the heavenly to the earthly sphere. Reaching his hand into the treasury, the angel would take out the first soul that came to his touch. At that point, the soul separates from the collective congregation in order to continue its individual descent toward life on earth and begin its unique journey in the manifest world.

Having been separated by the touch of Gabriel, the individual soul would be handed over and entrusted to the Angel of Conception, who would nourish and protect it until the time came for it to be born. Lailah is the name of the guardian angel who sets the embryonic soul in the dark well of the human womb. Lailah means "night," yet she is the one who places a lighted candle at the head of the nascent soul once it rests in the mother's womb. By the light of this inner angelic flame, the soul is said to see from one end of the world to the other, as if the light of the womb offers a preview of the world waiting outside. Under the glow of the inner light of the womb, the Angel of Conception is said to teach the soul about the world outside and the distinct role it will play after it has been born.

When the time comes for the soul to leave the inner realm, the angel Lailah extinguishes the light and the child is born from the darkness into the light of the world. In the instant that the newborn emerges from the womb, the angel lightly strikes a finger to the infant's lip, as if to say: "Shh." This touching of the mouth causes the newborn to forget everything it learned in the inner light of the womb. The knowledge of how it first came to life and what role it should play remains within the soul. However, it is sealed behind lips of silence, a necessary forgetting that continues until the day comes when a person awakens and finds their own true voice.

THE FIRST MIDWIFE

Most religious stories are derived from older myths and in this Jewish folk tale, something quite ancient and rich is being depicted. In Judeo-Christian traditions, angels tend to have masculine names as well as male characteristics. Here, the ripening soul is taken from the collective treasury by a masculine spirit, but is subsequently brooded over by a feminine angel. The name Gabriel means, "man of god" or "strong with god," as if Gabriel acts as an extension of the orthodox deity imaged as a male figure. Yet, for the ripening soul to make the transition to the mother's womb and on to life on earth, the nourishing touch of a feminine spirit is required. The angel Lailah appears and acts as intermediary between the divine treasury and the human womb. In that sense, Lailah appears not just as the Angel of Conception, but also the midwife of the soul who helps to give birth to the unique spirit of life that each human soul carries to the earth.

Since Lailah means "night" or "darkness," the angel who protects and nourishes souls about to be born seems herself to be born from the darkness of night. Typically, angels are creatures of the light; they exemplify the lightness of being that is in contrast to humans, who are born into gravity and bear the weight of being fully embodied. Even devils and demons tend to begin in the light, only becoming "fallen angels" when they slip from the light to the dark side of creation. The presence of a feminine angel that inspires and guides the soul is an essential aspect of myth that has often been omitted by orthodox teachings, but manages to survive in folk tales.

The Angel of Conception and archetypal midwife of the soul not only operates inside the darkness of the womb, but is herself a product of the dark. Then again, she is the source of the light that shines within the darkness. She comes from the eternal night and brings a light that not only shines in the dark, but secretly offers a view of the entire world. This capacity to bring light out of darkness connects her to the ancient tradition of Sophia, the source of all wisdom found on earth. Sophia was one old name for the embodiment of heavenly inspiration by virtue of being deeply in touch with the ground of inner truth and touching the underlying unity of being. Sophia was known as goddess and guide, the muse and knowing nurse of those who truly seek for knowledge and wisdom. Sophia is the wise nurse who nourishes our deepest thoughts and helps to heal any alienation we might feel from our deeper self.

In many old stories, the light of creation must also exist down below in the common world. Typically it becomes the role of humankind, often guided by angels, to find and reveal the light of ongoing creation in the darkness that surrounds and penetrates the world. In the ancient world, wisdom was known as "dark knowledge." That is to say that whoever would be wise must come to know both darkness and light; for each gives birth to the other in this world made of nights and days.

Whoever would find the light of wisdom must search for it in dark places where most fear to go, including the darker areas of one's own psyche and soul. Lailah is the lifelong companion of the soul who nourishes us with the kind of knowledge that can illuminate a person from within and light a path during the bleakest hours, in the dark night of the soul.

When the story of Lailah says that the soul sees by the light of the womb, the whole world from one end to the other, it reveals that each person has their own world view. For, besides prefiguring the world outside the womb, the light of Lailah serves an inner education of the soul. On this intimate and metaphysical level, the womb turns out to be, not simply the instrument of genetic transfers, but also the first school and original temple of education as well as the source of enlightenment in the human soul. In the mysterious darkness of the womb, not just life is conceived, but knowledge as well and a world view that can orient the soul in both worlds. By the light of its angel—or genius—the embryonic soul learns its own history and sees its natural place in the great scheme of things.

ESOTERIC AND EXOTERIC

For those with eyes to see, the seemingly innocent tale of angels, often used to teach children to be quiet, reveals a deeper knowledge. The touch of the finger of the Angel of the Lip reveals something even as it hushes; for it hints at a darker knowledge, a true wisdom sealed within the seeming silence of the soul. To be born on earth means to enter a world of elemental pairings: light and dark, higher and lower, inner and outer. Thus, there is a necessary division of knowledge into exoteric, or external, and esoteric, or internal and hidden. Anything essential and symbolic will have an external and accessible form of knowledge, but also an esoteric or inside story that must be sought through insight and deeper understanding.

There are many dimensions of this esoteric knowledge, mysteries within mysteries; after all, there is no end to knowledge. In the ancient world, essential knowledge would often be hidden, given only to initiates who would be under a seal of silence not to reveal what they had learned. In Hebrew, this deeper aspect of the sacred texts is called sitrei Torah, "the secrets of the Torah," or nistar, the concealed dimension of the holy book. This esoteric level or Kabbalah is comprised of secrets relating to the Creator, the creative process, and the hidden light of ongoing creation.

The esoteric level and inside story of creation includes the understanding that creation is not simply an event in the past, but rather something that continues to occur. When understood at a deeper level, it becomes evident that we are in the midst of creation all the time. The lost garden exists not simply before birth or after death, but right here on earth, whenever a person reconnects to the deeper self within the self. Whenever we are truly awake, we become agents of creation ongoing and students of the esoteric knowledge set within the soul just before birth. The old idea of being born again is not simply a religious practice but an esoteric instinct to awaken to the destiny secretly set within the soul.

This world is certainly a mystery, but it is a mystery trying to reveal itself. The story of the Angel of the Lip, most often interpreted to mean that children must be quiet while they learn the commandments of god and the laws of proper behavior, has an esoteric side that shines a light on the pre- history of the soul and the nature of creation. The outer laws and forms of belief serve as one kind of education, but the impression left on both body and soul by the touch of the Angel of Conception is there to remind the soul of something much deeper and much more important to the world that can so easily become a place of darkness and confusion.

In the clever way of creation stories, the tale of the Angel of the Lip serves to explain the origin of the strange indentation everyone has between the upper lip and their nose. Yet, the angelic imprint on the body also serves as a reminder that something important but now forgotten has been sealed in silence within each soul. Officially called the philtrum, the groove most humans have above the upper lip actually forms during embryonic development. Some have deemed it a useless vestige leftover from our earlier history as lower primates. Yet, like the inner patterns of the soul and individual fingerprints, philtrums differ from one person to the next. As recent studies have shown, this small grooved area is essential for proper speech and mouth development.

On the exoteric level, it helps humans to speak clearly and precisely. It also allows for the extensive and intricate facial expressions through which humans communicate their inner feelings. On the esoteric level, the indentation above the lip is a reminder that each soul has something meaningful to express, whether the chosen language turns out to be shaped from words, sculpted from stone, or composed as song. One of the oldest meanings of the practice of teaching and learning was "to sing over."

According to Greek mythology, the philtrum is one of the most sensual parts of the body and the name for this depression above the lip comes from philtron, which surprisingly means "a love charm or love potion." The related verb is phileo, meaning "to love, to kiss, to have affection for," and not far way is philo, which can bring us to philosophy. On the exoteric level, philosophy is treated as the history of ideas, often becoming a dry affair of abstract theories. The esoteric level of philosophy reads as philo-sophia, which translates as both a love of knowledge and as the knowledge of love. And that brings us back to the womb which serves as both the birthing place of the body and the inner temple of life. Before birth the soul is exposed to a body of knowledge that makes each of us unique and never to be repeated on this earth.

How often has a finger to the lip called people to be silent; the gesture is universal, even archetypal. It does not need to be explained, it makes immediate, evident sense. Yet, a deeper meaning is concealed within the common command to be quiet. The outer form calls for silence, but on the inner level, it reminds us that essential knowledge must to be sought within the silence of the soul. Loss of this inside story, and the esoteric level of knowledge right under our noses, can leave us in a horizontal world that lacks meaningful depth. It also denies us access to the unique world view that is the natural inheritance and guiding light for each individual soul.

An old meaning of the word soul was "the light found in darkness." The essential and necessarily esoteric knowledge set within the soul must be forgotten at the time of the birth of the body. Yet, each person, body and soul, secretly awaits a second nativity intended to be a psychic birth with revelations of the esoteric knowledge hidden within. An intimate knowledge that comprises an entire world view waits to be brought out into the light of day. Thus, a genuine education must include a self-revelation of knowledge intended to be born into the world through each of us. The soul expects a second birth and a further initiation into the mysteries of life.

Just as the holy books must present both a revealed and a concealed level, each person can be an open book at the level of ego of persona; yet each has a deeper, wiser self within. The deeper self holds the true treasury and collective inheritance of the individual life. Not only are we unwise when we fail to find the inner knowledge of the soul, we also fail to see the world in the way we are intended to view it. Not only do we lack the esoteric presence that our souls long to redeem, we also contribute to the increasing lack of presence in a world dominated by blind facts and surface data. The brightening of the inner light involves an intensification of being and a growth of soul that strengthens both the presence of genuine individuals and the natural connections of humanity to the Soul of the World.

ANOTHER CANDLE

This method of first viewing the exoteric level and then seeking for the esoteric message can be applied to many things in this world of literal thinking and soulful understanding. The ancient Romans had a practice for honoring the genius of the soul that continues in the modern world in a mostly exoteric way. Candles on birthday cakes derive from an ancient practice intended to honor the inner light of spirit that dwells within each person. As part of the remembrance of a person's birth, a candle would be lit to represent the invisible fire at the core of each life, the presence of the genius that comes to life with each soul born, regardless of age, gender, status, or sexual orientation. Instead of a candle for each year of life, the flame of a single candle represented the invisible fire at the core of the heart. The idea was to encourage the shining genius within each soul; so birthday gifts were not given to the person, but to the spirit born within them. In this old sense, birthday gifts served as reminders that each person is already gifted; each having an inner genius as well as god-given gifts intended to be brought to life and be given to the world. One's birthday served as a reminder of the inner inspiration of one's life and the hidden message trying to become known. The point was not simply to make a wish and blow out a candle. Rather, the aim was to consider what the candle of each life burns for. As guardian angel and nurse of the soul, Lailah might prefer a little silence after the birthday wish has been made in order to honor the inside story seeking to be lived out into the world.

The story of the Angel of Conception does not end at the birth of the infant with its curiously impressed lip. The tale goes on to tell how Lailah watches over each child and serves as a guardian angel throughout their life. As true midwife of the soul, she is there when the time comes for each person to leave this world. Since the life of the soul continues after the body has given up its ghost, the Angel of Conception leads the newly deceased back to the divine realm from which they came.

People continue to believe in the presence of angels because we intuit that something watches over us. We know it each time we follow the little voice inside or heed the warning or inspiration that arrives as if on wings. We need the intermediaries that keep us close to the spirit of life, to the wonders of nature and to the subtleties of our own inner nature.

The mystical significance of the Treasury of Souls is that each person is important in the ongoing story of creation and that each has a role and a divine errand which only they, with their unique soul, can fulfill. The soul has always been the secret storehouse of mystical human inheritance, the repository of the Treasure Hard to Attain, which ever waits to be rediscovered and brought back into consciousness. Paradise turns out to be the divine form hidden in one's own being, the secret image through which the divine knows itself in each of us. In the depths of the soul, in the center of each heart, the garden of paradise exists. The knowledge we most need in life has been sealed within us all along. The womb of humanity harbors an inner light and spark of genius that can serve as a world view, a way of understanding both the world and our individual place in it.

II

THE EDUCATION OF GENIUS

CHAPTER 7

A HIDDEN MESSAGE

*Our environment does not alter our essential nature
though it may condition it.*
- William Blake

To be alive at this time means to risk feeling increasingly isolated and cosmologically dissociated as the disenchantment of the world leaves humanity alienated from both nature and the cosmos. It means to live in an accidental universe ruled by chance and increasing uncertainty. Traditional views of both science and religion no longer hold a firm vision or containing story, yet no coherent new worldview has formed. The earth, once seen as the center of the known universe, became replaced by the sun around which it circles. Then the sun was removed as the center; but no new core took its place. Instead of a celestial nucleus around which we wheel, the middle of it all became the lack of any center at all.

The postmodern world is not just fluid and fast changing; it is also disoriented and increasingly fragmented—a tangle of endings and beginnings amidst a cosmic turning of undetermined duration. As we stumble through a troubled time between the end of one era and the beginning of the next, we also wander in a place betwixt one worldview and another. We rush about amidst the deconstructed flux of an unredeemed world, impelled ever onwards by technological inventions, yet increasingly unable to find solid ground on an intellectual, emotional, or spiritual level.

"As above so below" suggests the old wise saying. If the macrocosmic universe is empty of meaning and direction, so too must be the microcosmic human beings born into the swirling midst of it all. Under the rule of the accidental universe, each person is but an accident; each living soul the product of chance, circumstance, and some inherited genes, but otherwise blank. This modern notion of an accidental universe combines condemningly with the old idea of tabula rasa: a blank slate or vacant soul. Lacking any sense of inner meaning or genuine orientation, human life becomes devoid of all purpose and meaning. How we grow and what we grow into seems only to be determined by outer forces, not by inner meaning or character.

Lacking any sense of purpose and destiny, life on earth becomes the mere surviving of circumstances rather than a unique adventure of self-discovery. Humans become reduced to being but random consumers in an accidental world where they have nothing essential to learn and nothing meaningful to give. The instinctive expectation of a calling or meaningful vocation in life diminishes to merely an anxiety over the choice of a job or career. Each person is nothing much to begin with and must "make something of themselves" or else be another nobody in the midst of "a tale told by an idiot, full of sound and fury, signifying nothing."

ORIGINAL TABLET OF THE SOUL

The idea of an accidental universe stands in stark contrast to old notions of an ongoing creation and a secret center that holds everything together. And, the concept of tabula rasa stands in stark opposition to the idea of a uniquely formed soul that harbors a genius self, laden with talents and gifts to give. Tabula means "table or tablet" and rasa means "to scrape away, to erase;" thus, the idea of a completely blank slate within each person at birth.

Over time, tabula rasa and the idea of a clean slate within us has become the accepted way to view the inner life of humans on earth. Empty of all content at birth, the receptive inner tablet of mind or soul can only gather meaning and content from impressions made upon it by other people and the outer world. On the surface, the blank slate theory is a compelling metaphor; as an idea, it has trickled down through all the cultural layers so that the emptiness it implies has become rather commonly accepted.

This old idea-image of blankness originates from ancient methods of writing and sending messages between one place and another. The Roman tabula were wax tablets which were once the primary surfaces used for writing. After being used, a tablet could be heated and the softened wax would become smooth and clear. Having been made blank again, the tablet could be used over and over. The same basic notion led to the term blank slate when describing sheets of slate that could be written upon with chalk, be cleanly erased, and used again.

Yet, the metaphor of the wax tablet itself has been simplified and misunderstood. Something of the original meaning has been lost in the translation. Fortunately, what becomes lost at the level of daily life can often be found again at the level of myth and story. Important elements of life and knowledge may become lost, but they cannot completely disappear. In the great lost and found of the world, ancient understandings wait to be rediscovered and brought back into currency.

The lost message about blank slates can be recollected from a tale told by Herodotus, the old historian who once said: "Men trust their ears less than their eyes." He was trying to point to the fact that appearances can be sorely misleading and what you see is rarely the whole picture. In this world, there is often more than meets the eye. That was certainly the case with a cryptic message sent during an ancient time of conflicts and war. The story of the hidden message is part history, part legend; a tale of espionage that seems to prove Herodotus' point about not blindly trusting what appears before our eyes. It might also help us understand how something that is only partially true can come to be believed as the whole story.

Herodotus also once offered that: "No one is stupid enough to prefer war to peace; for in peace sons bury their fathers and in war fathers bury their sons." That idea did little to stop ancient Persia and the Greek city states of Sparta and Athens from engaging in a long period of almost uninterrupted wars. During that embattled time, a man named Demaratus wandered in exile with nothing but the clothes on his back. He had once ruled as king of Sparta but due to political intrigues, he had lost the throne and been stripped of all power and possessions.

Eventually, Demaratus landed in Persia where his political experience earned him a position as advisor to King Xerxes. In the course of events, the former king of Sparta learned that the war-like Persian ruler was planning a massive invasion of his old kingdom and native land. Despite having been exiled, Demaratus' heart remained connected to his birthplace and he felt an instinctive need to warn the people of Sparta. At the same time, he also feared the painful death that would be his reward if anyone learned that he tried to warn his former countrymen.

Adversity tends to encourage genius if a person can hold the tension of opposing instincts long enough for a third element to appear. One day, Demaratus observed someone removing a message from the common writing instrument of the day, a folding wooden tablet covered with a layer of clear wax. As he watched the wax being heated and made clear and empty of markings, something occurred to him. If he etched the warning message on the hard wood underlying the wax surface, the missive would appear to be nothing but a blank tablet.

According to Herodotus, the hidden message was carefully inscribed under the blank surface, so that when the tablet arrived at the court in Sparta, no one knew what to make of it. Although it was delivered as a message to the court of the king, there was no writing to be seen at all. The episode may have ended there, with no one ever grasping the hidden message within the seemingly blank tablet. However, the queen of Sparta happened to intervene.

It was not common at that time for a woman, even a queen, to be intimately involved in matters of the state; especially if the state was Sparta. Yet, sometimes exceptions are made even in the strictest of societies. Queen Gorgo had proven herself an exceptional person at a young age. At only eight or nine years old, the future queen had her first influence on matters of the state and the course of history. She happened to be present at court as her royal father conversed with a foreign ambassador. Sensing something devious in the man, she spoke right up, warning the king that the ambassador sought to intrigue him into an unwise war. The king saw the wisdom of the child's words and sent the ambassador packing. "Force has no place where there is need of skill," Herodotus once said.

After the telling episode, Princess Gorgo became invaluable as an advisor to her royal father. Later, she counseled her husband when he became king, and as a wise mother she guided a third ruler when the time came for her own son to take the throne. At the time of the arrival of the seemingly blank tablet, Gorgo was sitting at court as the queen of the land. Sensing that there might be more than meets the eye, she had the insight to look more closely at the wordless message. She scraped away the wax to see if there might be anything beneath the surface. Once the wax had been removed, the hidden message scribed upon the underlying surface was revealed for all to see. The people of Sparta were forewarned of the impending invasion and able to prepare for it, as once again the instinctive insights of Gorgo saved the day.

Although presented as history, the tale has elements of myth woven within it. Gorgo comes from the same Greek root that gives us "gorge" and "disgorge." As a name, it translates as "loud-voiced" or "roaring," as when someone shouts across a chasm or a gorge. Legend has it that even as a newborn baby, Gorgo came into the world roaring loudly. Thus, the infant's demeanor and the child's name held clues to her inner nature and the kind of person she would become. It makes sense that a person intended to have important words to say at critical moments in public life would be born with an intense urge to speak up and even roar out a warning.

ACORN THEORY

The ancient Greeks had a metaphor for understanding how it could be that a child would display genius-like qualities at a very young age. They called it the "Acorn Theory," for it drew upon something hidden inside the seeds of their revered oak trees. The theory, which seems more of a mythic imagination, suggests that inside the small seed there resides an entire tree. If the seed takes root somewhere and the shell cracks open, what will be revealed is a living shoot that can become a deeply rooted, widely branching tree. In other words, the full-grown tree is hidden inside the opaque seed.

Not just any tree, not an average tree, but an exact inner shape waiting to take root and bear fruit on the earth.

To the metaphorical eye, the seed can be seen as the inner kernel of genius that waits within each of us, waiting to one day crack open and become seen and known. The Acorn Theory helps to explain how children will suddenly display a talent or wisdom beyond their understanding and their years. The inner genius often appears at a critical time in a young person's life only to disappear and become latent. Genius works like that, giving portents of its presence for those who have eyes to see it. Notice the similarity of the word "talent" to the word "latent;" simply switch the "t" and the "l" in latent and you have talent. Each person has latent abilities and talents waiting to be revealed and delivered to the world.

Genius is the hidden message in the soul that wants to become known and be recognized as an agent of growth and a seed of purpose. Often a child will demonstrate the inner nature and qualities of his or her soul between the ages of eight and ten. In the case of Gorgo, her native intelligence and gift of insight came suddenly to the surface while about that age. She spoke up with knowledge beyond her years and disgorged some critical advice that affected everyone around her.

The other hidden message in the story is that the blank tablet only appears to be empty. For those with eyes to see, the slate is not blank. Essential knowledge has been hidden under the surface and appearances of life. In fact, life-defining information has been precisely etched within the soul of each person brought to life. Those who only wish to see the facts of life can easily overlook the esoteric message that has been inscribed within their own souls. Those who look only at the surface of the world miss the inner story and the underlying truths that make each life meaningful, precious, and potentially revelatory.

There are levels of perception and layers of understanding under the surface of everything that happens in this world. It is necessary to look deeper into the notion of tabula rasa in order to grasp the hidden message of the soul. At the surface, each life does appear to be a clear layer of wax upon which the impressions of the world make their mark. Children are quite impressionable and early life experiences can leave deep and enduring marks that affect our character and our view of the world. In that sense, we do begin life as a blank slate, unable to defend, protect, or explain ourselves. As any caring parent knows, there are signs from the very beginning that mark each child as uniquely shaped from within. Parents see and sense something distinct and defining in the nascent personality of their child.

What has become forgotten and overlooked in the modern world is that the inner message and defining pattern of each person's life needs to be uncovered and become known in order for them to become a genuine individual. The plotline inscribed within the soul is intended to be discovered despite all the impressions and instructions received from one's family and the circumstances surrounding our birth and our growth. There is and must be a deeper message and inner script waiting to be uncovered under the often scarred surface of each life.

Once the hidden message of the soul becomes known, a person has their own voice and good reason to learn to speak up and even roar out if that be a part of their inner nature. For, each soul has something meaningful to express and something valuable to offer in this world where we are continually under threat of becoming misled and increasingly under pressure to conform to collective ideas. The idea of a blank slate makes sense, but only at the surface of life and only during the period of childhood dependency on others. It used to be better known that at the end of childhood a greater adventure begins and a deeper identity must be found if a person is to become themselves. The source of many "identity problems" can be found in the idea that most people now believe human identities are shaped entirely from random experiences in the outside world.

A CONCEALED MISSION

Meanwhile, much of modern thought, as well as modern education, rests upon the idea that each person enters life as a blank slate upon which family and society make their marks. Under the rule of reason and the statistical worldview, it has become difficult to accept that there is a seed of individuality and a core of imagination already set within each soul. Under the blank stare of tabula rasa there can be no inner purpose or soulful pattern for us to draw upon. Instead of being seen as a gift-giver with a unique pattern waiting to unfold from within, we each become reduced to a biography written by circumstances in a universe developed by chance.

Empty of any intended personality or core qualities, life also becomes devoid of specific meaning. Deficient of signs and symbols and lacking portents of purpose and destiny, humans are reduced to vagrant consumers of a world in which they have nothing essential to give or to learn. The simplistic application of tabula rasa holds young students to be empty receptacles into which whatever collective ideas that prevail at the moment can be poured. To many this seems an ideal arrangement for educating obedient citizen-consumers; for others, it bespeaks a violation of the soul of humanity that precipitates a steady slide into the vacancies of nihilism.

The dominance of blank slate theories and behaviorism cause not only the error of seeing only some children as gifted, but also the lack of understanding of how and why all young people struggle to become themselves. The depression, alienation, and violence of many young people reflect the blank slate philosophy and the growing states of nihilism that characterize modern mass cultures.

In many ways, mass culture becomes anti-cultural; it fails to cultivate the essential elements that sustain true community, especially the essential need for awakened individuals who can live with purpose and meaning. An old maxim that considers the size of things applies in this case, as in most things: the bigger the front, the bigger the back. If the front of life becomes more and more massive and collective ideas and mass-produced products become greatly overvalued, a huge shadow falls heavily on that which is opposite and kept in the background.

In the case of the accidental universe and the theory of tabula rasa, the thing becoming more and more overshadowed is the sanctity and uniqueness of each individual human life. In order to sustain and grow the ideas of mass culture with its mass marketing, those on the receiving end of all the mass production must continue to feel empty inside. The great failure of mass culture becomes the diminishing importance and constant devaluing of the individual—the exact element that modern culture claims to value and constantly aims all its marketing and advertising at.

When it comes to the inner genius and the hidden message of the soul, modern beliefs offer a double whammy. Since we are considered to lack innate elements of character and purpose, we can simply be whatever we wish to be. However, in order to believe that we can be what we want to be and do as we please, we must accept that we are empty to begin with. Under the rule of an accidental universe, you can feel that you are nothing but a tiny speck of disappearing dust. Under the theory of the blank slate, you can be whatever you wish to be. The modern psyche can become caught in a collective form of mania and depression, swinging back and forth between an inflated sense of self and a crushing sense of self-doubt.

In a culture theoretically ruled by reason many unreasonable things can come to seem completely logical. Although most parents can perceive the subtle qualities and inner uniqueness that separate one child from another from the very beginning, children are being shortchanged by the shortsightedness of a society that does not recognize their innate giftedness and pre-rational orientation to life.

If the genius in the soul has a deep interest in a specific vocation, then having unlimited choices misses the point of having a true calling. We are most happy and inventive, most useful and effective, most satisfied and life-embracing when we fulfill our lot in life and bring our genius self to the world. We are lucky if we turn out to be who we are supposed to be based upon the seeds of genius set within us when we arrived in life, certainly helpless and seemingly empty inside.

The great visionaries and creative geniuses, the genuine leaders and teachers, the most respected healers and guides are all models of what occurs when the core of the soul and the thought of the heart awaken and reveal their inner meaning and intended purpose in life. The real issue in life has always been the need to reveal ourselves to ourselves in order to uncover the hidden message and undertake the concealed mission set within our souls.

Like the little kernel that can grow to be a broad shade tree that protects people or a wide-branching tree that bears abundant fruit, we are each born with a defining pattern etched within us, waiting to unfold. As soon as we have a body, we embody an inner blueprint that has unique qualities as defining as our fingerprints can be. If we do not live out the life seeded within us, no one else will ever do so. Many other seeds will come to life, but none will bear the distinct mixture of talents and gifts, of values and aims, trying to come to life through us.

This inner imprint of the soul is the hidden message we each carry into the world; it is the source of a unique identity that is reflected in both body and soul. Each birth begins a once-in-a-lifetime adventure, and each life presents the question of whether we awaken to what is unique within us or not. The much-heralded idea that "you can be anything you want to be" is not true now and never has been. Imagining that you can become anything you wish misses the greater and deeper point that each person is already aimed and shaped from within.

The human soul is a living paradox—neither a predetermined personality nor a completely open possibility. The point in this life is not simply to "become somebody," but to become who we were each intended to be when we first entered this world. For each of us has the most to give and contributes most meaningfully when we become who we were intended to be from the beginning. That is the inside story and the hidden message that has been etched upon each soul.

YOUR GENIUS IS CALLING

Uncovering the underlying message and hidden unity of our soul involves a lifelong project of self-discovery and the revelation of one's destiny in life. Rather than a simple product of personal and collective history, each person is a mystery trying to be solved; each life a puzzle that can only be deciphered by living out a pattern hidden in the soul from the beginning. This sense of an innate purpose and meaning cannot be proven in logical, scientific ways. Rather, each life becomes the living evidence of a story there all along, trying to unfold at each critical turn in life.

Amidst the onslaught of mass information and misinformation, it takes courage and determination to grow up and become oneself; were that not the case, more people would do it. To awaken to the living dream within one's life and remain awake in a world trying to lull everyone to sleep involves repeated struggle, yet also presents something truly worth fighting for. Given half a chance, most people will seek ways to be part of something greater than common levels of economic and social life. Something deep within us instinctively seeks to be part of something "larger than life."

The individual soul must have its share of genius and an exact core of imagination that can transcend the collective attitudes and the flattening of the world. Yet, we cannot truly believe in ourselves until we reveal to ourselves the hidden message and inner purpose of our lives. If we fail to use our innate gifts and god-given qualities, we leave the field open for those who have little self-awareness and narrow aims to determine the course of history. If we fail to live out the allotment of genius given to us, no one will ever live it. Our real job in life is to become our true selves in such a way that we contribute presence to the world and are seen as irreplaceable.

To become nobody but your true self and to struggle against the tide of sameness and the false security of simply fitting in is a fight worth having. To become oneself by contributing one's native gifts and talents to this troubled world: that is the job to keep applying for and a work worth spending an entire life doing. There may be no greater time to awaken to the calling of the true self than at times like this, when the world around us has become increasingly chaotic and ruled by great uncertainty.

What truly calls to us speaks to the personal myth and the innate purpose seeded in our soul from the beginning. Responding to the call of genius involves a process of awakening as well as a path of redemption from the oblivion of forgetting the inner dream that brought us to life. Some might ask whether the path is before us or within us. The answer is: Yes. We are both driven from within by our resident spirit and something outside calls forth the genius within us. The genius is what we aim to know and it is the force that drives us to awaken. Because each person has seeds of genius sewn within their soul, each also has a calling to follow and a purpose to pursue. The call creates a threshold, an opening through which the timeless thread of destiny tries to pull us further in life than we would otherwise choose to go. A chance experience, a blunder, a challenge or a dream; anything large or small can serve as the opening and prompt the call to awaken. A mistake or an accident, that after all is no accident at all, can shift a person's life towards a destiny that was waiting to be found. Following the call of spirit leads not simply to character development, but to becoming the main character in a life-long story of self-revelation.

Either we awaken to the true nature and inner spirit of our life and learn to express it or else we will live out a distortion or perversion of it.

Once we accept the calling that resonates with the pattern woven within us we wander rightly, we find a path and enter a pilgrimage that suits our soul. Yet, such a life-path requires that we risk ourselves continually in order to find ourselves more fully. Each time we awaken to the genius in our soul we become chosen again.

The idea that each person is called in some way to awaken and learn to give the gifts that are set within their soul is of such great importance that the calling keeps calling. Although the period of youthful experiments is often when we first hear the call, the calling keeps beckoning throughout our lives. We may be closest to hearing the call when we feel most alone or in trouble, for genius hides behind the wound and one of the greatest wounds in life is to not know who we are intended to be or what we are supposed to serve in life.

The genius that brought us to life is tied to the eternal and does not fade or grow old. It can be the source of renewing our life at any age. Growing old can mean more than slowing down; it can be a time of truly growing down and incarnating further. Because the inner genius tries to incarnate through us will keep calling for us to awaken further until we come to the end of our life adventure. After all, to be successful in life does not mean to reach an outer goal, but to reconnect to the source of one's life and the hidden message found on the ground of one's being. That reconnection can happen at any age and no matter what conditions the world might be in at the time.

CHAPTER 8

THE EDUCATION OF GENIUS

I am not a teacher, but an awakener.

– Robert Frost

"There are only two lasting bequests we can hope to give our children. One of these is roots, the other wings," advised the poet Goethe. The roots may be the rudiments of learning that each person requires in order to become established in life. The wings must be the extension and expansion of each child's inner spirit, core imagination, and way of being uniquely present in this world. We must offer each child and all young people ways for establishing themselves in life; yet we must also offer them meaningful ways of fulfilling their dreams and rising above the daily grind of life. For, no matter how poor or untutored a person may be, each of us carries a dream of life that seeks to awaken and carry us to an as yet unseen destiny.

A genuine education must somehow serve the wings of spirit and imagination that each child brings to life and each student brings to school. If not, it can be like the tale of the man who came upon a large egg that had fallen to the ground on the side of the road he was walking along. Seeing that the egg had not been broken and being a thoughtful person, he carried it to a nearby barnyard. Along the way, it occurred to him that it must be an eagle's egg because of its impressive size. Arriving at the barnyard, he deposited the sizable egg in the first nest he found, which happened to be in a chicken coop. In due time, a hen came along and settled on the eggs in the nest. She brooded steadily on all those eggs and soon enough the large egg hatched right along with a gaggle of little chicks.

Surrounded by chickens, the newborn eaglet began to emulate whatever they did, soon enough becoming able to scratch up enough food to stay alive and grow. The eagle-chick scraped the earth for worms and insects and it learned how to cluck and cackle, just like all the other birds in the barnyard. Over time, the little eagle came to think that it was just like the others. So, when it came to using its wings, the eaglet simply learned to thrash in the air and fly but a few feet before coming back down to familiar ground again. Despite an inner capacity to soar and rise above it all, the eaglet felt more connected to the common ground than to the sky above.

One day, when the shadow of a great bird flying high in the sky fell across the barnyard, all the chickens quickly ran for shelter. The eagle-chick looked up and saw a magnificent being circling far above the earth in the blue brightness of the sky. Instead of hiding, the eagle-chick became enraptured, in awe of the high-flying bird that glided with graceful majesty on the wind's currents, scarcely moving its strong golden wings.

"Who is it that flies so high with such power and grace?" asked the eaglet when the others returned from hiding. "That's an eagle," said a nearby hen, "it's the king of all the birds. It belongs to the brilliant sky, while we chickens belong to the scratching earth. Don't look at it too long or it will swoop down and take you off and devour you whole."

The eaglet never forgot the vision of the wide-winged eagle soaring effortlessly above. However, like the others, he soon learned to hide when the great shadows of soaring birds came overhead. Despite having the heart of an eagle within and visions of spreading wings and soaring flight, the true nature of the young one remained hidden and over time any dream of flying became forgotten. The eaglet continued to grow, but also continued to act like all the others and lived the life of a chicken. For that is what he thought he was and that was how others saw him and how they treated him.

Similar tales of an eagle that thought it was a chicken appear in many cultures. They serve as brief reminders of how easily we can settle for a life in which we simply scratch out a living and learn to cackle and complain about the condition of the world we are in and the limits of our lives. Not to say that life cannot be unfair, for it certainly can be. Initially, the aim of education should be to establish a level playing field so that all students have a chance to make a living and forge a basic dignity of life. Then there needs to be meaningful opportunities to nurture dreams and visions that allow each person to find their wings and see the world with the expansive eyes of spirit.

The point is not simply that everyone should fly as high as possible; remember what happened to Icarus when he flew too close to the sun. Not everyone is intended to be a high-flyer; yet again, no one flies too high who flies with their own wings. The second level of education involves helping to awaken the dreams of each young student and encourage their genuine visions of life. For a culture that rejects or dismisses the dreams of its youth will lack the imagination and vision needed for shaping a meaningful and inclusive future. Given the radical changes sweeping through the world, young people will need a more psychological education as well as encouragement to look within to find the resiliency of their genius nature.

A TRAGIC EDUCATION

One of the tragedies of modern life occurs when education becomes limited to collective instruction and the dreams of both teachers and students fail to find their winged ways. The loss of dreams leads to a genuine tragedy because this world is not neutral and repressed or suppressed dreams can become severe depressions, can surface as troubling delusions, or even explode in acts of violence and despair.

After waves of mass shootings in schools became an almost predictable form of modern tragedy, I received a copy of a letter sent by a student who had suddenly left high school and disappeared for a while. By all typical measures, he was a successful student who would easily matriculate and graduate on schedule. However, something was not computing for him and he tried to articulate the nature of the problem he had with modern education. He began by stating that if you are shocked by mass shootings in schools, you probably have not been in school for a while. He went on to argue that the shootings were a symptom of a sickness in society that now pervades the whole system of education.

"In high school I had dreams of destruction every day I was there. After the shootings, I never heard once a word about reforming the school system. The main message I received over and over was that it is not the system that's broken, it's you. The unhappiness, resentment and hate you feel is your own fault. This was told to me every day; usually not directly, but you feel constantly undermined. Your dreams are shot down by those who didn't follow their own dreams and are locked in jobs they don't enjoy. They failed to follow their dreams; they only took what was handed to them.

So many people grow embittered and tell you that's all there is; because that is all they know. This is the 'real world' they say condescendingly each time you dare to speak of your dreams. And how could they think it otherwise? If you break out of their 'real world', and find more than what is handed to you, that means that they have failed…failed in their lives.

Your dreams force them to confront their own unhappiness which is covered over, but vented onto students who step out of line or defy them. This is why I left high school, but couldn't put it into words. My feelings and emotions were trampled upon and labeled INVALID. Even if I could have spoken them, who would have listened? My parents, yes to a certain extent; but they too shared the fear because I wanted to stop something that was only an imitation of life. Who would have listened?"

This insightful young writer speaks for many others; for I have heard similar laments from students in the halls of higher learning as well as those who have dropped out altogether. In visiting various schools, I have discovered that most students know which of their teachers have learned to open their own wings. If I ask students who the true teachers are and who are simply employees, they will answer in quick agreement. The eye of the pupil readily sees the awakened spirit in the teacher and also notices when it is absent. We all carry a natural expectation to have our dreams and visions reflected back by those who have already awakened to their own dreams.

Regardless of the loss of vertical imagination and the flattening of the world that now characterize modern societies, each person is still guaranteed at least one experience of awakening to the true nature of their being. This inner vision may be brief, it may not be easily understood by others, yet it is an indelible inheritance of the human soul and it is ultimately necessary for human society. How easily and how frequently the instinct to spread our wings and fly can now be reduced to a fluttering that barely lifts us above the familiar ground of our unlived lives.

The notion that the ups and downs of youth can be attributed to the flux of hormones in their bodies has some truth in it; however, it fails to recognize the intensification of dreaming that also defines youth. Along with helplessly falling through space, dreams of flying are universally experienced, especially during youth. Like the fledgling bird that struggles to open its wings and master flight once it leaves the nest, the human spirit also bears an inborn expectation to fly and soar and awaken to a vision that encompasses the entire world. Not that a person would know everything; rather that each person should learn how they are intended to see the world in order to find their place in it.

Dreaming offers the universal evidence of the great imagination repeatedly visiting and secretly operating within each of us. The dream is a mystery that happens to us whether we acknowledge it or not. In a way, the dream dreams us more than we dream it. Flying dreams may be the most commonly remembered type of dream as even the most unimaginative, self-limiting person might take flight in their dreams. Yet, some people are afraid to fly, even in their dreams. Like the little eaglet in the story that has the potential of flight and the heart vision yet remains tethered to the ground. Our dreams place this uncanny sense of flying and the panicky fear of falling right in the center of our deepest place of sleep and rest. If no one recognizes and blesses the dream we bring to life, the fear of falling can heavily outweigh the longing for flight and freedom.

The modern science of dreams now agrees with ancient ideas that in order to live and not go insane, each of us needs both deep sleep and deep-seated dreams. Human life, with its strange arrangement of body, mind, and soul, must somehow balance itself and often only manages to do so in our dreams. Flying in dreams not only lifts us above the gravities and burdens of daily life; but also gives us a bird's-eye view of our psychic condition. As we peer down from above, we might perceive what holds us down in life, what entraps us and prevents us from rising above our circumstances and using our natural gifts and innate genius.

Hidden within the egg of the little-self is a genius self that longs to awaken fully and learn to express its true nature. Thus, an inner brooding and a second birth is required for a person to begin to become truly themselves. The second birth involves the awakening of the individual soul and the spreading of the inner wings of spirit that make each person unique in this world. A person who does not awaken to the true nature of their own life can become like the eagle-chick who has a vague vision of flying, but never really leaves the barnyard level of life.

TWO LEVELS OF EDUCATION

There are two levels of learning and two schools of thought when it comes to teaching. There is the common school, where everyone becomes socialized and each must fit in somewhere and find their place in the collective pecking order. And there is the sanctuary or temple of learning, where a person seeks to awaken to their inner nobility and true nature. The first level aims at fitting into the immediate cultural environment; the other sees with a sweeping vision what might be possible in life. While basic education can give a person some grounding in life, it also brings the danger of everyone learning to act in limited ways, only ever flying a few feet off the ground, never moving far from the beaten paths and the agreed upon limits. Deeper levels of learning depend on revelations of inner powers and gifts that lead to vastly wider world views and capacities to reach greater heights.

In the metaphor of the chickens and the eagle, all the little chicks need the same nourishment and basic instructions for surviving. They need to learn the local mores and accepted social hierarchy. After all, everyone starts out in the barnyard of life, even those who have the good fortune to be born to a higher perch. Even a student who aces every test and rises to the top of the class may be caught within the limiting framework of the barnyard of learning. Rising to the top of the pecking order does not necessarily lift a person out of the yard where people scratch out a living and fail to awaken to a purpose beyond survival or simple achievement. A person can be a "good egg," a successful rooster, a beautiful chick, or ruling hen, yet remain unaware of the greater potential and unique purpose hidden in their life.

The point is not that the first level of living and learning has no value; rather that there is a deeper revelation and higher standard waiting to be experienced. The eagle-chick has an inner nature already aimed at higher values and greater knowledge. Yet, something or someone must help the eaglet awaken to its own inner nature. When the time comes for really trying one's wings, a true awakening of the inner spirit becomes the primary point of learning. While everyone needs to become socialized, the deeper function of education involves the inherited human need to become aware of a greater sense of individuality and genuine purpose in life.

General instruction properly concerns itself with basic levels of learning and practical considerations. At this level, most students need to be taught the same basic curriculum. Survival and the needs of society require that children learn what it means to become a good citizen and a productive member of society. However, the education of genius goes another way altogether, as what wants to be learned has its basis in something that was present in the student before any instruction began. The genius within us already knows the dream trying to come to life through us; it naturally seeks confirmation and blessing from those who appear as teachers.

The genuine point of deeper knowing and higher learning involves an inner awakening that can lead to a true matriculation of the individual. The verb matriculate carries this double sense of education. On one level it simply means, "to register, to become enrolled;" on another level it means to tap into the "matrix" of life and the womb of one's origins. Each young person is pregnant with a precise knowledge that already resides within them, and education at a deep level means to "lead out" what is trying to be born from within. The job of a true teacher is to help awaken the inner pupil that has its own way of being and unique way of perceiving the world.

Since the genius in each person is unique in some way, each student requires some specific education in order to grow from within and flourish. When it comes to the ground of being, each person is already seeded with ideas and images that need to be recognized and nurtured so that these inner conceptions can blossom and produce the fruits of knowledge. There is an education of the heart that fosters the growth of ideas as well as the imagination needed to bring the gift of life to a place of fruition.

Learning is a sacred task, not necessarily in a religious sense, more truly in the spiritual sense that each student enters the world with an inner spirit that can awaken to a meaningful purpose and genuine destiny in life. Amidst all the arguments about testing and accountability in schools, the real meaning of education becomes routinely lost. So lost has the deeper sense of education become that many now believe that the easily bankrupted ideas of the marketplace can simply be applied to public education. Amidst the collapse of vertical imagination, which has left everything seemingly fallen into the soup of "the economy," education increasingly comes to be a production line where learning is just another product and students are prime consumers being prepared for life in the barnyard of materialism.

Parents and authorities may lament the negative effects of "peer pressure" on young people, yet they often fail to address the damages caused by the pressures of collectivism and the excesses of materialism. Attempts to redesign education using business models are not only unwise, they are also insulting to the inner nature of children and the spirit of young people. The sense that education should simply produce "contributing citizens" with acceptable careers represents a collapse of imagination and a loss of essential ideals. In a world of great uncertainty that is changing rapidly, the education of genius, with its surprising capacities and persistent resiliency may become more a necessity than an option.

The genius is an inner figure that personifies the deepest powers of each person's imagination, which is the living source of all forms of human achievement. The greater the absence of personal imagination, the more we seek to fill the void with banal substitutes for the things of the soul. Intellect alone may trap us in a world too narrow for growth; while fantasy may entrap us in illusions that are simply out of this world. Genuine imagination includes insights into the nature of oneself as well as the outer realms of both nature and culture. Imagination creates liberation by revealing secrets of nature and the nature of the inner life of the individual. Imagination is itself a thing of genius and the deepest power residing in the human soul.

When education becomes a business something sacred has already been lost. When education becomes learning by rote and teaching only fixed ideas there is a loss of soul as well as a lack of spirit. Rather than an adventure of learning, education can become a weight and a burden for students already discouraged by the lack of authenticity that pervades mass cultures. The focus upon basic instruction in institutional learning often fails to acknowledge or support the distinct spirit for life already present in each child that enters school. As Aristotle warned a long time ago, "Educating the mind without educating the heart is no education at all."

Education comes from the Latin educare, meaning "to lead out, to lead forth, to raise up." The old Latin verb is behind many of the conflicts and arguments in contemporary education. To truly educate would mean to raise up to awareness and lead out into the light that which already exists and is waiting to awaken inside each student. In this old sense, education involves a revelation of the innate qualities of the student, not just a honing of his or her ability to mimic or adapt outer modes of learning. What wants to be led out of each child is the unique spirit embedded within.

INSTRUCTION, DESTRUCTION

The other big word in the semantics of learning is "instruction." Instruction comes from another Latin verb, instructare, meaning "to pack in, to pile up, to give structure." Much of what we now call education is actually collective instruction. Modern mass culture tends toward mass indoctrination and standardized instruction, which packs the same knowledge into each young person, often without learning the true nature of the student. Modern education often reduces all students to learning the same information by rote in order to produce normalized and productive citizens; instruction packed in leading directly to production carried out.

For a society to truly prosper, remain innovative, and develop resiliency, it must balance social instruction with a deeper education. Instructional learning is not for the genius in a person, but for the common intelligence within them. In this view, it becomes more important to lead out and recognize the inner nature and qualities of the student before packing in too much information and too much instruction. An inner genius resides in each soul, its nature is surprising and unpredictable. That is what makes life worth living. When it comes to genius there can be no "one size fits all."

We all must grow up in the circumstances we are born into. We all become, to one degree or another, the products of our environment and of the times in which we live. Yet, we also carry within us something that is timeless and able to transcend our immediate circumstances and commonly accepted limitations. Eternity is interested in the productions of time and something eternal hidden within us aims to produce beauty and meaning in life. Each person has a potential appointment with their own potential, as that which naturally belongs to us tries to become consciously our own. The inner genius, the spirit already present in each young person and every student, needs to be awakened and allowed to spread its wings. The deepest meaning of education involves the awakening and leading out of the inner genius of each person.

When teaching becomes primarily transferring information and instilling rote behavior, both teachers and students fall away from the promise of life and the appointments with genius. If the natural genius goes unrecognized, a child can resist instruction and become more destructive. Their genius becomes obstructed and they resist further "packing in" until the resident spirit can be led out and confirmed. The opposite of instruction is destruction, meaning "to tear down," literally "to un-build." Denying a person meaningful opportunities to express what is most natural and self-defining in them can cause their genius to turn towards destruction.

Education that becomes too general or overly indoctrinating can un-build the natural confidence of students and undermine the sense that they have innate gifts to give and a genuine inner life that needs attention. Hence, many students find modern education uninteresting or nonapplicable to their struggle to "become themselves." As Einstein warned, "Any intelligent fool can make things bigger, more complex, more violent. It takes a touch of genius—and a lot of courage—to move in the opposite direction." And, as Mark Twain put it, "I have never let my schooling interfere with my education." General education can prepare a person for daily life, but a genius-based education is needed to awaken a person to who they are intended to become in the course of their life.

The intrinsic potentials of the soul belong to the "inner pupil" that looks out from the eyes of each student who enters school. In that sense, it can be said that every student is a genius—not in the sense that each is a potential grandmaster at chess, virtuoso on violin, world-class inventor, or a brilliant scientist; but in the sense that they are born with a distinct spirit for life, that there is something of value born into the world with them, and that there is something unique within them that would become known, that can become creative and truly generative. Genuine education seeks to bring into conscious awareness and put to greater use the inherent gifts, talents and qualities that the pupils already carry when they enter school.

The second level of education involves learning the nature of our own genius, how it is aimed at life, and how best to live with it. The inner genius already knows where it needs to go and what it longs to express. In genius education, that which is most naturally ours becomes consciously our own. While this involves an awakening from within, it also requires recognition and blessing from others. Therefore, awakening genius requires both individual effort and collective attention. Assisting students to develop their inherent gifts and qualities can lead to greater personal fulfillment; it may also be crucial for adapting education to the intense pressures and needs of the troubled times in which we live.

EAGLE VISIONS

In the story of the eagle born among chickens, the contrasting of the two birds works on many levels. Both have wings; yet one soars above everything, and the other can barely lift off the ground. Because chickens have long been domesticated and cooped up in pens, they develop a tendency to focus on the immediate ground before them. Metaphorically, they become representative of the part of culture that reduces the individual to nothing but a number or a dull member of a statistical group.

Meanwhile, eagles rise far above surface concerns and entrapments. They fly to great heights and soar effortlessly, as if being carried by the breath of the world. They ride on worldwide currents and see both nature and culture with penetrating vision. They see with a broad sweep that encompasses the breadth of the world; but they also gaze with the eagle eye that can zero in with exceptional accuracy.

As a traditional symbol of brilliance, eagles were identified with the radiant spirit of the sun. Eagle feathers were worn by tribal chiefs and holy people, often radiating like halos around their heads in imitation of the sun's brilliant rays. Or, in the case of a young brave, a single feather might rise from the back of the head as if to indicate the awakening of imagination, courage, and newborn nobility. Imagine that when someone talks of getting a "feather in their cap."

Having essential connections to both the elements of air and fire, the eagle becomes a proper symbol for lighting the flame of education. As it used to be better known, education is not so much "the filling of a pail, but the lighting of a fire." Living in the full light of the sky, eagles represent the light of consciousness as well as the dawning of new knowledge and the burning desire to spread the wings of our spirit for life.

In antiquity, people imagined that eagles had the power to gaze directly and unwaveringly at the sun and that the eagle mother would turn the eyes of her eaglets until they looked into the burning source of light and life in this world. Of course, if humans literally stare at the sun, blindness rather than vision will be the result. Symbolically however, to gaze deeply into something means to become identified with it, as Shakespeare knew when he wrote, in Henry VI: "… if thou be that princely eagle's bird, show thy descent by gazing 'gainst the sun." This old idea of a symbolic test of one's spiritual connection to the sun survives in ceremonies like the great sun dance of Native American tribes and in solstice traditions found throughout the world to this day.

Like many native peoples, the Pawnee tribe of the Great Plains revered eagles above all other animals. After the birth of a child, they held a ceremony intended to connect the newborn with the great bird of spirit. In the midst of the ritual of dedication to spirit, a puff of white eagle down would be placed upon the head of the infant. Ancient people felt they could touch and see the spiritual breath that gives life to each of us still moving through the body of the little ones so recently delivered from the great world of spirit. So, the soft down feathers would rest exactly upon the fontanelle, the tender spot where the child's skull remains open after birth.

The down feathers would be gathered from under the wings of eagles, right where they moved as the eagle breathed, right close to the beating heart of the great creature. Thus, each child would become symbolically connected to the breath and heart and spirit of the soaring bird. "With the spirit of your wings I soar, with your eagle eye I see," went an old song sung by the tribe at the blessing of a newborn child. The ritual would also connect the inner spirit of the child with the source of life in the sun that lights and warms the earth. Likewise, the child would be invisibly tied to where the immortal life-breath was forged. In a sense, the little one became one of the children of the sun and the protected offspring of spirit.

Important ideas were woven within old ceremonies as the inner nature of the child would be recognized as both spiritual and transcendent, and thus not simply derived from its earthly parents or limited by whatever ideas might be current at the time. This distinction helped to distinguish the potential life path of the child from the expectations of the parents and the common concerns of the group. One day the little one will grow old enough to try his or her own wings and will seek a vision that might reveal a view of the world as precise and encompassing as that of an eagle. It is in this sense of awakening that the concentration of mind and scope of vision of a person's genius can be understood.

Something in the child has its source in the center of life and that inner something will one day become necessary for the young one to know, and important for the rest of the tribe as well. This is true of each child born regardless of family circumstances or social conditions. The least among us can be carrying the exact vision that can lead to a new path for everyone.

During times of difficulty or disorientation, eagle ceremonies and symbols would be employed, as eagles were widely believed to have the power to bring new life or to renew a life that has fallen into darkness. Imagine the difference if contemporary education involved the blessing of the native spirit in each child, or if we returned to the ritual processes that could restore a sense of nobility and inner radiance when people become lost, depressed, or deeply discouraged.

TECHNE VS GNOSIS

It may seem hard to believe that the great majority of people would miss the opportunity to try their own wings of inspiration and imagination; but that has become the case. The story of the eagle that lived as a chicken tells a sad and common truth increasingly found in modern mass cultures, where the rule of literalism and the collapse of vertical imagination weigh heavily against the growth of genuine individuals. The awakened individual has always been somewhat at odds with society's need for conformity; but now an increasing tension pits mass culture and systematized education against the genuine spirit trying to awaken in the individual child.

As the reach of technology becomes more valued than the surprising and sudden pathways of ascension provided by one's own wings, the symbol of the barnyard can also stand for the realm of technology, which can be more limiting than liberating. We see those limits clearly in the myth of youthful Icarus, who ascended to the realm of the sun on manufactured wings fashioned of feathers and wax, yet fell just as quickly when that artificial method exposed him to the genuine heat of life. That is not to say that all technology is misleading or harmful; more that it can take people far off course and lead to a false sense of being connected to life. Like any system or collective process, technology can restrict us at the same time as it promises to free us.

Techne is an old Greek term that includes the sense of both "making and doing" things. Technology has been with us from the beginning, or at least since we have been making things and doing things. Originally, techne involved the kind of knowledge bound to issues of basic necessity, while gnosis was the contrasting term that involved higher knowledge as well as deeper thinking. Whereas techne applied to practical knowing in the outer world, gnosis referred to deeper ways of knowing, the kind of knowledge that gave people genuine insights and could make them wise. The difference now tends to be that people believe that technological inventions can solve problems that exist on much deeper levels. The problem now is that young people become attached to personal devices that substitute horizontal connections and endless streams of information for deeper relationships and a truly awakened inner life of the soul.

When we say we want to help students develop their potential, we are essentially saying that we want to assist them in awakening their inner genius and support them in finding the pathways that can lead to personal fulfillment as well as the benefit of those around them. When genius becomes involved, learning can occur suddenly and swiftly, the way a bird flies. A seemingly effortless sense of transmission can happen once the native intelligence and genius qualities have been engaged. A true education awakens the living spirit in the student and helps to reveal the calling already set within them. For, the inner pupil knows what course it needs to follow and how it is already oriented and aimed at life.

Seen this way, education does not introduce something completely new and unknown to the student as much as it involves a leading forth of something already present but not fully recognized. True teaching, then, would lead a person to self-knowledge as well as to a love of knowledge and an instinctive sense of self-discipline. With the idea of an innate nature and resident genius comes the sense of an inner life that can shape the pupil from within. Each student already carries an inner dream that tries to awaken and become known. Revealing the shape of the inner pupil will best determine how the student can become a genuine disciple of knowledge and a lifelong learner able to help awaken others to their own genius self.

CHAPTER 9

SURVIVAL MENTORING

The most common form of despair is not being who you are.
- Kierkegaard

At each turning point in life, there is a chance to look back before trying to push ahead. If we look carefully, certain events stand out like landmarks while most things fade in the distance. I was almost fifty years old when I first tried to write a book. For me, it was a meaningful turning point that forced me to look back over my life. For years I had kept copious notes on the things I studied and on key events in my life; but I did not think of that practice as "writing."

When a journalist asked me when I first knew I was a storyteller, the answer came immediately to mind, though it wasn't an answer I expected or had prepared in any way. It was more like a vision in which I saw myself as a teenager with a book in my hand and a light in my mind. It was the night of my thirteenth birthday and the book was the only gift I recall and, in some ways, the only thing I needed at the time. Of course, I had all the neediness of youth; but I also had a longing to know why I was alive and why I felt trapped in my family and in our neighborhood. And, I needed to know firsthand if I had anything meaningful to offer the world around me.

I did not understand it at the time, but young people need to know both—if the world has something to offer to them and if they have something to offer to it. Surprisingly, the book in my uncertain hands answered both of those questions. To this day I am grateful for that gift and the fact that it was also an accident. What I mean is that I didn't choose the book as much as it chose me, and that makes all the difference in this daunting and surprising dance of life. It is one thing to have choices in life, but another level of meaning altogether to be chosen.

I had asked for a history book in the hope that I could find an explanation for what I felt was a world that lacked meaning and a future that might serve no real purpose. My maternal aunt, who encouraged my education and somehow sympathized with my sense of anguish, bought what she thought was a history book and gave it to me. When it turned out to be a book on mythology, she wanted to take it back and exchange it, but I would not let it go. Once it was in my hands, I knew I had something intended for me despite and because it appeared to be the wrong book. It was not what I thought I wanted; it certainly was what I needed. It was mine by mistake and by accident on one level, and it was no mistake and no accident at all on another.

At the time, I did not understand that my life was changing forever. All I wanted to do was to read the entire book from beginning to end and, in what I now know to be true mythological sense, to start from the beginning all over again. I had found my life language, or it had found me; my aunt had given it to me without knowing what she was doing, as if some other hand had a hand in the matter; as if Ariadne was silently handing me the life thread and clue to what I longed for without knowing it.

That night, I was on fire and the memory of it is burned into my heart and soul. Each occasion of looking back reveals more of what happened in that open moment that opened the world to me in a new and, at the same time, ancient way. When the reporter asked when I became a storyteller, I was transported back into that moment that I only later realized was a genius occasion. Only through moments like that do I truly understand the radical meaning of the old idea that genius must be born and cannot be made. That was the crowning moment of my thirteenth birthday; yet it was also the beginning of a second birth in a psychological sense and in mythological terms.

When the opportunity to write a book appeared I was not sure that

I could do it; but I was also unsure if I should do it. The word author can simply mean "maker," but it has roots that go back to "authority" which also connect it to "authenticity." It seems a good idea for an author to have some genuine inspiration and authentic reasons for writing and publishing. I found both challenges daunting and might have put it off longer had it not been for a pattern that developed at night.

It didn't happen every night, but often enough, I would awaken in the dark to see sentences and even full paragraphs right before my eyes. Sometimes I would hear them being spoken as well. Not like an outside voice that might awaken others, but an inner voice only speaking to me. Each time it happened, I had the choice of getting up to try to capture the words or fall back to sleep and lose the nighttime script. As the pattern persisted, I realized that something was trying to be written through me whether I liked it or not. A part of me was writing, even while I was sleeping. Eventually, I had to find out what the inner voice was trying to tell me and if the text could be made into a book.

After a year of very little sleep, I had a manuscript that tried to bring mythic stories to bear upon issues at play in contemporary life. Like the burning questions I felt in my youth, the nightly script focused upon the lack of meaningful initiations in modern life. Writing the book became a kind of initiation for me, just as the book tour afterward also turned out to be. I was surprised that the inspirations that pushed me to write in the first place stirred again on the page each time I read from the book. It was as if I only learned after it was published what the manuscript was all about.

At book events I could talk about the themes intelligently and connect them to contemporary life, but the act of reading what I had written sparked additional sentences to appear on the spot. On one level I would be reading from the page, at another I would be adding spontaneous sentences like those that woke me at night and forced me to write. One definition of an initiatory event is it pulls us further into life than we would choose to go on our own. I felt that the book was continuing to pull me into places I might not choose to go otherwise.

A core theme of the book involved the ancient initiatory pattern of birth, death, and renewal. Although the stories in the book were ultimately encouraging, they required an understanding that for something greater to be born, something else must die. Because death was in the middle of any genuine transformation of life, I felt I had to speak about it directly. Since denial of death is a characteristic of modern life, I had to expect some discomfort and resistance in each audience. What I did not expect was that I might be taken as an authority on the weighty subject of death. Furthermore, I did not anticipate in any way the intensity of the questions that would come, often at the end of the evening, and especially in college towns or other places where young people showed up to listen.

After each reading, there would be a line, long or short, some people with books to sign and others with distinct questions to ask. Often there would be students who would stand at the end of the line, clearly waiting until everyone else had departed. I was delighted that young people would attend these events and often found their perspectives and questions less studied yet more provocative than their elders. They were intrigued to hear stories about rites of passage and the search for meaning in life; they were also compelled by ideas of death.

Eventually, there would be one young person left who would ask the last question and typically the subject became final things. "What about death, you mentioned death... What if someone thinks about death… a lot?" "What do you have to say about suicide?" Or, as several young people in pain simply blurted out: "I'm thinking about killing myself." Or, "I tried to kill myself." As the lights in the bookstore were going out and the streets outside becoming empty, one troubled soul demanded: "Why shouldn't I kill myself, tonight?"

I was shocked at first, and if it had happened only once or twice, I might have considered it an oddity, like the strange questions asked by those who seemed to read a different book from the one I wrote. But, it happened frequently, over and over; girls and boys, freshman and juniors in college, the poor and the rich. I began to keep an eye on whoever was lingering at the back of the line, anticipating that every evening would end with young people thinking of ending things for themselves.

As the tour wore on, the accumulated weight of these heavy questions coming from young people began to weigh on me. It felt as if I had taken on some heavy responsibility, another role beyond that of author. It was clear that the young people needed to talk to someone and were willing to take a risk on me. Instinctively, I felt that I had to listen with all my ears in order to find an answer attuned to what was in their souls. Regardless of how late it felt or how much I needed rest, I tried to listen for what was really being asked of me. I felt responsible to relieve them, at least momentarily, of the mortal burden they struggled to face and put into words.

Ultimately, I felt if they took a risk with me, I had to take a risk for them. Yet, I also felt uncertain that I had any real authority or right to answer what clearly could be life or death questions. I thought of the mythology book I had held so tightly when I was young and feeling so uninvited and unwelcome in the world. I thought of young Telemachus in the story of the Odyssey who feels isolated and overwhelmed as he wanders in anguish on the shores of his homeland. Even though he is the prince of the realm, he feels defeated and unable to stand up to the challenges of life on his own. Along comes Mentor, an old sailor who knows the rough waters of life and offers him some sage advice. He inspires the youth to find his own voice and take a stand in his life and for his life.

Had I inadvertently stepped into the role of mentor while worrying over the issues of being an author? Had I not unwittingly moved from being opposed to all the authorities to having to speak with some authority? Not for myself, but for the sake of those wanting and needing some voice from outside themselves to confirm something as yet undefined in themselves?

When the somewhat aggressive young man asked why he shouldn't kill himself that night, there was no way I could abandon him even though I had never seen him before that moment. There was no time to earn a degree in psychology or get some credential that might make my answer more valid or more meaningful for him. I had to draw upon some unseen authority that might help us both out of the situation. In the old myth, it is Athena, the goddess of wisdom, who speaks through Mentor when he advises the anguished prince. I simply said what came into my mind in the moment.

"You shouldn't kill yourself now because you don't yet know who you are; that's why." I wasn't lecturing him, but trying somehow to meet him at the edge of his anguish. I could sense that he was caught in a tension between defiance and fear, a place I knew well from my own youth. He seemed to want ideas, as if saying, "Give me a reason not to and I won't do it." I thought I heard the familiar challenge: Someone tell me why I should live and I might try to live. People tend to live on ideas and young people can easily die with a wrong one.

"Right now," I said, "death knows you better than you know yourself; that's why you think dying might be the only answer. When you know yourself better, dying will be less attractive. Right now, something you've outgrown or outlived might need to die so that you can go on living. Listen, you don't want to die; you just don't want to live a life that's not really yours." He clearly took that in and no longer looked as defiant. "Are you sure?"

"Pretty sure," I said; then went further down that road: "Besides, you wouldn't ask me unless you wanted some arguments from the side of life. So, the question is not should you die, that is ultimately inevitable. The question at this point is what in you really wants to live? For that is something that even death must respect."

He became even quieter, this time in a more settled way. Not just thinking, but seemingly remembering something. Suddenly, he acted as if he had something important to do or had somewhere else to be. He didn't explain it and I hoped there wasn't a bridge involved or something else dangerous. It was clear that we were finished with our conversation on death and I wished him well as he hastily departed. I gathered my books and things, which seemed heavier now and wondered if he felt less burdened.

I never saw him again. Yet, he showed up in a different form at the end of the line at the next reading. "You spoke of purpose in life, are you saying we are more than an accident waiting for death to happen?" I was becoming more alert to the presence of suicidal ideas, even if they were veiled. "Do you think it's simply an accident that you are asking me this now?" I asked. "No," she didn't think so. But had I thought of suicide when I was young? I told her I had and that most people had suicidal thoughts when they were young.

"Really?" Something in her seemed to wake up as if she needed to know that she was experiencing something understandable, even meaningful. I went on: "It's only part of you that wants to die; the rest of you wants to live more fully. It's a signal that it's time for you to enter life more fully."

She nodded, almost enthusiastically. I nodded too. I was beginning to get used to this. I was especially realizing how important it was to give death a place in each life, to relate to death in a way that makes sense for that person. Youth need to let parts of themselves die in order for other parts to begin to live fully. However, the young psyche is prone to feel the extremes of "all or nothing," and the death of one part of them seems like the death of the entirety of them. The avoidance of the subject of death in the collective mind and culture makes it haunt youth who know it must be there somewhere. Important things need a place... and death is vitally important, especially for the living.

As the conversations about death continued, I began to understand my role better and trust the "mentoring moments," when an earnest question seemed to draw a telling answer from me or from somewhere beyond me. To another young woman who asked if I ever felt like dying, I answered that I did. When she became awkwardly quiet, I found myself asking: "Have you tried it?" She said she had, more than once. "Recently?" "Yes…" "Looks like you're not very good at that," I said. That's not what I would say to someone else; but somehow it felt as if a little humor might lighten things up for her. "I think your talents lie elsewhere. What if the issue isn't letting go of life, but finding what you're supposed to do in life? You need to find something you're good at. What do you want to do?" "I like to write." "Well, that takes time. It took me almost fifty years to live enough to write one book. You need to live in earnest in order to write and feel the things that will feed your writing. You need time to learn how you write and what you really need to write about."

"Can you get into a writing program?" "I could." "Please do that. Do you have people to talk to?" "Yeah." "Write about what you feel and talk about it. Trust someone; you are here to do something just the way you came here this evening to find something. Will you be ok?" "I think so. Thanks."

What was I supposed to do? Was I saying the right things? What was my responsibility to these young people? Why wasn't someone talking to them? It was clear that they felt enough pressure in their lives to ask a stranger how they should deal with depression and death. I felt I had to offer something and was surprised at their willingness to accept my thoughts, consider my advice, and even take my direction. Clearly, they sought a kind of authority they could not feel in themselves at that time. Unfortunately, in a culture that constantly misuses authority and often avoids essential issues, young people might miss the opportunities to get some guidance when they most need it.

Meanwhile, I felt I was living through moments that proved the old Irish proverb that said that "death was the middle of a long life." If the presence of death could be handled in a meaningful way, then life could go on in its intended way. The end of another reading came and another young man stood, quietly waiting his turn. He was tall, angular, and forthright. "What about suicide; you mentioned death, but not suicide?" I asked right back, "Have you tried it?" "I'm thinking about it." "Have you figured out how to do it?" "Yep." We stood there silently, almost hanging between words. The shortness of his answers was troubling. He's ready to do it, I thought, and I became afraid for both of us.

I thought, I'm leaving here in the morning and this kid is in real danger. What can I do? Now, I looked around for help. A man was sitting at a nearby table and I realized that he wanted to be the last one. He was listening while trying to appear as if he wasn't paying attention. I asked: "Are you from here?" "Yeah, I live here." "Listen, this kid's really in trouble. He's going to need someone local to help him. Can you find some help for him, like a therapist or counselor?" I'm staring hard at him so he'll realize that this is serious. Finally, he nods.

I turn back to the youth: "Listen, I'm afraid you're about to make a big mistake. Will you talk to a therapist about this?" More silence. Now, I'm staring hard at him. Finally, "Yeah, yeah I will... I'm scared too."

Back to the man: "Do you know a good therapist?" "Well, I am a therapist." To the boy: "Will you talk to him." "Yes." Now, to the therapist:

"I don't know what to say about paying; I don't know his situation." The man said, "It's alright, I'll work it out."

They sat at the table and began to talk. The young man seemed to relax; the therapist was direct and calm. I looked at him again as if to say: "You were going to ask me something...?" He shook his head, as if to say, "Now there's no need." Maybe they needed each other; I certainly hoped that would be the case.

As the death conversations continued to happen, I felt I was learning how to listen in ways that caused the young people to feel they were truly being heard. That was clearly something that they needed in order to begin to trust themselves. Until a person has truly been heard, they don't know what to trust and can suddenly accept the idea of letting go of life. The other aspect of the mentoring moments involved them hearing an authentic response. Modern societies offer young people endless distractions and many inauthentic experiences. This leaves youth with a heightened sense for the inauthentic and a desperate need to be in genuine situations that can confirm their lives.

That point was driven home in the next conversation with death, when a disheveled-looking college student awkwardly asked what I thought about suicide. When I asked him if he had tried it, the answer was a shake of his head: No. "What then?" I asked. Well, he was thinking about it a lot. "Is there a plan?" Another nod came: Yes. "What's the plan?" I asked.

Now, he looked wildly confused, almost insulted, as if to say, "You can't ask that; that's secret." But, I was asking, feeling that he asked me for a reason and might not ask again before doing it.

"Alright, there's a bridge I go to at night," he answered. "Do you have a time or a date?" "Yes."

Now, I'm feeling confused and scared; yet I have no choice except to keep going. As I look at him, I can see him going over the edge. He is not well put together and looks as if he has been slipping for a while.

"Alright, who will be hurt the most if you do it?" Now, he softens and seems to pull back a little. "My niece, she looks up to me." I could feel how true that was and could feel an agony in him that must be present in the whole family. Tears were forming in his eyes; in mine as well. "You can't do it," I said. "You can't leave her with that burden. She loves something genuine in you; you need to love that too." Something like that; I don't remember clearly, for suddenly I was holding him as he fell into my arms like a child and just cried.

I needed an agreement from him before I would let him leave. Would he agree not to kill himself? Yes. Would he get some help? Yes. Would he go and hug his niece and tell her that he loved her? Yes, he would, and I believed him.

After that I was angry. I was sad; but I was also angry at the realization of how thoroughly abandoned young people can be in the midst of a culture that promotes public education, yet fails to offer genuine guidance and understanding. Young people can have great flights of imagination and they can also take things quite literally. For them, thinking of dying is very close to doing it. Sometimes it turns out that thinking of living is very close to doing that too. The world of youth can be like that, immediate and extreme, magical and tragic almost at the same time.

What good is a higher education if you have no idea who you really are? What good is a career if you have no real idea what to live for? There needs to be opportunities for young people to sort things out and genuine guidance when they have the courage to seek it. The fact that these were brief conversations seemed to suit most of them; as if some philosophical assurance and spiritual encouragement in the moment can be enough for them to take the next step on the road of life. There is a way in which being willing to pick up the weight of death, even for a few moments, helps young people be released to enter life further.

MENTORING MOMENTS

Eventually, the book tour came to an end; but it was not the end of events where I found myself facing life and death dilemmas with disaffected youth. I had learned that a person becomes a mentor, not so much by choice, but more from being chosen when someone needs them to be truly present.

Over time, I found myself working more and more with young people who were on the edge of either violence or self-destruction. I came to think of these encounters as mentoring moments, intense exchanges that formed part of a developing practice of survival mentoring.

Unfortunately, young people at all levels of society are increasingly exposed to disorientation and uncertainty. Whether the situation arises from a slipping-down life on the streets, from unbearable pressure to perform at high levels in elite schools, or the lack of meaningful opportunities in marginal areas, more young people feel unable to take the next step in life. Most young folks lack the blessing from others that remains an expectation of the human soul. Culturally, there needs to be an education about death that gives it a place in life. And, there needs to be more opportunities for mentoring moments that confirm the inner worth and value that each young person carries within.

A general type of mentoring can happen when someone simply acknowledges the presence and value of a younger person and offers them some encouragement or support. What I am calling survival mentoring puts both mentor and student on more demanding and sometimes dangerous ground. It demands that the potential mentor takes a genuine stance with regard to the life of the young person needing help. It could also be called crisis mentoring in a similar sense to the instinct behind "hot lines" for suicide and other crises that are increasingly prevalent in modern societies. At critical moments, young people need a lifeline, and mentoring is the age-old and instinctive way to help pull them further into life.

Youth are naturally filled with longings they cannot understand. As they step away from childhood, they long to belong to something; yet the answer cannot simply be a social group. For, there is a deeper longing for genuine recognition that can make them antisocial if it fails to be fulfilled. Each young person is a problem trying to solve itself, a mystery trying to be decoded by facing obstacles and genuine challenges in life. Something attempts to come to conscious life in youth and come into the world through youth. Youth carry archetypal energies that favor risk and seek transformation as something "other" in them tries to awaken and become known. In definitive ways and at critical times, young people become unknowable to others in order to become known to themselves. Their breakouts and breakdowns are symptomatic of a hidden identity trying to break through the skin of normal attitudes and behaviors. Whether poor or rich each young person will remain a mystery unto themselves until they come to grips with the mysterious spirit trying to awaken within and live through them.

Regardless of their appearance or life circumstances, young people are on a path of discovery that becomes most meaningful when it turns to self-discovery. They gravitate toward trouble because they are troubling over who they might really be. The point in youth, and at any turning point in life, is not to avoid trouble at all costs. The point is to find the right trouble to be in; for when in trouble we are closer to inner resources we did not know we had and nearer to the knowing spirit that brought us to life in the first place.

It was the Roman poet Horace who advised: "Adversity reveals genius, prosperity conceals it." Genius is waiting to be revealed in each of us and, in the right kind of trouble, a person can transform their entire life. The right trouble will provoke the tension and at times the turbulence between a person and their life purpose. Youth are the troubled and gifted, living opportunity for a society to remake itself. But, the troubles of youth become the problems of culture if they are not confirmed as unique individuals and truly welcomed into collective life.

Modern cultures tend to deny the presence of death as part of life and that makes genuine transformation more difficult. Ancient cultures, being closer to the cycles of life and death in nature, knew that for something to grow, something else must die. A second and psychological birth is the unconscious need which drives youth to extremes and the water of this rebirth becomes anything in which they can lose themselves in order to find more of themselves.

The archetypal sense of initiation implies both the need for something to die and the potential for rebirth at another level. When a culture fails to address the mysteries of life and death and does not offer genuine images of transformation and renewal, youth will be more at risk than they need to be. Lacking consciousness of the inner genius and spirit for life trying to awaken within them, young people will seek forms of oblivion and dissociation. Drugs, alcohol, sex, speed, power, anything that might offer the sense of touching the unseen, even at the cost of health and well-being.

A culture faces the essential problems of human existence when it faces its youth. Suicidal fantasies so common to modern youth stem from a collective confusion about the underlying instinct for radical change as opposed to the developmental process that applies mostly to children. At the end of childhood, the human soul has an expectation of an archetypal passage in which a "little death" leads to a rebirth in a greater life. Youth can easily confuse the need for a little death with a sacrifice of their entire life.

The turmoil that marks much of youthful experience is also the necessary labor of the next generation trying to be fully born. When adults cannot understand that youth are trying to give birth to themselves, it is an indication of the suppression of their own youthful longings and an attempt to impose that suppression upon the next generation. Modern youth tend to be a separate social class—self-enclosed, largely uninitiated by elders, and increasingly communicating only amongst themselves. Young people are increasingly isolated in their separate class and overburdened with cultural weight that older people refuse to take responsibility for.

In fact, many adults simply envy youth, wishing they were young again, imagining youth to be the time of no worries and limitless potential. Modern tendencies to remain immature, self-involved, and narcissistic throughout life, grow from an omission of the death and rebirth passage, that helps to dissolve childhood attitudes and opens the psyche to the immensity of life as well as the presence of death.

A mentoring moment can be a chance to plant invisible seeds that will grow throughout life. Some seeds fall on fertile ground and sprout immediately; others may lodge somewhere and go unnoticed until they sprout unexpectedly at a time and place distant from the original sowing. Often other people enjoy the fruits of mentoring without knowing who nourished the seeds or inspired the effort to begin with. It is similar to the effect that loving, caring parents can have on children with the difference that a mentor helps awaken and foster the life project of the student.

On the other hand, the lack of mentoring leaves many seeds of genius dormant. The abandoning of young people right at the time they are ready to awaken and transform themselves is another tragic condition of modern life that ripples through the world with disastrous and deadening effects. Mentoring becomes essential at certain points in a life. When it does not occur, other lives are affected as well, as everyone suffers the diminished spirit for life. Meanwhile, much good can happen in a single mentoring moment; not just recognition, but confirmation and even a blessing can occur. There can be a transmission of knowledge and the flipping of an internal switch that lights up the soul and opens a path for it to follow. All human beings long to learn before they die what they are living for and what their souls are aimed at. Yet, in order to grow from within, we each require that our inner life be blessed by someone that we trust and respect if only for a moment.

CHAPTER 10

MEETING AT THE EDGE

Being authentic is a requirement for becoming wise.

The Odyssey of Homer remains one of the best known examples of a myth that continues to speak to modern people. The epic tale of Odysseus suffering endless obstacles and tortuous dilemmas on the long journey to find home continues to offer a basic metaphor for life itself. Home may ultimately be found in the depths of our hearts; yet we may have to wander far into the world and become lost in many ways before we reach the place of origin within us.

The actual telling of the Odyssey begins closer to home and far away from the heroic scenes of war as it focuses upon the hero's youthful son who has been left behind. Young Telemachus has come of age during the absence of his father, the king. He assumes the role of prince of the realm; but he lacks support and faces tremendous dilemmas of his own. He watches as an unruly horde of warriors and would-be leaders take over the realm. They recklessly begin using up the resources of the land and threatening to leave everything in chaos and he feels unable to stop them.

He is old enough to grasp the state of affairs that has developed in the absence of the rightful ruler. Yet, he is young enough to sorely miss the guidance and counsel of his noble father. Telemachus, whose name can mean "far from battle," unsuccessfully attempts to stand up to the marauders. Feeling isolated and overwhelmed, the prince wanders alone on the shores of the island, anguishing over the condition of the world and his inability to change it. He laments the loss of the grandeur that once was and the absence of the ideals that made life meaningful. He suffers a loss of innocence and fears no meaningful future exists before him. He laments that the gods have inflicted heavy cares upon him and moans that the weight might soon break him into pieces.

It is in this moment of great disorientation and deep doubt that Mentor comes upon the scene. Neither parent nor ruler, Mentor comes to play a different role. Described as an old sailor and friend to the missing king, he enters from the other end of the shore and from the opposite end of life. Mentor and youth both seem to be driven to the edge by the chaos at the center of the realm. Opposites in both age and life experience, they meet at a place betwixt and between one thing and another, where the solid earth meets the flowing tides of change.

While the young prince questions whether he can stand up to the challenges of life, Mentor represents lived experience and brings a body of knowledge to the situation. As an old salt, he understands that "smooth seas make bad sailors" and that trouble attends all meaningful enterprises. Instead of the complicated attitudes of a parent, Mentor brings the steady hand of an old sailor. Mentor fills the absence of father with the presence of an advisor and teacher.

THE SPIRIT OF MENTORING

The meeting of Mentor and the troubled young prince is an archetypal event, a mythic occurrence that gives us the term "mentoring." Yet, in mythic terms, the third thing is always a charm, and so in order for real change to occur, a third element is required. In this case, the third and most telling element appears as Athena, the goddess of wisdom and protector of the center of culture. The goddess becomes attracted to this meeting of the old salt and the young person feeling lost and at sea in a tumultuous world.

Grey-eyed Athena tells Zeus that she will go to the home of Odysseus to stir up his son and put some confidence in him. She speaks of awakening his life-force, raising its presence in him, and stirring the voice that attends his spirit as well. At first the goddess appears as Mentes, a young oarsman who tells the prince that he must stop clinging to childhood and learn to speak boldly against those ruining the realm. Then, she enters the psyche of Mentor and speaks words of encouragement and wisdom through him. Thus, when the original mentor advises the troubled youth, he is being inspired by the goddess of wisdom. This scene remains of great importance for anyone who would consider the essential meaning of education and understand the inspiration needed to change a culture that has lost its way.

Athens, and all that it comes to represent in terms of culture and learning, takes its name from Athena. It also takes its core imagination from the olive tree which Athena created to symbolize living peace and prosperity at the center of human culture. The practice of mentoring arises as well from something eternal and wise that can help awaken the life spirit in each young person; but that also serves to renew the spirit at the center of a culture. The role of mentor becomes a practice for the making of genuine elders who understand that young people need to be welcomed into the heart of culture.

When Telemachus pours forth the issues burning within him, Athena speaks through Mentor, telling the youth that he will have to find his voice and speak his mind to the congress of marauders. She advises him that the things he needs to know will be found in his own heart or else some divinity will put them in his mind. Mentoring intends to call forth a spirit that can encourage the human mind and embolden the human heart. Genuine mentoring has a spiritual component, as it is the spirit of life that seeks to become known and be heard in each young soul.

The young prince must take a further step into life that can help him reveal himself to himself. He stands at the edge of childhood and at the threshold of awakening to a greater self. The child in him wants his father to return and stand by him. Yet, his fate requires that he take his own steps and take a stand for himself. In order to become himself, he must shift from being trapped between heroism and passivity to speaking out and finding his own voice in the drama of life.

Telemachus is not simply "saved" by his meeting with Mentor; he is moved to enter the world in a greater way. Once again, the issue is not simply heroics. In fact, all the famous heroes are absent and at war when the original mentoring occasion occurs. With the encouragement of Mentor and the inspiration of Athena, Telemachus manages to take a stand and deliver a passionate, inspired speech. The marauders listen to his fiery words and even congratulate him. However, he is unable to move the assembly of usurpers or alter the troubling conditions that threaten the realm.

The prince is still young and faces troubles beyond his abilities. He cannot forcefully change the world in which he lives. Yet, having stood up for himself and found his voice, he can now take greater steps on his own two feet and stand in the power of his own spirit. Freeing the speech of the soul helps release him from the spells of childhood and allows him to enter his own life adventure. In a sense, he fails at the heroic task; yet his own life moves dramatically forward. He assembles a group of youth and prepares to set off with Mentor on the seas of life.

The act of mentoring helps youth search within for meaning and genuine identity, but it also helps initiate a greater search for knowledge in the world. Mentes can mean knowledge, wisdom, and guidance, and mentoring instinctively involves us in old, wise ways. Within mentoring moments, utterances can become oracular and influential, taking on the urgency of inspiration, even the feeling of revelation. It was in this inspired sense that learning was considered to be a sacred activity attended by guiding spirits.

The young prince represents the nobility of youth and the crisis that faces all young people regardless of race or gender, economic status, or social background. For, each young person tries to awaken to the innate nobility and inherent genius of their own soul. Like Telemachus, the inner spirit of each person tries to break into time and space during youth. For, each girl or boy has inner nobility and something to contribute as well as a great need to feel necessary to life.

Mentor acts as a vessel through which a divine intelligence speaks and stirs the life spirit of young people, but he also seeks to respond to the historical and cultural issues of the day. Mentoring is a creative work in the sense that something is being born or fashioned that can alter the world. Mentoring is an art that brings otherworldly knowledge and inspiration to a situation that otherwise seems overwhelming, unjust or even hopeless.

The initiation of Telemachus is set within metaphors of inspiration and an education of the spirit intended to give hope and a sense of purpose to a young person in a time of crisis. The hope that comes from Athena arrives in the form of knowledge that stirs a person's life spirit and awakens their inner voice. For there are words written on the heart and scripted in the soul of each young person, just waiting for the breath of inspiration and the invitation to be expressed in the world. Speech is a key part of the genius of humanity and in order for a thought or a vision to become real it must be given full expression in some form.

Mentoring represents an invisible continuity, something ancient, meaningful, and enduring being passed on, in the old way of person to person. To mentor means to enter an age-old practice that aims to reveal the true nature and natural genius of youth while awakening the inner elder in mentors and teachers. Mentoring can build a bridge between young and old, between existing traditions and current needs, between past and future. Mentoring gives coherency to learning and offers an age-old way of making and keeping continuity amongst generations. Creative mentoring is the way culture becomes renewed, as well as a process through which youth encounter their own genius and unique spirit for life.

THE TURMOIL WE'RE IN

Thousands of years have passed since the tragic tales of the Trojan War and the epic story of the Odyssey were first told aloud and elaborated by Homer. The journey of the hero trying to find a way home continues to play out in a world continually plagued with wars that promise heroic rewards. Yet, the epic adventure, often considered the defining story of Western culture, begins with an abandoned youth trying to find his footing in life and a meaningful way of contributing to the heart of his culture.

The initiation of Telemachus takes up a third of the entire tale of Odysseus, and it too prefigures the conditions that persist throughout the world at this time. Chaos at home, wars abroad, and youth despairing at the edge of life are not simply aspects of the past. Given the current conditions of life, it makes great sense that the story of the human odyssey begins with an absent father, a missing king, and a queen and mother who must struggle night and day to keep the wolves from her door.

Absent fathers abound and it can often seem that there are no proper leaders in sight. Gangs and homeless people roam the streets, troops as well as refugees appear everywhere, and corporations exploit the earth and often lay waste to the land. Mothers are beset from all sides and aspiring youth become weighed down with heavy hearts as they must question not only their future, but also the future of this troubled world.

Youth must grow up within the atmosphere of the times in which they live. The dilemmas that troubled the heart and mind of the ancient prince have become multiplied and intensified as modern youth inherit global issues and planetary problems. Rather than the issues of an island kingdom contemporary youth must face a worldwide wasteland that forms before their eyes as great forests fall to feed common greed and ice caps melt for lack of foresight and loss of reverence for the balance of nature. The anguish of modern youth includes growing up amidst fears of worldwide chaos and decline, as the turmoil of culture is paralleled by great disturbances in the balance of nature.

We live in extraordinary times, amidst extreme conditions, as both nature and culture undergo great disturbances and radical changes. Not simply extreme weather changes, but religious extremists abound and the politics of extremism pervades everywhere. Amidst the intensification of oppositions and the polarization of many groups, young versus old may easily become a basic split and a widening gap in cultures all over the world. Cultures tend to fall apart from two ends at the same time. When the dreams of youth are not welcomed and nourished; when the wisdom of elders fails to develop, culture can unravel rather than cyclically renew itself.

It was conditions of chaos and greed that brought forth the archetypal presence of Mentor to begin with and that might again give mentoring a key role in imagining solutions for the seemingly impossible tasks that trouble the heart of the earth and threaten the center of human culture. Like so many things of enduring value, the word mentor and the idea of mentoring come from the timeless realm of myth. When time seems to be running out and the end of everything seems near, it is not more time that is needed, but the touch of timeless things and the presence of mythic imagination and a trust in the nature of life to renew itself.

THE ARCHETYPE OF MENTORING

Mentoring is an archetypal activity that has timeless elements which can connect us to the universal ground where nature renews itself and culture becomes reimagined. Just as the original mentor and the troubled youth meet at the edge of the realm, elders and youth are each on the edge of life. Youth and elder meet where the pressure of the future meets the presence of the past. Old and young are opposites that secretly identify with each other; for neither fits well into the mainstream of life. It is the dynamic meeting of opposites that draws the goddess of wisdom to the troubled ground of the earth.

More than conditions of age, elder and youth are each symbolic states in which imagination can become heightened and wisdom can become more available. In a mentoring moment, a young person can become wiser than their age while an elder can experience a renewal of youthful dreams and the core imagination of life. When we say youth, we refer to an ideal, a symbolic condition more than an age limit. The same is true of the elder, which is more a symbolic state than a guarantee that comes with advanced age.

Youth and elders each carry aspects of an essential and timeless gift that only becomes visible when the parts are joined. On their own, youth cannot quite evoke the meaning they carry within; by themselves, the elders cannot quite establish meaning in the midst of life. The weird gifts and strange legacies of both youth and elders are both required to make the road of life meaningful. The awakening of genius that first occurs in youth naturally leads to lifelong learning and practices that develop "olders" into elders. Rather than retiring from life, awakened elders become the guardians of meaningful education as well as the protectors of cultural wisdom.

The distance between elders and youth in modern life becomes emblematic of the loss of continuity so characteristic of modern mass cultures. Wherever the generation gap expands, the continuity of culture diminishes further. Both youth and elders become isolated and at risk of rejection where mass societies are dedicated to simple materialism and excessive practicality. The roles of both youth and elder conflict with the insistence on productivity and the reduction of life purpose to short-term goals. Elders and youth share a natural longing for the nobility of life and for transcendent ideals.

The grandness of life must be represented to young people through someone other than their parents. In that sense, mentoring is a natural replacement for parent-child relationships. Parents must nurture the life of children and nourish their physical and emotional essences. Mentors, on the other hand, nurture the gifts and purposes intended to grow a life well beyond the needs of childhood. Once the spirit of life and inner genius begin to stir, mentoring replaces the dynamic of parenting and shifts the base of learning from adapting to the family to adhering to something inherent in oneself. Mentors awaken the spiritual nature of youth. They parent on a spiritual level what the parents have unknowingly nurtured physically and emotionally.

Mentoring involves a mythic sense that individual life repeatedly transforms as well as the understanding that with each generation the world must be made anew. Mentoring is a renewable practice with roots in the human soul, a prototypical way of learning and teaching that can bring into play genuinely inspired ideas and heartfelt dreams that can alter the conditions of the world.

Being more art than science, mentoring involves creativity as well as psychological awareness, an awakening of genius as well as a sense of survival. Genuine mentoring helps to recognize and awaken, uncover and release the genius in the student or pupil. In that sense, mentoring is not a social activity intended to make life easier for young people. Rather, mentoring involves an essential relationship that includes aspects of fate and issues of justice as well as an intensification of human presence in the world.

Mentoring aims to quicken and deepen the "interior life" of young people. Having an interior life becomes increasingly important when the world around us lacks continuity and coherence. As the outer world becomes riddled with trouble and uncertainties, the inner life must provide some sense of grounding and stability, or all can begin to seem hopeless and meaningless. A world lacking paths of purpose and meaning is a daunting prospect for those just starting the road of adult life. Youth are at greater risk when they don't feel much continuity with the past or a promise of a meaningful place in the present. Having no abiding past, they can fail to imagine an enduring future.

In trying to escape the past, the modern world has left much behind, including the instinctive practices of mentoring. Mentor begins as a mythic figure and mentoring is an archetypal activity that has timeless elements which can connect us to the universal principles in human life. Mentoring involves our natural inclinations to teach as well as instincts to guide and protect. In considering mentoring, we place ourselves in a stream of stories that arise at the back of time.

Mentoring seeks to reveal the natural genius of each young person, while also awakening the inner sage within. Only those who find their gifts and glimpse their own core can properly see the inherent qualities of others. The desire to help others to awaken happens naturally in those who feel acknowledged and empowered themselves. In attempting to awaken and guide others as mentors, we step into a stream of knowing, an age-old continuity which involves the exchange of wisdom amidst the struggle for the nobility of the human soul.

The word mentor comes from the same roots that gave "mental, mentation and teacher." It stretches back to metis, meaning "wisdom and guidance." Mentoring involves us in old, wise ways that depend upon remembering the presence of inherent gifts, not on the implementation of abstract systems. Genuine learning continually returns to revealing what is known and carried within the individual soul. Genius to genius mentoring involves a transfer of knowledge as well as bestowing of a blessing.

Mentor and pupil are part of an ancient lineage and a great love of learning. In the moment of learning, we truly know, as in the old sense of gnosis; we know in the blood and bone and in the heart. We enter a "different state," an "other place," a realm of inspiration. The divine breath of inspiration enters and life can become truly changed by knowledge. Genuine learning helps fit our outer life more closely to the inner life of meaning and purpose which is trying to live through us. In the shared state of knowing "inner authorities" awaken. In those moments, the natural authority and living presence within both teacher and student can grow.

In mentoring, being authentically present is more important than appearing wise or all knowing. Mentoring involves a mutual seeing into the life of the other. Where a teacher is inauthentic, they will appear transparent to youth, who have a high sensitivity for the inauthentic. Mentoring is not a matter of needing to know all the answers, nor is it simply a matter of age and experience. When teacher and pupil or mentor and student come together something else is at play, a third and mythical element that can shift the ground from simple advice or basic instruction to inspired speech. As the old myth suggests, the willingness to be present as a mentor can open the way for sudden inspiration and even for oracular events.

THE COURSE OF MENTORING

It is no accident that Mentor appears as an old sailor, for sailors know that ships are always off course. Sailing involves continuous adjustments and correcting to the course. Mentoring can be similar in the sense that the true course is being set by the genius in the soul of the student. The mentor does not have to set the course for the student to follow as much as help to keep things on course and aligned with the spirit of the young person. We accept what teachers and mentors say because they resonate with things residing in our own hearts and minds that need to become more conscious to us.

Innate talents and inherent ideas in young people expect to be activated and wait to be called upon. This natural expectation can be strong enough to awaken the inner wisdom of a mentor or teacher and draw both teacher and student into inspired speech. It is in this way that teachers can seem like oracles speaking directly to the hearts and minds of students. Specific things in each of us expect to be activated and wait to be called into awareness. Someone genuinely searching for an answer or a sense of direction hears exactly what they need to hear, as if an oracle has spoken. Oracular speech can be miraculously clear or may need interpretation or the passing of time to release its meaning. Yet, something occurs that shifts the direction when there seemed to be no hope of going forward.

Mentoring is an instinctive practice and a revivable tradition that can provide tools and tales of learning that can break down the walls of isolation and cynicism that often separate youth from elders. Mentoring is a renewable practice, but is not simply a program that can be organized and applied in a bureaucratic manner. It is a practice with roots in the human soul; a prototypical way of learning and teaching that works best soul to soul and genius to genius. As young people face increasing pressures in a world of rapid change, the ancient practice of mentoring can provide both inspiration and grounding that transcends common systems and programs.

Mentoring can form a bridge that allows genius to enter culture more fully and spirit to revitalize human community. At the same time, mentoring others helps clarify the purpose and meaning in one's own life. Genius fosters genius as both student and mentor awaken to a greater sense of meaning and purpose in life. Mentoring moves both the elder and the younger folks further along the path of individuation and fulfillment. Seen this way, the central task of educators, counselors and therapists, involves the awakening and refining of the genius of each person. Quite naturally, those who have been mentored tend to turn around and help the next ones coming along. The interlocking levels of learning and guiding can serve to hold a community together and lead to greater understanding from one generation to the next.

The ancient practice of mentoring is part of our universal human inheritance; as such it is endlessly revivable and able to help us find continuity and more stable cultural footing in the present. Mentoring involves learning ancient truths and ways of being present in life, but it also nourishes and supports the innovative and inspired visions of youth. Used in creative ways, mentoring becomes a living bridge between generations, a practice that invites youth into the true adventures of life while helping to generate healthy communities. Genius-based mentoring extends to all periods of life and all meaningful endeavors—the arts as well as the sciences, the spiritual paths as well as the critical work of helping nature heal.

There is great meaning in the idea that Athena, the goddess of wisdom and protector of the heart of culture, appears as the spiritual inspiration behind mentoring and counseling people. Genuine mentoring combines traditional practices with innovative ideas that can generate ways of helping to heal nature as well as re-imagine culture. Awakening the genius within each individual opens surprising paths to personal fulfillment, but also leads to innovative ways to solve the increasing number of problems we face as a global society. Teaching and learning both bring something eternal and wise to the recurrent human dilemmas and can help make the future more viable by drawing the mythical past into the present. Mentoring can invoke inspiration from the otherworld and protection for the ideals critical to the center of culture.

We live in a time of extreme events and the loss of holding institutions and unifying stories. There is a lack of genuine wisdom and a loss of cohering ideas. As things polarize and collapse, energies of the deep unconscious shift and raw emotions rise more readily to the surface of life. We live in a time of fear and disruption, when furious changes occur at all levels of life and blind fury can erupt anywhere in the world. The meaning of fury can range from "fierce passion" to "violent rage," and to "madness."

In myths this kind of rage was depicted as the Furies, or the Erinyes, meaning "the angry ones." Some stories say that the Furies dwelt close by the Gates of Hades and would be stirred to frenzy whenever blood was spilled on the earth or where injustice came to prevail. As primordial spirits of vengeance, they would rise from the depths of the earth to punish those who violated the rules of nature or spilled blood wrongfully upon the earth.

Whenever people of this world have forgotten the sacred nature of the earth and have turned to violating it, the Furies come to visit the world in many guises. By now, they must never return to the underworld, but simply dwell among us in all the forms of blind emotion, vengeful ideas, and fanatic beliefs that spread fear and anger all over the earth. Amidst all the churning, the world seems to have turned upside down so that the upper world has come to be the underworld.

Of course, a mythic view would suggest that this has all happened before and that remedies can be found. At a time when the Furies threatened to torment all inhabitants of the world and make all the land toxic, it was Athena who persuaded the Furies to break the cycles of blood vengeance instead. The goddess of wisdom gave them a place in her temple and offered them a new role wherein they serve as protectors of justice rather than purveyors of vengeance.

In a sense, Athena mentored the blind rage of the Furies and turned the raw emotions of the unconscious from toxicity to nobility. Once given a place of respect in the world above, the Furies became known as the Eumenides, or the "kindly ones." Once they assumed more benevolent aspects, they became the spirits who push edible plants up through the earth in such abundance that people began to remember that the spirit for renewing life dwells within the Soul of the World and resides within the soul of each person as well. Amidst the storms and furies that attend the great odyssey of life on earth essential things keep getting lost. Yet, in this world nothing completely disappears; if we allow for the presence and guidance of unseen spirits, we may find ways to correct the course of modern life and find again the capacity to renew our lives and assist the world to renew as well.

CHAPTER 11

MIDDLE OF NOWHERE

Genius seeks an edge that can become a center.

In order to work more closely with both mentors and at-risk youth, a group of us began a series of week-long retreats in rustic camps far from urban neighborhoods. A retreat would give youth a chance to be in nature and give us all a chance to work without daily pressures and neighborhood issues. We began inviting groups of mentors and youth from the most oppressed communities in America to gather in remote camps and work together. Because of all the difficulties of gathering youth for an extended period and arranging trips from various neighborhoods, we invited more than we would need for each event. Of course, we felt overwhelmed when, at one of the initial retreats, most of those we invited showed up along with some we had no prior knowledge of at all. All in all, we wound up with almost sixty kids from rough neighborhoods and gang-involved areas, and about half as many volunteer mentors.

Some of the youth had not been informed about the nature of the event and therefore felt no obligation to pay attention or even remain present at scheduled meetings. When we were able to gather them together, they remained poised on the edge of departure, always just about to leave the room. Sometimes, they would get up and walk out with no notice and no explanation. After all, most of them had dropped out of school and had opted out of the common culture, and many were quite ready to leave this life altogether. I say that because some stated that they would be dead by the time they were eighteen, while others revealed that they wished to die soon.

All young people find themselves in situations that feel like life or death; for these kids, life and death were daily issues. This reality left them on the hard edge of life, ready to throw down over almost anything or prepared to just walk out. Their sudden departures implied that there was not enough presence in what we were doing to keep them present; what was being said seemed false to them or too weak to stand up to the pressures they felt in daily life. In addition, anything they were unfamiliar with could be considered phony or insulting, and any confusion we might display could be felt as a lack of interest in them. It would be easy to miss the fact that, although they walked out many times, they never completely left. They showed up at times, particularly when there was music, especially drumming. They tended to listen when poems were read and openly commented on ones they liked.

More than anything else they liked to hear the ancient stories. During storytelling, they paid close attention to every word; afterwards they could repeat the details and even asked questions. Once, I was telling a long adventure tale and broke it up into episodes over several days. They appeared promptly for each telling and kept asking when the next installment would occur. As they surrendered to the rhythm and plotline of the mythic adventures, they looked younger and became more open. Many would actually become childlike, completely dropping the hard poses and outcast mannerisms they adopted when living on the streets. In those moments, you could see they were just kids on the inside, made old before their time by neglect, abuse, and hard living.

When I finally reached the end of the story, the young hero we had all been following had completed all the dangerous tasks and not only survived, but wound up winning the love of the princess and receiving the crown of the kingdom. The whole room burst into applause and almost joyous appreciation, as if the success in the story somehow ameliorated the pain and alienation of daily life. We were all glad to be in that room; we were all in life together despite our contrasting experiences and palpable differences.

Even the failures we were having in coming together seemed worthwhile, as for a moment we were all in it together. Then an even more surprising thing happened. Out of sheer enthusiasm, one of the kids ran right up and jumped into my lap. He was about fifteen and had already lived on the streets for some time. He was one of the smaller kids, but had as many tattoos and as hard of an attitude as anyone present. But, here he was sitting in my lap like a seven-year-old, hugging my neck as if he were my son. I felt a little embarrassed and feared that the other youth might insult and humiliate him for acting like that. However, after he got back to his feet and thanked me for the story, everyone else just went on talking about the story. It was as if they understood at some level that they had all missed out on simply being children and feeling the joy of being alive.

It was a remarkable occasion for all of us, but it affected one of the mentors most deeply. He had grown up hard in a Latino neighborhood, had gotten into trouble and joined the army in order to escape the situation. Now, he was running a wilderness camp for troubled youth and trying to combine his knowledge of street life with the survival skills and discipline he had learned in the military. Being impressed with the way hardened street kids responded to mythic stories, he asked if I would come to the camp and work with the hardest kids of all. The idea intrigued me, I agreed to try it, and a plan was made.

When the time came, I was driven to an area of high desert and dropped off in a place that seemed to be in the middle of nowhere. All I could see was a rough camp sitting in the midst of an endless expanse of desert. After being oriented to the lay of the land and the need to avoid the sun and drink lots of water, we set off to meet the kids. I was expecting to meet a crew of truly hardened kids who came from the streets and had been in prison or at least in juvenile detention. The first surprise was that all the girls and boys were white and looked pretty young. But, I was truly shocked when it was revealed that the camp was a last resort, a place where wealthy families sent their children after they were kicked out of elite private schools. The remote desert camp turned out to be a last ditch program for what I decided were at-risk rich kids.

The unwilling members of the group shared two common elements: they stood to inherit great wealth and they had been in trouble both in school and after school. They had all experienced some involvement with drugs and alcohol and had acted out in a variety of ways. The wealth and position of the families had allowed the troubled kids to be moved from one exclusive school to another until there were no options left. Now, about a dozen of them were living in a wilderness camp beyond the pale of all social life. They had managed to exile themselves from elite schools and opulent homes and were reduced to camping out in an almost barren wilderness. They were out in the middle of nowhere, having to learn to conserve food and water rather than living the high life and doing whatever they pleased.

Each had their own small area, defined by a scrub tree, rock, or depression in the land where they camped out in army surplus tents. They dressed in used, poorly fitting army fatigues, and each carried a bag with a few essentials and just enough food for one day. They looked like survivors after a great calamity, or a troop of homeless people who had wandered away from civilization, poorly prepared for the elements of nature. They were like reverse refugees, the orphans of extreme privilege with nowhere to go.

As refugees from abundance, they seemed to be the direct opposite of all the young sisters and brothers who lived in poverty and oppression, those who scrape a living out of the mean streets and partly deserted inner-city neighborhoods. At first, I could not fathom how these could be considered "hard kids." In fact, they looked more like lost souls. The lost kid in them was sticking out all over as they carried their little bags the way a child might drag a blanket or a stuffed toy.

Strangely though, their eyes defied their state. If you offered them compassion, you'd be in for a shock. For they did not accept or even fully feel the harsh reality of their forlorn state. They looked to all the world like outcasts and seemed like orphans; yet, they considered themselves somehow above it all. The glare of defiance harbored an inner state of denial that barely held them together as they stood against the wilderness. Despite the fact that their parents could afford anything they desired, or maybe because of it, they simply could not afford to be present. They were not present in the midst of nature just as they had been mostly absent at school. They were truly lost because they were lost unto themselves.

They were dressed like refugees but acted like jaded nobility that would one day be restored to the high positions due to them by birth. Draped in surplus army clothes and out in the middle of nowhere, they would speak of being able to be anywhere they wanted to be. As if the wilderness did not count, as if a limo might arrive at any moment and whisk them away. Despite their evident neediness, any offer of sympathy was treated as an affront. They seemed to have an unshakeable belief in a future place of high status and their anointed right to assume it at some point. They were lost souls carrying a wilderness within them as they stumbled about in the middle of nowhere.

Their disdain for the world around them reflected an absence of anything real inside themselves. The inner emptiness turned out to be what made them seem the hardest kids to work with. But that did not become clear until after I became so frustrated with them that I refused to even speak to them.

I had been telling them a story in which a person left behind all that they had in the world and all the people whom they knew in order to follow a dream that had come in the middle of the night. The dreamer had been told that a golden treasure waited to be found and that it was time to go and seek it. I stopped the progress of the tale at a point where the wanderer appeared lost and threadbare and had worn through the soles of his shoes without finding any reward. The scene seemed to parallel their homeless situation, and I wanted to know what dreams they were carrying beneath their ill-fitting fatigues. I asked them to consider what the dream of their life might be, hoping to have a conversation about things that mattered more than wealth and status and other people's expectations of them.

Their answers both surprised and troubled me. I was asking for images and dreams of what their souls desired; but they described estates, vacation homes, even business holdings. I could hardly believe it and could not accept that to be the genuine language or the longings of their souls. They were old enough for their souls to speak the language of genuine desire, not the jargon of brochures and portfolios. When I challenged the nature of their supposed life dreams, they became quickly offended. I pointed out the rank materialism and elitism of the stuff they offered as dreams. They said I had no right to tell them what their dreams should be.

I said I was not telling them what to dream, just pointing out that those could not be genuine lifelong dreams. I wasn't asking about their parents' materialistic dreams for them; I was asking about their deeper selves and their own dreams of life. They claimed the right to desire whatever they wanted. I argued that they were parroting things that other people wanted them to want.

We were at an impasse over the meaning and purpose of dreams, and they began to dig in their heels as if they had something essential to defend. Before I began the story, they had been bickering about various things and insulting each other, behaviors that the camp staff insisted were their only pastimes. Now, they were united and even willing to defend each other. They would not follow the rules at school, nor would they try to learn from nature; yet, they would band together to defend what were clearly received ideas planted in them by their families. Their fixated sense of privilege kept them from having any genuine sense of who they were at the core of their lives and that made them hard cases indeed.

Now, they had a new focus for their collective complaints: If I say it's my dream you must respect it; you have no right to judge what I say because it's my choice. The collective complaint became more heated when they accused me of acting just like the other adults in the camp, trying to tell them what to do and already betraying them.

In the heat of the day, we sat uncomfortably close together, in the middle of nowhere, heatedly arguing over dreams and imagination, over wealth and privilege and who was betraying whom. All my sympathy and empathy seemed to escape through the cracks in the tent as I began to feel hollow within myself; but also offended and mistreated by their misplaced defenses. As I began to feel alone and really stuck in the middle of nowhere, they were becoming unified around their desperate defense of false dreams. They had accepted their parents' plans as substitutes for their own dreams of life. This left their dreaming selves shrunken and small, angry and sad, leaving them with little capacity for truly feeling or expressing themselves. Now, I could feel my own soul shrinking and getting smaller by the minute. That's when it hit me: I could not reach them while the plans of their parents overshadowed the innate longings of their souls. I was not really talking with them, but with the programs their parents had placed on them at such an early age; their sense of self was well-hidden behind their families' plans and programs. Despite the current outcast condition they were in, they remained programmed in ways that made them feel superior to others.

I was beginning to understand what had seemed at first an unnecessarily harsh attitude amongst the camp staff. They appeared to be fed up with the orphans of abundance and I was just becoming aware of why that might be. I was becoming angry and on the verge of saying things that would add to the pain and would be hard to take back. It was time for me to get out of there. I told them I was leaving and would not talk to them until they could speak honestly about themselves. They became appalled at the idea that I would walk out on them and became incensed when I got up and left.

I was so glad to be out of that overheated tent of frustrations that I walked straight off into the desert, oblivious of the blaring sun. When I finally stopped, I realized that I now felt trapped in the middle of nowhere. I felt a wilderness of pain and confusion inside myself as I realized that I had nowhere to go either. It was as if I had become fifteen again and wanted to break something in order to dispel the feeling that I was trapped in a wasteland of misunderstanding, or imprisoned in someone else's life.

One of the inevitable results of working with young people is that they will cause you to relive your own youth and especially revisit the most intense emotions and frustrations of that stage of life. The dreams of our lives do try to surface during youth, and those lifelong dreams typically put us at odds with family and friends and our own ego-driven attitudes as well. As I wandered aimlessly away from the camp, I recalled a day when I burst out of my family house screaming in my mind: "This is not my family, I was not born to these people. I am from somewhere else. This is not the source of my life. They don't even know who I am!"

I had to get out of that house and get at least physically beyond the stultifying limitations of my family. If I couldn't feel myself, I would go crazy. Or worse: "I would become them! No!" I could hear my mind screaming. On one level I was in the middle of nowhere, on another I was back on the street in front of my house, wanting to scream "No" at the top of my lungs.

Back then, I had run across the street where a vacant lot stretched between our block and the next one. For the kids on our block, it was simply an empty lot we crossed through to go from one street to another. It was mid-summer, but I didn't notice the coolness of the weeds and bushes. In my anger I stared at the old unpainted house that leaned on one side of the lot, seeming about to fall over. The lateral slats of wood were worn and almost bare of paint, so that it looked like no one lived there. But, there was a family there and a son named Billy, a little older than me. He was not as big as some of the older guys, but he carried something that made him seem bigger. In my current state of searing anger I thought about him.

No one in the neighborhood thought much of him, except to repeat stories of how crazy he was and what he had once done. Everyone was actually afraid of him because he had a legendary capacity for rage. At an age younger than I was at the time, he had killed another kid and had done it with one punch. It happened before we moved there, so I didn't know the dead kid and only knew Billy by sight. The neighborhood story always focused on that single punch and the fact, if it were in fact true, that he had done it right there, in the lot by his house; the same lot we played in and walked past on the way to school every day.

That day, I stood there, just steaming inside; looking at Billy's house, possibly standing right where the kid got killed with one angry blow. In the fury of that moment, I felt more like Billy than the kid. No one talked to Billy; there was the fear of his rage, but also a sense that the stain was transferable. Yet in that moment, I could see myself tear a piece of stained wood from that house and smash something or someone with it. I could see how it could happen in a moment of blinding fury and I began to understand the anger and rage that seemed to well up in most of the kids I knew.

Eventually, I did talk with Billy a few times. At first I made a point of saying hello; then small conversation. I was leading up to asking him about killing the kid. I wanted to know if he really did it and why. And one day I just asked him straight out. Despite his reputation, he didn't get angry, but suddenly looked sad in a way that seemed beyond his years. He said it had been an accident. They were playing and had a fight. He got angry and punched the other boy. The kid fell back and his head hit a rock there in the lot and he died.

Because it was an accident, Billy was not punished by the law; but he sure was judged and punished by all the neighbors. I didn't ask him anything else because the darkness that had fallen over his face was enough reason to end the conversation. There seemed to be nothing else to say.

Now, standing on edge of the open desert, I felt more sadness than anger. I felt sad for the alienation that happened to Billy and even a little sad for the orphans of privilege lost in their foolish delusions. I had wandered amongst the rocks and scrub trees of a small outcropping. It was strangely beautiful. Although I could feel the sun pouring its heat down, it no longer seemed to dominate everything. My anger had also diminished, as if it mixed with the air and became cooled by the shadows and green patches of life within the rocks. It occurred to me that nature had a capacity to absorb anger and ease other emotional states as well. I didn't know that when I was fifteen, exploding onto the street, needing to be held by something greater than my own anger. Now, I could sense how nature openly accepts the flood of strong emotions in the same way it accepts the excesses of the sun, the scourge of winds, and the downpouring of rain.

The more I became present to the spirit of the place, the more I could see its subtle elegance and gather in the pungent fragrances that hung in the overheated air. Amidst the sharp shadows, there were subtle and understated signs of beauty. Beneath the glare of the sun and under the covering of dust, I could begin to make out the varied colors of lichen, even tiny flowers hiding between rocks. They fairly danced in the air and, once noticed, they seemed to intensify and hint at other invisible presences in the landscape.

I began to feel sympathy again for the orphans back in camp who were so lost and alienated within themselves that they couldn't find a way to be present in the midst of nature. I felt sorry that I had lost my compassion for them and thought how easy it is to judge and alienate each other and wind up exiled within ourselves and out of touch with the beauty of the world.

As I began to wander back toward the camp, I realized that the whole group needed to be out in the land in a way that would make everyone more present, inside and out. They had to feel that the place of exile could become the center of everything if we could find a way to be more genuinely present. There was a reason we were all out in the wilderness, and there had to be ways to reorient our lives from within. We needed to make a center in the middle of nowhere so that they might feel something essential and centering in their own lives.

The desert had been talking to me and I was beginning to understand the language of the situation. I had wandered into a camp of refugees who were experts at keeping themselves in exile and in quickly exiling others. What we all needed was a genuine sense of unity and acceptance. The direction was becoming clear even if the method was not. Now, an idea began to form as I looked at the rock formations in the desert.

In mythic terms, even a single rock can symbolize the omphalos, or navel at the center of the world. "Upon this rock I shall build a church," goes the old saying that turns a common stone into a rock of ages. Stones formed the center of the world in many ancient traditions, just as they did in sweat lodge ceremonies that would have been held for young people in places like the desert we were in. While there wasn't time to make something as elaborate as a sweat lodge, there were some rock formations that began to look a lot like altars to me.

What if we built an altar out in the middle of nowhere and made it a unifying center? Placing things on altars is one of the elemental gestures of human ritual, and ritual is one of the genius things for all humanity. One of the problems with the modern world is that we lack exactly the rituals that we need to make ourselves whole. We especially lack rituals that can help young people find the deep center of self that can give them psychic stability as well as a genuine sense of orientation in life.

I now wanted nothing more than to build an altar in the middle of the desert, and to build it with the orphans of abundance. Of course, they might not be as excited about carrying stones in the heat of the desert in middle of nowhere. The whole thing would seem foolish to them; they barely acknowledged the presence of the desert and the exiled condition they were in. A ritual can't really work if people don't desire to participate in it.

To do it right a lot of stones had to be carried and everyone would have to help. It had to be all or nothing; everyone pulling together or else there would be more exile and drifting apart. The altar would have to rise up from nowhere and become central to them. They had already lost everything, except their false notions of who they were inside. Now, they would have to make something from nothing in order to let go of the false sense of self that was keeping all of them from entering the next stage of their lives.

While I sat in my tent humbling myself before the idea that we were going to build an altar in the wilderness with no shared beliefs or social agreements, something had crystalized amongst them. Their desire to hear the rest of the story and have another discussion had begun to outweigh their resentment of how they were perceived and treated. They sent emissaries saying that they would have better things to offer if we had another discussion. I was happy to try it all again on the condition that we endeavor to make something together. It was quickly agreed with them and with the camp staff.

When the time came to gather, they arrived promptly and looked almost eager for something. Just one problem: one of the boys was under a disciplinary restriction that required him to stay at his "spot" for the remainder of the day. Everyone else was prepared to go on. But, I couldn't do it. If a community ritual is developed and someone has been left out, they will not be able to rejoin the group very easily. The group would have reformed around a central experience that they were not part of. Rituals can either be exclusive or inclusive, and this one had to include everyone.

In a way, the excluded one would be the only one left in the middle of nowhere, and that could be truly damaging. We had to bring the most recent exile back into the fold and that seemed to require settling the matter that caused the disciplinary action. That is often the way with making a creative ritual, once you start you have to go wherever the process might lead. It happened that the youth had tried to run away despite the fact that we were miles and miles from any place to run to. Mostly, he had endangered himself and upset everyone else with fears of his injury or death. Now, he was refusing to speak to anyone or accept correction; thus, he was in solitary detention at his spot.

The camp director was willing to lift the discipline if the youth would at least speak up and explain why he had run off the way he did. Meanwhile, the missing member did wish to rejoin the group, but he refused to talk to the director. I went to meet with the young man. It turned out that the issue involved the manner and attitude of the camp director and the youth's acute sense of injustice. He felt that the director had misjudged a situation and had mistreated some of the group. When the exiled youth stood up for those falsely accused, he became the one to be punished. I asked him to return and speak up for himself. He refused to do it. After further conversation, he revealed that while he could stand up for the others, he could not take a stand before the director on his own behalf. He felt he really couldn't do that.

It was evident that this was a core issue for him and in that sense, he was already in a symbolic condition. His inability to speak for himself was the wound that kept him isolated, and it represented a key issue for the entire group of refugees from abundance as well. He was the epitome of the exile they all shared and was the likely key to shifting the entire situation. Thus, he became the pivotal piece in a rite of reorientation. In a sense the ritual was already underway and he would become the first rock that had to be moved.

In the earlier attempt to discuss dreams of life, he had spoken of his father owning many companies that were all over the world. I imagined that the father was gone often and was a powerful presence when he did appear. That could leave a child with some authority issues and a heightened attention to injustice. I didn't inquire about the particulars because the situation seemed to speak for itself. I asked if he could speak if all the youth supported him. He considered the idea and said he would try if I agreed to come to their aid when things got desperate. We made an agreement and I went to inform the director that we needed to have a communal meeting.

The banished youth sat with his friends and began by defending the one who had been wrongly accused to begin with. The director suddenly challenged him for not explaining his own actions. I began to realize that part of the trouble lay with the forceful manner of the camp director, who had barely listened to the anguished youth. As he struggled to speak up for himself, I quickly moved behind him, giving him reinforcement. Suddenly, he burst out with a tirade against improper authority. He spoke directly to the head of the camp and accused the director of having it in for him from the beginning.

The director began to defend himself and accuse all the youth of being disrespectful and self-involved. Tears of anger and frustration began to fall from the eyes of the boy. Yet, he did not stop; he cried out with an unmistakable passion that made him seem older all of a sudden. You could feel the unity of all the young people forgetting whatever their own issues might be and becoming unified behind the pained courage of one of them. You could also feel desperation in the air as the camp director now seemed to be the one who was cornered.

The situation had reached a breaking point where things would either break into a new plane of honesty and relatedness or else break down even further. The camp had been dividing along the lines of the authority of the staff as opposed to the resentments of the youth. Underneath that was the question of what the young people really needed in order to feel fully alive and part of something meaningful. We were partway to where we needed to be in the sense that the youth were now unified and vitalized. If the banished boy was exiled again, it was clear the entire group would join him.

A genuine ritual needs at least a little sacrifice as an impasse often does as well. The burden of sacrifice now shifted to the camp director. If he fully defended institutional authority against the inner authority rising in the voice of the youth, all might be lost. These kids had an excess of privilege alright, but they also had a severe lack of self-respect and self-value. They had already been sacrificed to the family plan and the program outlined by privileged society. They were exiles of their own privilege and victims of their own isolation. If they were made to bow to authoritarian rules, there would be nothing accomplished through the exile in the desert.

In our little camp in the middle of nowhere, the authority to close the invisible door or leave it open to the inner voices was residing with the director. If he insisted on abstract rules, things would collapse to an even deeper level of mutual antagonism. However, if the director could manage to yield some positional power, the young people might find some genuine authority in themselves.

The youth had made their case for justice and for unity, illustrating that there cannot be much unity where justice is lacking. In this case, we were lucky. Despite his military background and the hard-edged model of the camp, the director painfully managed to acknowledge that the youth had spoken some true things and that he may have overreacted at times. That was enough to not slam the door on the spirit of the young people and leave the situation open for greater change.

There was still a good deal of tension; but you could feel the increased vitality and forward motion of the kids. We had found a preliminary unity that might be enough to launch the bigger project of building an altar in the middle of nowhere. We had stepped across an invisible threshold and could enter both the vibrant realm of nature and the world of making and creating something beautiful. Or so I thought.

By the time we left the tent with our newfound sense of enthusiasm and purpose, it was already late in the day. When I explained my idea of a unifying ritual to the staff and camp director, there were some serious logistical problems. For one thing, the time for meals was set and dinnertime was not far off; for another, it would soon be dark. The rules stated that everyone had to be on time for dinner and safety concerns argued that no one should be out of camp once it was dark.

Once again, it became rites of change versus rules of order. The kids quickly insisted that they did not want dinner and that they desired to be out in the desert landscape. Everyone was shocked enough to allow the strange project to proceed. With no more plan than that, we moved into the desert and toward an area where loose rocks could be collected. The excitement of the kids diminished once they grasped the idea that they would have to carry rocks and build something sizeable. What was an altar anyway? They had neglected to inquire and they were not used to working hard or having to achieve something on short notice. It was as if they expected to have the rocks moved for them.

When instructed to go into the darkening desert and bring back stones, they halfheartedly wandered off, returning with hand-sized rocks that they dropped at my feet. When I asked for more and larger rocks, they moaned as if they were falling into exhaustion. Now, it was my turn to feel defeated and despairing. They had just begun to work, but the idea of work exhausted them mentally and spiritually. Some of them considered physical labor below them; they would rather bear the burdens of privilege than build something meaningful with their own hands.

I had to explain that in making something beautiful, each act and each piece became meaningful. In addition, once a ritual has begun, everything we do becomes a part of it and can affect it in positive or negative ways. So, the idea was not to blindly carry and stack rocks; rather, the sense of it was to let certain rocks pick them, then find the right place for each stone to rest. Moving the rocks could be a chain gang of enforced labor or a willing effort of creative involvement. Surprisingly, that seemed to do the trick and they set off to find or be found by just the right rocks. I found the idea so compelling that I set off myself to see which rocks most intrigued me.

We all began to wander about in the desert as it became a little darker with each passing minute. If you stood by the altar place and looked out, you would see a troop of earnest young girls and boys who would suddenly disappear into the surrounding darkness only to return carrying big rocks, like miners returning from an unseen world. The pile of rocks began to grow as if it were made from the dark or gathered from the void, the way any ritual or work of art seems to appear from the unknown.

Once the basic table-like shape could be seen, the kids could place their rocks however seemed best to them. It's surprising, the human interest in and capacity for distinction in almost any act once fully engaged. Each kid became a journeyman stone mason on the spot and each displayed their own style. When one would hesitate or seem to be stuck with their rock, I offered help only to be told that they were just considering the right placement of "their" rock. The same kids that wouldn't pick up rocks under orders now wouldn't put them down until they found the proper place to rest them. They no longer complained and they did not need help; they were willing to stand, holding heavy rocks until they were sure where to place their rock and their energy.

Youth who are supposed to be incapable of caring and believed to be "out of it" can care intensely once they are engaged and have become part of making something meaningful. And, almost anything can become meaningful when one sees with the eye of imagination. Once the act of creation has begun, everything takes on creative proportions. The world changes from being a place of inert objects to being a realm of distinct entities requiring discreet handling. "Common" rocks become unique elements of a living work that can have magic and meaning for those involved. It's a little known fact; but the knowledge of how to make creative rituals resides in the bone memory of each of us.

Ironically, it could be said to be a biblical case of "upon these rocks I build my church." But, it is more than irony since many creation myths begin with stone from which life breaks forth. In myths, things that come to life can originate from an inert state that needed the breath of life to stir it into full existence. In the desert, we were carrying inert stones from the dark void in the middle of nowhere—and beginning to love doing it.

Eventually, a large and somewhat charming altar was taking shape, and now we had to breathe life into it. With the light fading fast, I asked the kids to go into the desert and bring back anything that spoke to them about their dream in life or a burning desire that could help ignite the altar. Again, the point was to let the environment speak to them and help symbolize what they longed for or dreamed about. At this point, there were no arguments about dreams. Under the spell of nature and the delight of creating, everyone was now ready to go hunting for symbolic gifts from the darkening desert.

Only one problem: the camp rules stated that the kids could not be away from the camp after dark. Not only that, but a thunderstorm and lightning were predicted to strike the area any minute. Those were the rules, and the camp director insisted that there was no way these kids would be allowed to get lost in the dark or, god forbid, be exposed to the danger of lightning. In complete contrast, time had stopped for the kids and they were tuned into the pulse of the desert. The idea of thunder and lightning seemed more like a gift from nature than a threat to their well-being. They were all in quick agreement that they needed and wanted to continue their search for symbolic gifts.

For a moment, it seemed as if the old conflict of rules and resentments might flare up once again. To my surprise, the kids asked for permission in a heartfelt way and promised to be careful and quick. More surprise came when the staff and director gave in pretty readily. By now, we were moving with spirit and when that happens, even obstacles can become allies. In order to secure the new agreement, I taught everyone a simple chant and we sang into the night before turning back to the desert.

As the thunder began to rumble in the night sky, everyone headed out into the desert, eventually disappearing into the darkness. Then, a flash of lightning would bring the entire desert into blazing relief and you could spot the wanderers scattered across the landscape. In the sudden light of discovery, searchers would bend down and collect some highlighted item from the rocks or the desert floor and raise it toward the sky. It was a thrilling sight, not to be forgotten.

Each person found something that spoke to them and carefully placed the item between the rocks of the altar as the alternating dance of darkness and sudden light continued. The surprising array of offerings included twigs and branches, several kinds of flowers, a few feathers, and the entire skin that a desert snake had shed and seemingly donated. Of course, the whole thing took much longer than anyone anticipated and we had to wonder if some of the kids had not become lost in the dark.

As the lightning continued to flash in the distance, we began singing the little chant we had learned earlier. The song grew stronger as missing members would appear and join in. Eventually, the last person returned and we stood together singing under the night sky that seemed endless as stars flickered brightly in the primeval darkness. There was nothing that needed doing and nowhere else we would rather have been as we stood in the middle of nowhere and sang as if we all belonged right there together.

When the song ended, we knew instinctively that we should be silent and head straight to bed. Strange and beautiful, the way some things make total sense with no need of discussion, as if we had all done these things before. The whole evening had been surprising, healing, and deeply gratifying. The last surprise came when the kids, following their own instincts, lined up in order to give each adult who was present a sincere hug before slipping off to bed. We were left shaking our heads softly in wonder and awe at the presence of love where before there had been so much anger, fear, and resentment. The same kids who were by turns detached and rebellious, resistant and cynical, now lined up of their own unified accord to embrace their elders before going to bed.

When morning came, most of the youth were already gathered at the altar. It was abundantly clear that it was now our center. Even if it looked less grand in the harsh light of the desert sun, we had built it together and it represented things central to each of our lives. The details that could now be seen where we had placed twigs and flowers and feathers were intricate and beautiful. Once everyone was present, I asked if anyone wished to say anything about the personal object they had placed on the altar. I did not expect that everyone would want to speak, or that we would all cry as the stories began to pour out, or that the staff members would slip off into the desert to gather their own items in order to join in the sharing.

But, that is what happened. The first one to speak was a girl who had been adamant the day before that her dream was to have several houses. Now, she stood next to a little flower she had found and placed between rocks. She tried to say what the flower meant to her; but instead of words coming out, tears began to fall. After a time she did find words, and she said that when she saw the little flower in the desert, she had thought of her grandmother who had died. She felt that her grandmother had offered her the flower in the same caring way she had given her things when she was a child. More tears came as she struggled to state both a painful and important truth in her life. She said that her beloved grandmother was the only person in the world who had ever truly loved her. The flower represented her grandmother's love, but also her own desire to be an artist; for that was truly her dream. We could have stopped there; her honesty and courage moved all of us closer to our own hearts and dreams. There were tears in everyone's eyes and there would be no way to stop the new part of the ritual, which now had become twofold.

Each speaker that now stepped up to the altar would tell something about the person they felt had loved them the most in their life. Each story was poignant in its own way, and each revealed something profound in the life of the speaker. Then, they would each try to put words to the longings in their soul and at least point to something they desired to live for. Each one revealed some heartfelt and genuine truth, and the overall truth was that all of them suffered from a lack of love when they sorely needed it.

That was the common thread amongst the statements of the kids. They each spoke of an experience of being loved and loving back; as if they had found a loving center that had been lost. For a while, no one was lost and we had found things to love and respect in ourselves and in each other. It was clear that the earth held us and the desert gave us eloquent gifts; the primeval night had accepted our song, the stars had shone down upon us and the lightning blessed us in its startling way. For a while we were unified and connected to our dreams and standing in the middle of our lives.

CHAPTER 12

GENIUS IS THE STAR IN MAN

Our birth is but a sleep and a forgetting: the Soul that rises with us, our life's Star, hath had elsewhere its setting, and cometh from afar.

– William Wordsworth

People all over the earth suffer expanding exposure to threats of natural disasters and nightmares of man-made destruction. Increasingly, it seems that the whole thing might come to an end either from a mistake of culture or an accident of nature. Disaster comes to us from the stars, from the old Latin *aster*, which gives us astrology, astronomy, and asteroid, meaning "star-like," as well. Astrologists throughout the ages have predicted a disastrous end to the world, just as some astronomers now calculate the likelihood of a large asteroid destroying life on earth. Major religions, which often disagree on core issues of life, seem to agree that the end may be close at hand. To be alive at this time is to face the threat of disaster from many directions.

Yet, the more common and seemingly more preventable disaster involves the sense that most people fail to learn what their life might be for and that many die without having truly lived. For, to live truly means to become one's genuine self and that requires an awakening to the uniqueness woven and set within one's soul. Disaster can mean "to follow the wrong star, to follow the wrong gods home," meaning to follow a plan or a map made by others while all along there was an inner design waiting to be discovered. The instinctive sense of wonder proper to viewing the world comes from the uniqueness of the individual soul which has been increasingly replaced with blind literalism, dutiful creeds, and narrow ideologies. The greatest disaster of all may be that most people never learn what their lives were secretly aimed at, as far too many fail to embrace the core pattern that was set within them all along.

Not long ago, an old burial mound was discovered in Italy. Within the mound there was a tomb, and set within the tomb the skeletal remains of an ancient man. Placed carefully near the head of the deceased, there rested a thin and folded sheet made of beaten gold. Clearly etched upon the golden sheet could be seen the following words: "I am a child of earth and starry heaven but my race is of heaven alone." Scholars speculate that the golden sheet was a kind of passport for the dead used to gain reentry to the place of origins in the world beyond this world.

What happens after death has always been an intriguing mystery and most cultures imagine some form of afterlife. Yet, there is more here than the issue of whether the soul continues its journey after life or why ancient people would bury gold with the dead. The golden passport also says something about the living and where we stand in life. We are each a child of the fertile earth below our feet and also a descendent of the starry heavens above our heads. The issue is not just where we go after we die; but also how often we are asleep while seemingly awake; how often we forget the inner connections between our souls and the starry universe.

We live in two worlds and always have done so, yet half our being is often asleep. We belong to more than one dimension of life and our souls are secretly attuned to other levels of reality. One level is visible, palpable, and readily observable to the human eye; the other is mostly invisible, seemingly ephemeral, and more difficult to come to know. Yet, this second level is most essential to our well-being and critical to our understanding of both life and death. This inner and other realm of the Unseen that often goes unrecognized holds the missing elements we need to become truly self-aware and more fully realized.

The point is not to become inflated with an exaggerated sense of the overriding importance of humanity in the midst of the immensity of the universe. The point involves the interconnectedness that places us, like it or not, and stretches us, believe it or not, between the dark earth and the heavens above. We are star born and at times star guided; yet our birth is also a sleep in which we continually forget our otherworldly origins and our subtle connections to the living cosmos and the starry heavens. The hidden light within our souls is the star-spark that connects each of us to the cosmic origins of life. The soul is the connective tissue of life and the star in mankind is the spark hidden in the soul of each person born to this earth that is itself a star rolling through the universe.

RESIDUE OF THE STARS

We live in a time of collapse and discovery, in an age of loss and remembrance. Ancient tablets that speak of stars are discovered in earthen mounds at the same time that cutting-edge scientists studying the starry skies rediscover evidence of our star-born inheritance. As life all around us seems to make less and less sense to us, we are rediscovering our cosmic origins and our mythological inheritance. For, even scientists now must agree that we are each star born and carry star matter in our very cells. We are children of the increasingly troubled earth and we are both literally and mythically made of star life and carry star energy in every cell of our being.

We may increasingly act as separate islands of life, only connected by technological devices, but our souls remain star born and our bodies are continually remade from the residue of stardust falling from ancient times, only now reaching the earth. Our consciousness includes an infinitesimal spark of cosmic light waiting to be revealed and become known to us, its often unconscious host and bearer.

The notion that we are threaded to the stars and drawn to destinies set within us may seem like lines from a poem of a long gone age when things were more fanciful and facts were less prevalent. Yet, at times fact and myth approach each other and the star in man, which once seemed an unearthly idea, becomes the conclusion of many modern scientists. Hard-nosed physicists find themselves waxing metaphysical as they encounter the mysteries of life at the extension of powerful telescopes and penetrating microscopes that reveal the pure and continuing wonder of the world.

Astrophysicists, some of whom are geniuses in their own right, now consider that a bit of the original star has to be in everyone. They reason that if it all began with the explosion of a star, in the surprise and brilliance of an original Big Bang, then anything that appears afterward must have some of that original star in it or else it could not be part of this existence. Consciously or not, they are following the old dictum from mythology, which states that "everything is at the beginning." If we are here now, we must have been there then in some shape or form when things first began. Thus, the shape that shapes us from within turns out to be both astronomical and mythological, a speck of cosmic star hailing from the very beginning of time, which can also be referred to as "once upon a time," since the time assigned to the beginning cannot be easily fixed or agreed upon.

We are made of the remnants of stars, our bodies still connected to and derived from massive explosions in distant galaxies, everything in us originating in cosmic combustions beginning billions of years ago. We live upon a star and everyone is a star by birthright, simply by being born into this cosmic dream and swirling galaxy of stars. Physically and metaphysically we are made of the stuff of dreams, the residue of dying stars, and the dust of the original star that exploded and became the big cosmic bang that kick-started the whole universe that continues to expand to this day.

The idea that we are made of the stuff of stars is both literally and figuratively true, as every few years the bulk of our bodies is created again, partially from the stardust that falls upon us even as we sleep. We carry the residue of stars within our earthly frame as each ingredient of the human body is formed from elements first forged in the inner furnaces of ancient stars. It is as if we rediscover our innate connections to the stars and to the cosmos from the literal residue of stars within us as the scientific approach reveals what the ancients knew when they prepared the dead to return to the place of cosmic origins.

In this age of statistics, everything must be counted and the latest estimates suggest that 40,000 tons or more of cosmic dust falls upon the earth each year. The stardust finds its way into roots and plants, and from there into the nutrients that we need to move, to think, and to grow. We are stardust and like the universe, our bodies are in a constant state of decay and regeneration. Not just the building blocks of our food, but even the metallic bits that drive our electronic devices owe their existence to and derive energy from the birth and death of ancient stars.

Planet is the word now commonly used to refer to our earthly home and planet means "wandering star." It's as if we need to remind ourselves of our cosmic connections as many of our man-made institutions rattle and even nature undergoes radical changes. If there is to be a renaissance of some kind in the midst of all the worldwide disturbances and global troubles, we may have to find the sparks of inspiration and the glint of innovation in the speck of star we carry within ourselves.

Genius is the star in man, the irreducible spark of life hidden in the depths of each living soul, like a star waiting to be discovered in the dark expanse of the unconscious. In Italy during the time of the Renaissance, Marsilio Ficino stated: "Whoever discovers his own genius will thus find his own natural work and at the same time find his own star and daemon." Ficino, in true Renaissance fashion was a priest and a doctor, an accomplished musician, but also a humanist philosopher and an avid astrologer. He found his own genius to be multi-faceted and felt it to be necessarily star formed and star born.

In the Renaissance they may have thought in terms of the star in "man" as in the male of the species. By now it should be clear that the star dust falls upon everyone alive, woman or man, girl or boy. The speck of star that makes each of us unique appears in each and every soul regardless of how a person might identify their gender. If there is to be a true renaissance of humanity it will have to include everyone and value each as having something to contribute that might be needed at this dramatic time of both collapse and discovery.

Genius appears as an original inner constellation that holds the key to understanding the meaning and purpose inherent in each life. Whoever finds that spark and speck of star within finds their natural way of being and their best way of contributing to the world. When we feel most alive, we are closer to that inner star and can thank our lucky stars to be in an altered state that connects us all the way back to the origins of the universe. Whatever within us might be deemed original and unique is a manifestation of our secret connection to the original star of creation.

In these dark and uncertain times, there can be great value in imagining a bit of star in each human soul. Not just that it gives some hope for humanity at a time when man's inhumanity to man seems ever on the increase; but also because it points to an inner brightness that can light the way in dark times. The disasters of modern life include both the loss of imagination about the mystery and wonder of this world and the lack of understanding of our essential place within it. At critical moments, a person must follow the light of the inner constellation or they will miss their star and "follow the wrong gods home."

STAR QUALITIES

The speck of stardust implanted in each of our souls is another and perhaps deeper way to consider the old statement of "dust thou art, and to dust thou shalt return." We may feel small and insignificant in terms of the cosmic expanse and the growing uncertainties of life on earth, yet we are directly connected to the stars and it is the very nature of the human soul to bring the stars down to earth.

We come from the stars and the diamond dust of ancient stars continues to float through us as we wander the earth in search of our true destiny in life. For, destiny is another star word, from destinare, meaning "of the stars." Destiny is the eternal irritant in us, the hidden speck and spark in the human psyche that makes us long to be part of something great and meaningful and even transcendent. Destiny can also mean "to stand out, to stand apart;" especially to be seen standing in a visible relation to one's inner spark of genius. Our true destiny sets us apart from others because our genius self becomes visible and shines for others to see.

In this older, deeper sense, becoming famous meant something closer to being "known well," rather than simply becoming "well known." Thus, the true sense of fame relates more to the unique quality of one's life than to the simple quantity of one's renown. The older sense of fame depends upon moments of revelation in which the inner genius becomes evident and can be celebrated. In mythic terms, the bit of star that links each person to the cosmos also connects each soul to the great Soul of the World, to the living, breathing Anima Mundi. This inner connection to the origins and creation of the world gives each person some cosmic essence that can in turn become the source of personal creativity and originality. We are truly original when we act from the inner spirit of our lives.

Genius names that inner spirit and spark of star that makes each person bright in their own way. Everyone has some genius in them and each can shine in some way when that genius spark is recognized and given a way to express its inner light and creative heat. For the genius spark within us carries the vitality of our lives as well as the brilliance. When the inner genius is not recognized or served, we still leave our mark upon the world; but only as the footprint of a consumer who lived on the residue of stars, but failed to give back to the cosmic exchange in the unique and life-enhancing ways that were possible.

The diamond in the rough that begins to shine like a star reminds everyone that the human soul is naturally gifted with talents and an inner light trying to incarnate and become known. Genius is born and not made as the inner spark or flame of genius names the "star quality" in each person that enables them to shine in some way and bring the lights of intelligence and beauty to this world. We can see it in those who effortlessly "light up a room" simply by entering. Some compelling inner quality shines from within them; it both sets them apart from others and attracts people to them.

The loss of the intuitive sense of a gifted self within each person causes many modern people to obsess over those who possess or seem to possess the brighter lights of genius. Of course, this psychological imbalance suffers a radical redress when those who were the greatest fans tear down their chosen idols for failing to meet the impossible star standards and expectations projected upon them.

When people fail to awaken to the spark in their own soul, they tend to project their innate star qualities on others in the form of adoration. The older meaning of adore had to do with "beseeching or asking in prayer" for something needed or longed for. The sense of casting one's adoration upon distant rock stars, sports stars, or movie stars misses the point of becoming conscious of one's own inner spark and hidden genius qualities. The question lost in the collective adoration and fanaticism of modern 'fans' is what kind of star was born in me?

People would be less obsessed with the stars of film and stage and even business if they understood that projecting a sense of genius and talent onto others is an instinctive step towards discovering the hidden brilliance within oneself. Those deemed the latest "rising stars" and "rock stars" would have fewer demons and less dramatic breakdowns if they did not believe their own press and if they were less exposed to the mania produced by an excessive projection from their adoring fans.

Fan is shorthand for fanatic, which can mean a person acting out of "excessive enthusiasm and uncritical devotion." However, the Latin origin indicates something much more radical, as fanaticus can mean "insanely but divinely inspired." The genius in humanity involves divine inspiration and enthusiasm. Enthusiasm has something divine and potentially zealous in it as "theos" means "god." The genius bears something divine trying to enter the world through each of us and it cannot simply be denied. If it cannot find individual acceptance and expression, it will take the form of excessive devotion and fanaticism for sports teams, for political movements or extremes of religious fervor.

The genius may be a defining part of us; yet it is foreign to us as well. It is the "inner other," the otherness within us that would lead us to become something other than most expect us to be. The genius within us has its own pattern and indelible design; it has designs on our lives and would direct us from within. Since the spark of genius has a divine source, it has little concern with the health of one's body or the quality of one's relationships. The genius has its own light that can light the way for us; but it also bears an inner heat that can burn us out.

Under the rule that there is always more than meets the eye, the modern notion of charisma falls short of seeing the meaning and the purpose of individual charm and magnetism. Deeper than the fascination with attractive personalities and the appeal of popular figures, charisma originally pointed to the presence of grace and a touch of the divine. Charisma is the old Greek term for "a grace, a talent or divine gift," that glows and radiates light from within a person. This spark of genius cannot be said to be exactly human. We are descendants of the stars and bearers of gifts of the spirit that we cannot completely own and sometimes cannot govern.

When a person is able to live out some of their inner genius and inherent destiny, they become as a star, they shine before others and help to reveal a hint of the divine nature of this world. Yet, the brighter the lights of fame may shine on the outside, the darker the inside can become. Whatever shines the brightest and rises highest also casts a long shadow, and the modern fascination with wide fame and great fortune can just as readily endanger one's destiny as confirm it. The more that the inner genius becomes revealed, the more the individual must grow in character and in consciousness in order to carry their gifts and talents wisely. Thus, the problem shifts from not knowing the nature of one's inner star to having to learn how to live with it more consciously.

A TALENT IS A GIFT TO BE GIVEN

Most people think of a talent as an ability or capacity that a person has because they were born with it. Some wish they were more talented and many envy talents that others seem to take for granted and carry so effortlessly. Having a talent for something can make doing it look or seem so easy; yet the root meanings of talent include the verbs "to bear, to carry, to weigh." The weighty side of talent comes from the Greek talanton, meaning "a balance, a set of scales," hence "a weight or anything weighed." In ancient times a talent referred to a counterbalance, a weight used to measure precious metals like gold or silver on a scale.

People have always tried to put a price on talents and skills, often to the detriment of those who carry them from birth. A talent can carry a person far in life; it can also carry them far astray, think of all the stars and starlets who lose all sense of self when it seems that they have gained all they could ever want. A talent can become a heavy weight to bear. Most often people fall victim to a fate they cannot control, precisely because they don't know that they are controlled by it.

In ancient Athens a "talent of silver" was the amount paid for nine years of hard work by a skilled craftsman. Talents have always had a place in the marketplace; but by now, the marketplace has taken over everything and financial language is the currency of the land. Now, most people hope to "monetize" whatever gifts and abilities they might have in some industry. What were once fields of study or areas of discipline have simply become industries where it is easy to sell oneself short when it comes to the inner value of natural gifts and talents.

On the other side of the coin, the Latin talenta carries meanings of "inclination, leaning, desire." Natural talents can also be seen as indications of how our souls are inclined towards life. A god-given gift for doing something is proof of inner values we each bring to life. An innate talent reflects a golden aspect of one's deeper self and offers a vital ingredient of one's inborn genius for life. It may become an expertise that provides a way to make a living; but it is essentially a way to give forth and give back from what has been given to each of us.

A talent not used is not simply an opportunity wasted; rather it becomes a weight on one's soul. What could shine like gold can also become a dead weight, like lead. A talent is intended to be a channel through which our vitality and creativity can flow into life. Thus, a talent can enliven both the one using it and those receiving it. If it goes unused its host can remain inert where they could be enlivening. The root of a depression or stuckness in life can often be found in the growing weight of a talent not freely given.

Like an element in the periodic table, each talent has its weight and characteristic form. We are out of balance and in bad form if we fail to recognize the gifts we have been given and how they aim our lives, requiring us to give something to the world. On the other hand, if we simply trade our innate gifts for outer wealth or fame, we have given away our inner gold and can wind up feeling empty and worthless, regardless of the appearance of having high status or enviable success.

The weight of a given talent needs to be balanced with the growth of one's character. The greater the god-given gift, the deeper must be the character shaped to carry it. Not the simple sense of moral character, more the complications of a great and memorable character. The place of our greatest gifts should become the ground of our growing generosity. Whereas a talent not given becomes a weight on the soul; strangely, when given freely it tends to grow and not be diminished by being given away. A person is always more than the sum of their talents and innate abilities; yet a person remains less than themselves until they learn how to give freely what was given to them. Doing easily what others find difficult is talent; doing what others cannot even imagine, that is living genius being revealed.

TO BECOME IRREPLACEABLE

Genius is a compelling and necessary source of inspiration; but it is also a mystery and a puzzle and a source of consternation as well. Being human we need to bring the stars down to earth and also ground the star qualities and god-given genius within us. The point is not simply to become famous or widely known; that may gratify the ego in a person, but it cannot satisfy the inner star or genius. Far better is the older idea that each person is on a divine errand and the more we can express and deliver the unique gifts we have been given, the better we leave the world when we must depart. This sense of an irreplaceable star quality hidden within each person can be found in many traditions.

The ancient Bushman of Africa were legendary hunters who knew at a cellular level that they were the children of the great mother earth. Yet, they were also bold visionaries who lived close to the heart of Africa and felt themselves to be tied to the stars by virtue of "feeling strings." They imagined the thread of each human life to be a string of feeling and imagination that reached to a star in the heavens above. They further imagined that as a person dies, a star begins falling somewhere in the cosmic sky.

For once the heart ceases to beat, the feeling strings that connect it to its stellar origins become loosened, and the star begins to fall. At the same time, the wind which moves between all things and is connected to the breath of each person, feels that something has stopped and been lost from life. As the star falls silently from the sky and the person falls out of life, the wind begins to blow away the footprints of the fallen soul. After that the person who has fallen out of life continues to live in the stories told about them; how they brought a unique presence to life and even how the world feels less present without their living presence.

The Spanish philosopher and poet Miguel de Unamuno argued that "our greatest endeavor must be to make ourselves irreplaceable, so that no one else can fill the gap that will be left when we die." He went further than most in saying that each soul born is not only unique, but irreplaceable and "worth the whole universe...each one of us." Therefore, each person ought to give as much of themselves as possible, exceed the usual self and go beyond to make themselves irreplaceable. If a person comes to know and comes to give of the star qualities and unique genius nature they have been given, they will have shed some light in this world and they will have brought the stars down to earth. When they die, people will know that something is missing and cannot be replaced. For each one born is unique in some way and having lived and become who they were intended to be becomes irreplaceable and never to be repeated. As the Navaho saying reminds: "When you were born you cried and the world rejoiced; live your life so that when you die the world cries and you rejoice."

As the fabric of life loosens and the veil between this world and the otherworld becomes thinner and more permeable, we can begin again to align ourselves with the luminous ground of imagination, the inherited territory of the human heart and soul. Our minds can learn again to serve the deepest longing of our hearts and draw upon the wisdom hidden in our souls. Just as time seems to be running out on everyone, the eternal tries to slip back into human awareness. Things become both impossible and more possible at the same time. Amidst the theories about how it all might come to an end, the unseen thread of the eternal can be found again. For, we are all held by the threads of dreams and secretly tied to the cosmos. If we allow it, we are pushed by the inspirations of genius and pulled on by the stars.

The answers to the overwhelming problems and daunting global issues we all face cannot simply come from the limited consciousness of abstract reasoning and scientific attitudes that currently dominate the world. The problems run deeper than the simple facts of the matter; the answers must be found in deeper places as well. There is an increasing need for psychic balance, for both deeper intelligence and greater imagination that might reveal more of the ways we are each woven to the earthly realm and connected at the same time to the stars. Both at the quantum level and the mythic levels of understanding, we all remain connected to the dream of the cosmos and the wonder of the world.

On one level we are each insignificant, merely a speck of life in the immense darkness of a seemingly random universe. On another level, each soul comes to life as a unique torchbearer, each one bearing the eternal flame of existence for an indeterminate length of time. For each carries in their own way an inner spark of imagination and the flame of conscious life. On one level we barely matter, on another level what matters most to us also matters to the world.

When the dark times come round and great changes are afoot, it becomes more important that awake people remain awake and that more individuals awaken to the nature of the spark of life they carry within. In the drama of life the human soul becomes the extra quantity and distinct living quality needed to tip the balance of the world towards ongoing creation.

The loss of a felt connection to the divine spark hidden within each person may be the greatest curse of modern mass societies. Yet, the human soul, undeterred by the passage of time, retains its indelible birthright and a capacity to awaken to it and recollect the inheritance that keeps being lost. The idea that each person bears, from the beginning and in their own way, the flame of existence and a spark of genius is an open secret that keeps being forgotten. Yet, as the problems of the world grow massive in size and loom large around us, there may be no better time to reimagine the nature and purpose of human genius as a spark of individual light able to shine in the darkness of an unreconciled world.

III

A TALE OF TWO VILLAGES

CHAPTER 13

THE GENIUS OF IMAGINATION

If children grew up according to early indication,
we should have nothing but geniuses.

– Goethe

If we return to the image of the eagle as a way of considering the range of vision and broad scope of genius, it might be helpful to note that the eggs of eagles require the attention of both parents. Both male and female eagles help to incubate the eggs, taking alternate shifts during the brooding process. After the eggs hatch, the eagle parents continue with mutual care and feeding up until the fledglings attempt their first solo flights. The caring attitudes of the fierce and noble birds served as models for ancient people, who often considered both the natural and spiritual roles in parenting. Imagining that children have the spirit of an eagle also helped the process of letting go when the time came for the young ones to spread their wings and learn to fly on their own.

At the same time human parents seem to have always had trouble when it comes to recognizing the unique nature and inner purpose of their own offspring. Genius refers to a pattern and a potency that is indigenous to the person and not a derivative of the family or the society we belong to by birth. Genius is the exception to all norms and to most rules and therefore it can easily be at odds to one's family or community. Genuine independence involves becoming conscious of qualities and capacities that distinguish us from everyone else including the patterns and beliefs held by one's family.

The wings of genius will be present in each child born, yet the family of origins can be the last to recognize the originality and giftedness of their "own child." This is especially true where a culture lacks rituals that welcome the unique spirit of each child; but also the case when parents remain unaware of their own inner spirit and indwelling genius nature.

As some say, there is nothing completely new under the sun. What happens now has happened before in some way and there are stories that can tell the tale and offer insights. An ancient African story begins in a simple village where a young woman becomes a mother by giving birth to her first child. The birth went smoothly, the newborn was healthy and whole, and the new mother recovered quickly. It was a time when people lived simply and close to the earth. So, soon after giving birth, the new mother tied the little one on her back and went off to work the little plot of land that was the garden for her family.

The young mother placed the infant at the base of a tree and set to work in the garden. While the mother worked the earth in the heat of the day, the infant began to cry. Being an attentive mother, she stopped working and followed the instinct to suckle and nourish her child. Afterward, she laid the infant down in the shade of the tree and went back to her work.

After a while, the child began to cry again. The mother stopped to look at the infant and was startled to see that a large bird had come to the tree and had settled upon the child. The great bird seemed to soothe the child with its wings and, soon enough, the infant became quiet and fell asleep peacefully. However, seeing the great bird so near her child caused the young woman to become greatly alarmed. "What if that bird was to eat my child?" she thought. She ran towards her baby, which caused the bird to lift its great wings and fly away. Then, the mother suckled and held her child close before finishing her work and returning to the village.

That night, in the little hut she shared with her husband, she did not mention a word of the episode with the great bird and their child. She said nothing of the marvel that had happened, but kept her thoughts and feelings to herself. The next morning she went to work in her garden again and placed the infant by the tree. As she worked the land in the heat of the day, the same thing happened again. When her child began to cry, the great bird descended to soothe it. This time, she could see that it was an eagle and that it had an instant soothing effect on the little child who quickly fell into a deep and peaceful sleep.

The young woman had to accept that the eagle had no intention of harming her child. Just the opposite; she began to understand that the great bird settled the child and brought it peace and solace. At the same time, she still felt the need to protect and nourish the infant. So once again, she went to hold her child. This time, the bird rose gently, lifting itself to a limb just above where the mother held and suckled her child.

That evening, when she returned to the village and sat in the hut with her husband, she told him of the astounding thing that had happened to their child. She described to him how, two days in a row, the great eagle had come to the field where she worked. She told all the details of how the bird arrived exactly when the infant cried, how it settled on the child with its great wings, and how each time the baby stopped crying. She explained how it became clear to her that the bird was able to soothe the infant and deliver it to a restful sleep.

Not surprisingly, the husband and father of that child, refused to believe the story that his wife told so ardently. He insisted that no such thing could happen; that she was making it up or else seeing things in the heat of the sun. It simply could not be true. That night was spent the way you spend a night in a hut in which the woman believes one thing and the man sees it another way altogether.

With the dawning of the next day, the mother and child went back to the garden. Once again she placed her child in the shade at the base of the tree. After a time, as could be expected, the baby began to cry. Just as before, the eagle appeared and descended with open wings to the child. This time, the woman thought she would call her foolish husband and show him just what was true and what was not. She set off running to the village and when she drew near began calling for him to come and see the astounding thing that was in fact occurring again.

At that moment, it happened that the young husband was sitting with the other hunters, sharpening his arrows. When he left to follow his wife, he carried with him his bow and arrows. Soon both the mother and father of the child arrived and stood at the edge of the little field. When the father saw the huge eagle resting on his little child, he was both astounded and horrified. Quickly, he placed two arrows in his bow, took aim at the eagle, and without thought, let the arrows fly.

Seeing the arrows coming through the air, the eagle simply raised its great wings and lifted itself into the sky. As the great bird rose above, the arrows pierced the infant that it had been protecting and the child instantly died. The eagle settled on a branch of the tree and began to speak to both shocked parents. "Now, killing has begun and from now on people will kill each other. Now, kindness amongst people comes to an end because you have killed your child."

A METAPHORICAL EYE

It is a shocking story, especially if taken literally. The old tellers often used dramatic effects and traumatic events to provoke a greater sense of imagination in listeners. Although modern theories often claim that ancient people used myths to falsely explain how things came to be in this world, the old knowers used symbolic images and dramatic metaphors to awaken people to persistent human problems. People living close to nature would intuitively understand that the connection between the child and the eagle could not be literal and therefore must be symbolic and metaphorical.

Opposite from the literal sense of the matter-of-fact world stands the mythical and metaphorical sense of imagination, which opens everything in the world to greater understanding. Meta means "beside or beyond" and phora means "to carry or that which carries." Metaphors are intended to carry us beyond the obvious and past the literal level in order to see more than meets the eye. Metaphors are essential tools of imagination that can uncover hidden connections and reveal deeper understandings. Metaphors reveal facts of a different order and truths of a different nature. There is wonder in the image of a full-grown eagle coming to bring peace to a tiny infant; yet we can somehow imagine it. Our imagination allows us to see mysterious and hidden connections that make sense of things that seem otherwise unrelated.

In this case, the story points to a kind of killing that can happen inside families and in cultures where people forget that each child born is also born of spirit. The issue for this primordial couple is that their child seems to have a spiritual connection that they fail to understand or accept in a timely way. Even after the mother recognizes the soothing effect of the eagle's presence, she feels compelled to offer her own instinctive way of protecting and soothing the child. The father, despite being told of his child's connection to a great bird that soothes its soul, succumbs to his own instincts for defending and protecting with disastrous and tragic results.

Both parents wind up at odds with the spiritual nature of their own child. The mother was able to see how the great bird responded to the cry of her child. Her eyes were open to that mystery even if her mothering instincts went against the sense that a spirit or spirit animal could soothe and settle the child in itself. She becomes caught again when she tries to convince her husband that his child has a powerful spiritual connection that exists independently of their roles as parents.

The father then becomes caught between his natural instinct for protecting the child and the startling powerful sight of the spirit visitation. He seems even less ready for the wonder that spontaneously attends the life of his young child.

NATURAL AND SUPERNATURAL

The size and power of the eagle points to the nature and quality of something already present in the newborn child. The mystery of it includes the sense that something that can be fierce and dangerous could also have a soothing effect on that particular child. This dichotomy of a soothing spirit that can also be devouring depicts a key aspect of human nature with its inherent genius. The resident spirit of the soul is part of the nature of the child; but not simply human. Human nature includes something that goes beyond nature and connects us to the supernatural.

Our inborn genius shapes our natural way of being in this world and it is also one way that the supernatural appears in the midst of the natural world. It is the nature of genius to inhabit both worlds and be both natural and supernatural at the same time. The word supernatural combines all that seems most natural with that which seems to be "above and beyond nature." In this world, many things that first appear to be completely natural turn out to be far more than that. In Africa they say that nature is spirit wearing a green garment. Spirit can also appear in animals, especially in birds that seem to defy the common gravity of being on earth. What we casually call nature includes hordes of things that are not simply natural; just as the soul of mankind maintains essential connections to both spirit and nature.

The genius in us is autonomous and has its own reasons for being and ways of acting. Each person's life spirit has its own language and style; although native to a person, the genius must often be won over and a psychological container must be shaped in order for it to become useful. Once it has been uncovered or been discovered, a person must learn to live with the uniqueness and oddity of their own genius. Call it the devil within us or the angel looking over us; for that which is genius about us can appear to be devilish or angelic.

Close to the roots of genius can be found the old word genie, which carries more clearly the sense of a spirit that can be threatening or helpful, depending on how it is approached or treated. Old tribal traditions warn that a person needs to learn the nature and language of the spirit that accompanied them on their journey in this world. Not only that, but if one's inner spirit goes unrecognized or becomes rejected by their family or culture, it can become hostile to its host as well as the human community.

Being both natural to us and supernatural in its origins, the presence of genius intensifies the opposing energies and instincts in life. Thus, the human parents can easily become opposed to the mysterious spirit in their own child. The opposition or even confusion of the parents can trouble the spiritual nature that might otherwise settle and soothe their child. The greater the genius potential might be, the more intense the issues of character and meaning might become. If we keep the inner spirit bottled up too long it can turn against us and make our lives miserable. Something as potent and creative as human genius can appear as a godsend or else can become a source of hell on earth for all involved.

Daimon was an old Greek word for the unique spirit that inhabits each soul, and the word for happiness was eudaimonia, meaning "a satisfied daimon" or fulfilled inner spirit. In this ancient view, being truly happy depends upon discovering and living close to the pattern set within our soul before birth. On the other hand, if neglected or rejected our inner daimon can turn into our worst demons. The inner spirit of our lives cannot remain neutral, but must express itself in some potent way. If it is not welcomed or becomes rejected, as happens in the story, something dies or becomes seriously distorted.

For children, who cannot deny or completely avoid their connection to spirit and imagination, this can be experienced as a spiritual death. Notions such as "children should be seen and not heard" can do great damage to the natural spontaneity and spirit for life that exists in each child born. Because the inner genius of the child holds both the vitality and the uniqueness natural to them, repression of their spirit can wound both their natural ambition and their life libido. Those who would repress the natural spirit and spontaneity of children have already diminished and suppressed their own inner genius and spirit for life.

For those who see things literally and those who have not fully experienced the wings of their own imagination, the idea of a spirit that accompanies life will seem unbelievable and unreal. It will also seem threatening, as it did to the father whose child had a deep connection to the great bird of spirit. Not only individual sets of parents, but groups of people and even entire cultures can fall under the spell of literalism and become blind and resistant to the natural presence of spirit in life.

CHILD PRODIGIES

It is a condition of life on earth that human parents can rarely see the genius nature and god-given gifts of their own offspring. Typically, the job of teaching and helping the young to learn how to use the wings of their own spirit falls to unrelated adults who teach or mentor the young. Genuine teachers will perceive the signs of native intelligence in each student and read the potentials and portents of their souls. Genius comes full-blown, like the eagle that descends knowingly to the newborn child. Like a bird with feathered wings, the genius in a person exists as a whole to begin with. It is not built up from parts in the way that people often think of education. Genius comes to life fully matriculated.

A classic example of the full-blown genius occurs when a child prodigy appears. Prodigy means "a sign or a portent," a prodigious omen of something coming forth in its own time and on its own terms. Something in the child already knows what instrument to play, how to paint, or exactly how things work and how new things can be invented. However, the point of the prodigy is not simply that some are born with developed gifts; the real point is that something of a prodigious nature exists within each person born. In that sense, each person is at root a "child prodigy," for each carries an inner spirit and unique genius that attempts to announce its presence.

The appearance of a child prodigy also points to the fact that the genius is not simply human, but is rooted in the realm of spirit. Each child has its genius and each is a child prodigy with regard to their own essence. The issue is not growing the genius up; rather the issue becomes growing the character of the host so that it carries the genius well and delivers its gifts more fully. The inner genius arrives on wings already bearing its own knowledge, talent, and ways of inspiring us. The genius within us gives signs and offers symbols indicative of our essential nature and true calling in life.

Like the great eagle that attends the infant in the story, the genius within us arrives with grand images and already has big ideas; it has long thoughts that can take an entire life to think through; it also has feelings of uniqueness and longings for genuine expression. The genius bears a natural need to be seen, to be witnessed both by its human host and by others who might bless and confirm it. Seen this way, a key issue in the drama of life becomes awakening to the spiritual fact that each soul born bears within it a divine connection and a genius seed that makes it unique. The mortal body carries a divine seed that can awaken at any moment and grow and blossom forth at any point in life.

The presence of the genius calls each young person into moments of great exposure in order that the resident spirit of the soul can become known. Genius resides at the core of a person and tends to manifest when core issues have been touched, when core qualities are called upon, and when core gifts are sorely needed. The resident spirit of the soul carries a distinct "calling" in life, and the inner gifts and divine resources within need to be called upon in order for us to fully awaken. The resident spirit in our lives is also the taskmaster of our soul that sets for us the most difficult tasks that we can somehow achieve. It demands that we become fully alive and grow our soul.

The eagle is a raptor bird, specially adapted for seizing its prey and carrying it off into blue oblivion. The term raptor comes from the Latin raptus, which can mean "to seize or carry off." Close by can be found rapt, meaning "to be carried up in spirit." In the grip of genius we can experience being released from mundane concerns, but can also find ourselves being mercilessly driven. The genius of the soul would set us the hardest work among those things not impossible for us to accomplish. As they used to say, the first problem is that you have not found your genius and cannot yet grasp your purpose in life; the second problem is that you have found it.

THE POWER OF IMAGINATION

An eagle can swing its head around with enormous speed and even turn it upside down, thus achieving an all-encompassing vision of everything around it. Just so, the eye of genius can see the entire world from if its nest within the soul, giving each person a world view particular to them. The deepest potentials of the soul belong to the "inner pupil" who sees with an already knowing eye and which looks out from the inner life of the soul. Rather than the notion of the child as passive learner, the inner pupil actively sees into the world, shaping and organizing the space in which to make its inherent pattern of life both conscious and visible. The inner pupil is the pupus or pupa, the eternally young boy or girl of the soul, the inner disciple born into the world with us, already knowing which disciplines will best serve its needs and inherent goals.

Once awakened and encouraged, the inner pupil becomes both a natural disciple and a protégé. Protégé comes from the Latin verb protegere, meaning "to protect, to cover in front." The protégé and inner pupil need protection in the same way that a newborn must be nurtured and kept from harm. The inner protégé can be under the protection of the genius or guardian angel; yet will develop more quickly when also under the protection and guidance of a true mentor or teacher. Just as both eagle parents can nourish the fledgling eaglet, a person can become the protégé or student of either a woman or a man. When it comes to mentoring and teaching, aspects of gender can be far less important than the qualities of being fully alive and having a genuine vision to follow.

Imagination is the true spark of the divine within us. Upon this surprising, elusive, yet ever-present function depends the presence of dreams and visions as well as the possibility of inspiration occurring at any moment. Imagination is the key that connects us to the realm of all that is exceptional and creative in life, and imagination is the hidden power of genius. Imagination is the unifying force; the only function which precedes thought and follows the body's waking ways of knowing. Only a return to genuine imagination can lead us home to ourselves and our meaningful place in the world.

Everything that exists must first be imagined, and imagining is the primary activity of the psyche. We enter this world carrying within us a hidden core of mythic story and symbolic patterns. Imagination is the greatest power of the human soul and the core image at the center of our soul; the true sponsor of our being and the orienting force within our lives. Whether we know it or not, our lives are acts of imagination and the world is continually re-imagined through us.

Our innate genius offers the uncommon capacity and ability to imagine life in ways that people cannot see with normal vision. Genius can see ways out of dilemmas and into states of discovery because it is essentially visionary. Imagination sees with an eye for creation rather than simple observation; for there is always more than meets the eye. By virtue of imagination, we see with penetrating and creative vision; not the delusion of fantasy, but the surprise of revelation. As Mark Twain put it, "You can't depend on your eyes when your imagination is out of focus."

Imagination reveals what is under the surface, at the edge of the mind, and trying to enter reality at a given time as the unseen that seeks to become visible enters the world through us. With imagination we enter into each situation, penetrate it, and reveal what was otherwise hidden. In this sense, imagination can be seen as something that makes life more real, rather than as something connected to fantasy. Fantasy involves an exaggerated belief in the appearance of things. Fantasy is mostly appearance; it fosters illusion and tends to increase distraction and generate confusion.

Whereas fantasy tends to take people out of reality, imagination would have us add something to reality. Through imagination, we perceive that which can become real; for, whatever comes to be must first be imagined. Whereas fantasy plays with the ego's need for escape and distraction, imagination is connected to being more present in our lives. Whereas fantasy would lead us out of this world, genuine imagination increases our presence in the world. In the extreme, fantasy can lead to dissociation, whereas imagination leads to a greater sense of cohesion between ourselves and the world around us.

The soul naturally longs to break through to meaning and live with genuine purpose. But, too often our lives become trapped within fantasies of who we might become and how great we could be if only the world would change. Like fantasy, abstract thinking can also lead to dissociation and ultimately add to the sense of emptiness in the world. Fantasy traps people in an illusion of things, but abstract intellect and exaggerated rationality can also trap people in the appearance of things. Intellect alone cannot penetrate the appearance of things and unlock all the levels of meaning and understanding that exist below the surface of life's steady flow.

LITERALISM AND IMAGINATION

At times it seems that the entire culture has become shocked and scared, like the father who sees only the threat to his child and misses the mystery and wonder at hand. The sad fact is that until a person awakens to the presence of spirit and genius in their own life, they can reject it in the lives of others, including those they love the most. Under the rule of literalism and the demographic world view, statistical figures dominate the scene and the great figures of imagination are often replaced with fantasy figures that diminish our presence in the world.

Through the tyranny of facts and horizontal connections, we lose the surprising and mysterious presence of the imaginative view of life and the metaphoric mind that can find connections where none were visible, that can locate openings where all paths seemed closed. We lack the inherent, instinctive poetics of language and lose familiarity with the innate creativity of the human mind and soul. Language is a core element of human genius; a kind of poetic-making magic capacity that can wither for lack of use.

Words are also genius seeds that can be cracked open to reveal inner meanings able to nourish the mind and soul. In modern life, words move swiftly across the world and seemingly at no cost, yet language itself becomes increasingly diminished and impoverished in the rush to communicate. Amidst the collapse of vertical imagination, we fall into a diminished state, exchanging sound bites and text messages, where the unfettered soul would declaim great soliloquies and poetic pronouncements. We stack and store up endless amounts of data and information while the spirit of life and healing imaginations of the soul increasingly fail to find expression in the world.

Yet, while the surface world spins ever more digital threads and the worldwide web expands horizontally, the human soul remains securely connected to the roots of imagination and the unifying vision of metaphors like the Tree of Life. The great birds of spirit and imagination still visit the World Tree, where all the newborn souls wait to be inspired and to be soothed and settled into themselves. Unlike the technological innovations and personal devices that can suddenly breakdown or go off-line and leave people feeling wildly disconnected, the living tree of imagination provides endless ways of branching out while remaining rooted in oneself.

The key issue may be a rediscovery of the inner nature of the human soul that allows us to find and renew old connections to Great Nature. A reawakening to imagination makes conscious acts of participation in the ongoing creation of the world more possible. Poiesis was an old word for human participation in creation through the power of imagination and through the deep thoughts that can be found in the heart. The poetic sense of life quite naturally combines thinking with feeling and imagining with the unseen energies that continue to move the world. In acts of poiesis, the mind and the heart perceive as one so that feeling can arise in the mind and thought can be revealed in the depths of the heart.

The modern legacy can become a resentful passing along of an increasingly diminished world that has been too narrowly defined as well as overly exploited. Despair and cultural anxiety result from the increasing loss of soul and the absence of imaginative solutions to worldwide problems. Whatever the rationalists and seeming realists might think, if we try to remove the supernatural from life, we will be left not with the natural, but with a world that is markedly unnatural and despairingly incomplete. Take from this world all that seems to be incomprehensible, unreasonable, impossible, and irrational, and nothing much will remain.

Under the rule of literalism, some now believe that a "day of rapture" will come and save them from the troubles and iniquities of this world. Yet, rapturous visions are part of the inheritance of the soul and have always been a part of human experience on earth. The flights of genuine imagination and the raptures of both body and soul experienced while living in this world give full meaning to the metaphorical phrase "heaven on earth."

Humans live in the midst of all that can be deemed natural and are at the same time continually affected by things that might be termed supernatural. Our ancestors may have had fewer technological devices, but they lived closer to the unseen energies of nature, the invisible sources of soul, and all the uncanny possibilities that make up the otherworld, with its deeply natural roots and its nearby supernatural elements. The instinctive and intuitive capacity for metaphor and symbol cannot be completely lost or life itself would disappear. Each moment of life is a living genesis of ideas and images that remake the world, even when everything seems about to unravel around us.

The otherworld and the supernatural can be found in the awesome elements of nature as well as in awesome qualities set within our human nature. We are human by birth and divine by design and have natural recourse to the powers of imagination that we each brought to life. Metaphors allow us to see things anew and therefore to understand life as enduring and even renewable. Seen metaphorically, creation is not a thing of the past, but something surprising that continues to be present within each living soul. By following our imagination and having the courage of our innate thoughts, we find how and where we can be most present in the world and become an agent of change ourselves. When seen with imagination, all things shift toward meaning, releasing energies that are hidden within appearances, releasing the inner wings of spirit, opening wide the doors to healing and wholeness.

CHAPTER 14

A TALE OF TWO VILLAGES

It may be a global world, but we often live in a half-village.

Many people are familiar with the African proverb that states, "It takes a whole village to raise a child." Unbeknown to most, there is a second half of the proverb that adds, "If the youth of a village are not fully invited into life, they will burn the village down." By the time young people are ready to leave childhood, they are supposed to feel invited into the next stage of life. They also have an expectation of being supported by the community around them. However, if the underlying sense of the wholeness of life has been lost, the young will feel an emptiness inside instead of the fullness of life.

At the same time, the older people will forget how to act as genuine elders and not fulfill their half of the bargain. Something as yet unseen tries to enter the world through youth while genuine elders attempt to pass on those things that can sustain life and make it meaningful. For, youth and elders each hold a part of the dream of life and each has a role to play when it comes to finding a sense of wholeness on the road of life.

By now, the global village has arrived at a place where age-old divisions have become inflamed as disparities intensify, and hard lines and hardliners appear in all areas of life. Meanwhile, most adults, lacking a conscious sense of meaning and purpose in their own lives, become powerless to confirm and bless the lives of those in the next generation. Instead of a felt sense of the value of each young life, there is the confused sense of accidental lives in a random universe. The modern world may be seen as a comprehensive global village, but modern life increasingly leaves people feeling unwelcome, alone, and left out.

A village that is not whole will still raise the child; the problem is that a village divided against itself may only raise the child halfway. Of course, mythic tales suggest that this has all happened before and that the eye of imagination can see ways through all the fog and smoke, conflict and confusion. The ancient people of Borneo had an interest in the dynamic between the wholeness of life and the fact that the human village often becomes split apart and torn in half. They had a tale of two villages: one that offers only half of what people need and long for and another that must constantly be sought for at the edge of life.

Once upon a time, there was a village in which a woman was about to give birth to a child. After a time, her first child appeared and it was a boy. Well, to tell the whole truth it was actually a half-boy. Her labors brought forth only half of a child. There was a left foot and a left leg, a left hip and a left side. There was a left shoulder and left arm, and a left side of the head with a left eye looking out of it. But, where you would expect to see the same things on the right side… there was nothing there at all.

The newborn was only a half of a boy. Perhaps because only half of him was born, he came into the world screaming and crying; perhaps that was the reason that people turned away from him. Or they may have turned away because they did not want to see only a half-child. Since the people turned away from him, the half-boy cried and lamented all the louder, which caused the people to move even further away from him.

Somehow the half-boy continued to live and to grow—at least the half of him that was there was able to grow. In the course of time, he reached the age of adolescence or youth. At that point, even his family turned away from him as the half-boy began to act out the pain and the sorrow he felt. One day, it occurred to him that people would always see him the same way if he remained in that village. People would always see him as only half a person, as only half of what he could be. And, once he realized that, he decided to leave the village and go out into the wide world beyond it.

The next day, when the sun rose, the half-boy gathered himself together as best he could and dragged himself to the edge of the village. He reached the line where the familiar world came to an end and the rest of the world began. I have to tell you that when the half-boy dragged himself across the line that separated the village from the great unknown, there was no one there to wish him well, there was no one there to make prayers for him. There was no one there to sing for him the way people used to sing each time a boy or girl left the village to find themselves out in the world. When the half-boy left the village, there was no one there at all.

All on his own, the half-boy pulled himself across the line and out of the village of his birth. He entered the road that was said to lead to a distant village. He dragged himself along, the way a half-person drags themselves through life, and simply kept going, motivated by both the abandonment he felt and the longings he had. After a time—a long time or a short time—the half-boy came upon a road that crossed the path he was on. This road was made entirely of water—what people call a river. The stream of water poured continually between the banks on either side and seemed to divide the world into two sides.

The half-boy dragged himself up onto the bank of a river and began to look around with his solitary eye. As he gazed about, he thought he saw something coming down the bank toward him. He squeezed his eye down in order to better see what might be coming toward him, now that he was on the journey of his own life. Eventually, he realized that it was another person coming his way. In fact, it was another half-person coming along with a right foot and a right leg and a right side of the body. The other one had a right eye that was looking right at him as he stared back with his solitary left one.

Soon enough, the right half had come next to the left half and you may think that because one was right and one was left that they simply joined together and lived happily ever after. But, this is not that kind of story. Once they found themselves close to each other the two halves began to disagree and argue. They could not see anything eye to eye and soon enough, they began to have conflict about everything and that led to a fight. And before you knew it, they were in a great battle that raised a storm of dust, obscuring the sun and making everything seem occluded.

As the battle became more heated the two halves, unable to make a whole, rolled right down the bank and disappeared into the river. Because of the heat of their conflict, the river began to boil up. Soon, wave began to pile upon wave and foam gathered, and where the waves mixed there grew a great fog that fell over everything. After the waters settled, the fog dissipated and no one could be seen at all. If you happened to pass by you would see no indication of the great struggle that had taken place. You would see no evidence of the two halves fighting or trying to make things whole. All that you would see would be the river that flowed steadily along and ran its course the way it did any day in the world.

After a time, the river began to boil up again, and wave piled upon wave, and from the river there could be seen a boy rising and stepping onto the banks. It was a whole boy with a right foot and a left, with both sides of a body and with two eyes looking at the world. Although he was whole, he seemed deeply confused and completely disoriented. He stumbled about unused to having to coordinate two sides of himself. As he staggered about, he spotted what appeared to be a village and went toward it.

Coming closer he could make out what appeared to be an elder sitting at the edge of the village. The old one had one foot in the territory of the river and the other foot across the line of the village. The half-boy went to him and said: "I have been in a huge conflict and now I have no idea where I have come to or where I might be."

The elder said, "I can tell you where you have come to; you have arrived back at the village where you began. You have returned to the place of your origins and now that you have returned the village can dance again. For, no one has been dancing since you went away. I can also tell you that if you and I enter the village dancing together, then the whole village will begin to dance again. Are you willing to do that?"

The half-boy was agreeable to the plan. So, the two of them, the elder and the half-boy who was now made whole, entered the village dancing together. Then it happened just as the old man had said. People began to come out and join the dance. Of course, the children came first because it looked like fun to them. Then, the old people came. They moved a little slower, but possibly felt the joy of dancing a little more. Eventually, the adults left their tasks and responsibilities and began to dance as well. The only ones who remained outside the dance were the youth. For, they waited until it became clear that the occasion was authentic and real. Then, they joined in and even invented some new ways to dance.

Pretty soon, the entire village was dancing together; no one was left out or excluded for any reason. It was then that you could see that each person had their own way of stepping out and moving. At the same time, they were all in it together; the whole village dancing and the village made whole again. Some people say that the village is still dancing. Others say that they danced all night, but in the morning they stopped because a woman gave birth to a child. Actually, it was a half-child that came into the world crying loudly. That caused the people to move away from the newborn and that only caused the child to cry all the louder. And that created more distance and more crying, just as had happened before when all the dancing stopped.

HALFNESS AND WHOLENESS

It's a strange old story where even the ending divides into two ways of seeing the world. We live in two villages that exist side by side, like two different worlds. In one realm, the dance of life goes on and on and everyone is invited to join and each is encouraged to find their distinct way of being alive and contributing something to the great dance. The image and ideal of wholeness in life is part of the heritage of the human soul; it has to remain true at some level. Yet, right next to that sense of union we find the other realm: the half-village, where no one feels fully alive, completely welcome, or truly blessed. The conditions of a harsh and dismissive reality are also true and, increasingly, anyone can find themselves out in the cold or driven to some isolating extreme. There are more refugees in what we now call the global village than have existed at any other time in history. Amidst all the disparities and inequalities, whole groups of young people can be rejected and old people become neglected and can be forgotten as the communal dance keeps being lost.

We can only meet a story with what we know of life and the easiest way to enter a story is to identify with a character in it. Since the main character in this tale is a half-boy, each person must recall times of feeling the halfness in their own life in order to follow the tale. On one level, the story speaks of the problems created by a village that is less than whole. On another level, it speaks to the half-boy or half-girl inside each of us. For, everyone knows what it feels like to be undervalued, overlooked, or torn apart by circumstances beyond our control.

The story begins with the cry of the newborn soul just entering the world, as if to emphasize that something is missing right from the beginning of every life. The tale of the half-boy draws upon early life wounds and issues of abandonment that form some part of each of our lives from the very beginning. Each soul carries the wound of abandonment and no childhood turns out to be perfect. In this world, the longing to feel whole must be precipitated by the experience of feeling empty and torn inside. Each of us comes into the world full of longing; we long to be born, long to be held, and eventually long to know who we really are and what we are intended to do in this world. Sometimes we are cut in half and divided within when we remember what we truly desire.

The story creates a landscape of loss and longing that begins at birth and, significantly, places the drive to become a whole person at the center of each human life. The little folk myth aims at wholeness by wisely focusing upon the condition of halfness. For, the half-boy speaks to the part of us that has never felt completely loved, fully welcomed, or properly held by life. The half-boy stands for our incompleteness, our unconsciousness, and our repeated abandonment of ourselves regardless of how we may have been treated early in life.

We carry our halfness wherever we go as we each become as the half-boy or half-girl again and again during the course of our lives. Our inevitable birth-traumas and our unfulfilled longings travel with us all along the way and intensify at each crisis and critical turn we encounter in our lives. We find ourselves in the half-village each time we feel torn apart, rejected, or suffer some loss. The loss of a loved one tears us apart, a divorce tears both parties in half; an illness, loss of a career or nervous breakdown breaks us in half again. Some may deny it, but everyone feels less than who they really are at times and often only half of what they could be. As they say, everyone has their issues; but our core problems will tear us apart if we refuse to admit our inner sense of longing and feeling unwanted, rejected, or abandoned. Being torn in half and divided within is an unavoidable part of life and accepting the divisions within us becomes a necessary step on any path to wholeness.

People often try to hide the ways in which they are torn; but eventually it comes out. Even the most privileged person knows some lack within themselves; even the most gifted will find themselves empty and alone at times. The image of the half-boy indicates the size and importance of something essential that can repeatedly become missing in our lives. The only way to grow and transform is to be torn and driven to find wholeness again. This is the kind of story that people used to tell in order to keep everyone aware that the vicissitudes of life can reduce all of us to feeling less than who we think we are or what we know we can be. In order to find and touch our sense of wholeness, we must face our inner conflicts and painful divisions again and again.

This is the kind of tale that used to be told to young people about to enter the world in a bigger way. The journey that begins in youth is intended to lead to an awakening of the inner genius and the experience of being wholly and truly oneself. Yet, in order to become more fully who we are intended to be, we must first become acutely aware of our incompleteness. In hearing the story, young people instinctively identify with the alienation, isolation, and inner conflicts of the half-boy. It becomes clear to them that they are but partially seen, often unheard, and are typically only partly accepted by others. In the eternal drama of life on earth, each young person is not only an unknown actor in the eyes of others, they are also greatly unknown to themselves.

A second birth is required for a person to become whole. In the depths of the waters where life is begotten again and again, the half-boy becomes a whole person as he finds the inner genius and resident spirit that first brought him to life. Only then can the whole thing make sense; only then can the whole village be found again. For, the wholeness is hidden inside where we often fear to go because of the conflicts, abandonments, and betrayals we each bear. The transition from childhood to youth is but the beginning of a lifelong series of events in which we experience our own version of halfness along with our distinct potential for becoming a whole person in the fullness of life.

THE GREAT DISCONNECT

A key point in the story comes when the half-boy realizes that if he remains at home he will always be seen the same way; he will never be seen for who he truly is at heart. In that moment, he knows the time has come to seek the other half of life. When he manages to reach the line that separates the realm of childhood from the greater world beyond it, no one is there to wish him well or to sing for him. He experiences another level of being alone and abandoned. This detail in the story marks an important loss that permeates the modern world. For, we now live without meaningful rites of passage that could help all of us feel a greater sense of connection as we wander and struggle through the stages of life.

People used to have songs to sing for those taking their first steps onto the road that leads to the rest of their lives. The whole village used to come out to sing and stand at the edge supporting each girl or boy about to take steps into the unknown that exists right next to all that we deem familiar. The elders as well as the children and all the others would sing songs that imbued spirit into the heart of each young girl or boy about to begin the search for meaning and wholeness in life.

Once started, the song would be sustained until the young person disappeared from sight and be held even longer so they would hear and feel the singing following them into the world. So, they would remember the song and have the feeling of the whole village being behind them during the days and nights when they found themselves alone, afraid, or unwanted. In a spiritual sense, we are never truly alone in this world; yet if we do not have a palpable, bodily sense of support behind us, we can feel utterly abandoned and entirely alone.

The song sung for those setting off was intended to serve as a reminder that the fulfillment of each young person was meaningful and connected to the whole village. For, each person is unique and comes to life bearing gifts intended to be given. Without the genius gifts of awakened individuals there can be no village. At the same time, the gifted need a place to return to and give what was given to them as part of the gift of life. How the inner genius is experienced and how it becomes carried through life determines the uniqueness of that life. Refusing to admit this genius, denying it, or perverting it endangers both the host and the society. The real human village is made of giving and receiving. It takes a whole village to keep welcoming everyone and the gifts they have to give. It takes some whole people to give all that they have to offer and make wholeness visible to others.

Besides the secret longings of young people, the story of the half-boy points to what is often missing in the local community as well as in the greater culture. The trouble now is that even if a young person manages to find the courage to take a big step in life, there may be no one there to pray for their well-being, to wish them well, or to put a song at their back. In addition to that, those who enter the road of life now face a world that is itself torn apart, mired in conflicts and oppositions, and caught in a constant flood of changes.

The atmospheres of modern culture are not just literally polluted and subject to widening holes in the ozone layers intended to protect the planet. Young people inhale the depths of despair that can be found just under the rushing speed and constant connectivity of modern devices and mass communications. Young people now grow up amidst a mania of social media that leaves everyone increasingly more connected, yet also more alone than ever before. We may belong to a global village and be virtually connected to the worldwide web, yet we also find ourselves more and more disconnected all the time. The whole world may now seem to be at the fingertips of young people, yet that cannot stop them from feeling unseen, unheard, and mostly unblessed when trying to enter the great dance of life.

In modern societies, a disagreement goes on between parents and public institutions over who takes responsibility for the disruptions and conflicts inevitably caused by youth. The argument seems endless because neither their family nor the common community can give young people what they desperately require. Beginning with adolescence, youth enter a betwixt and between state; between child and adult, betwixt family and state. What we call adolescence is the beginning of a halfway zone that can easily turn into a "no man's land" where young people become lost altogether. When the village of life becomes intensely divided and polarized, the young feel more divided on the inside and more separated from others than they should be.

LEFT TO THEIR OWN DEVICES

It takes a village to raise a child; but once childhood is over, it takes a culture that blesses the dream trying to awaken in the soul of each young person. Children can be admonished and even controlled, but youth are on the edge of the great passions of the human soul that can burn toward destruction or else become a light that brightens and animates an entire culture. Young people are not simply awash with hormones, they are also imbued with dreams and the trouble with dreams is that they aim at higher goals like beauty and truth and they touch the deepest human senses like our sense of justice. A society is playing with fire if it denies the dreams of its youth in favor of a status quo that favors some and excludes others.

We live in extreme times during which the growing disparity in terms of wealth and opportunity adds more fuel to the fires of despair every day. As the distance between the haves and the have-nots grows ever wider, the state of despair inside the culture grows ever deeper and greater. Yet, it is not only that opportunities have been denied to so many for too long, though they have been; but also that human dignity has been systematically abused as injuries to the soul have been sanctified under the rule of bigotry, denial, and ignorance. A society is a living body in which hatred and despair can grow if the gaps in justice and understanding become too great.

Something I learned in decades of working with at-risk youth in the streets of America is that they are lost until someone can honestly recognize the unique genius they carry and often hide. Each soul, regardless of outer circumstances or appearances, is born with an inner nobility and sense of purpose that longs to be recognized and given a chance, or even a second chance, to manifest. Denying an individual soul, much less an entire group, the opportunity to find and follow their dream is not simply a mistake or a justifiable omission; it is also an assault on their natural nobility and an insult to their souls.

A society is playing with fire each time it rejects the innate nobility of its youth. For youth not only carry within them the dream of the future, they also tend to act out the imbalances and injustices of society as well as the deep grievances of their communities. Injustices that are not faced inside a culture will eventually be lived out on its streets as a kind of collective fate.

Good role models are important at all levels of society and genuine job opportunities can bring security and a level of dignity that can make life manageable; but a living dream brings forth the true nobility of the soul. What remains trapped in the opportunity gaps, in the divides caused by racism and bigotry, in the midst of failing institutions as well as in the shadows of dilapidated buildings is the long-deferred dream of freedom that can only grow when offered to everyone. Those who would deny any young person the opportunity to learn and find a purpose in life have already lost their own dream and are unconsciously contributing to the half village and the shadows of despair.

A SECOND BIRTH

People used to know better that the period of youth involves a necessary second birth, a psychological nativity through which one's inner life and true nature can become revealed. If it were only about "growing up," nature would take care of things. A person would simply become themselves over time. Natural instincts and the passage of time would make a person meaningful, purposeful, and ultimately fulfilled. However, human nature requires each person to find another passageway, a rite of change that separates them from everything before they can find a unifying path and fulfilling way of life.

What we call youth is more than a biological condition and it involves more than a temporary social category that we can outgrow. Youth is a meaningful, symbolic condition that presages the course of each human life. Youth, whether they know it or not, are trying to give birth to the "other half" within them. Re-birth and awakening are the inner needs that drive youth to extremes. Each young person is pregnant with gifts intended to one day be given to the community. Meanwhile, "coming of age" involves coming upon what is truly ageless within each of us. In coming of age, a person touches that which is universal and enduring in human life, the mysterious place where we are each connected to the wholeness at the center of life.

We are fascinated with youth partially because in youth each of us becomes touched by the eternal. The presence of the eternal is what makes youth so alluring yet so vulnerable; so purposeful yet so lost. Something inside each young person knows that they are wildly incomplete, in need of finding missing parts and awakening unknown resources within themselves. Something already developed but mostly hidden forces youth to go out of step with mainstream society. Call it the genius of the child; call it the inner spirit; call it the soul, the purpose, the fate, the destiny, the uniqueness—for it is all of those. It will have its day or, if denied, will waste many days and can lead to wasted lives.

In a mythic sense, youth is an eternal state in which everything can be experienced for the first time. As a result, everyone's youth has a touch of eternity in it. People may long for the time of youth that is long past. Yet, the past is anything but past. The past travels with us and after the literal time of youth has gone, the longing for the eternal is what remains. Each time we feel lost or torn apart by the troubles of life, we may be close again to the struggles of our youth, the time in which the dream of our lives first awakened within us. Genius becomes revealed in times of adversity making available resources and vitality that otherwise remain hidden in the soul.

When the human community fails to provide meaningful rites of passage and offer effective means of support to young people, they must set out on their own. Like the half-boy, they must one day cross the line and begin the great journey of life, with or without the support of others. The longing for self-discovery and the drive to seek some sense of fulfillment cannot be completely rescinded. In this world, the only solution for the incompleteness of our lives comes when and where we risk everything to become a greater version of ourselves. Yet, before any wholeness can be found the brokenness of life must be fully experienced. Like the half-boy, each person must become stuck in life and descend to a great depth in order to find the place of unity hidden within. Then, the turbulent waters become the baptismal font, and life becomes renewed from the eternal spark and unique spirit set within the soul before we were first born.

A GENUINE INDIVIDUAL

The half-boy story has survived thousands of years and continues to resonate because it reveals a basic human truth. We are each half or less than half of what we came to life to become and we long to be whole, even if for one brief moment. Like other mythic stories, the tale reminds us that what we are really searching for already exists inside ourselves. The trouble is that we must become as if torn apart, suffer some great loss, or begin a deep descent in order to find what was there all along. Any approach to being whole or feeling complete depends upon first realizing that something important is missing.

Being an individual means more than simply being recognized as "a single human being" amongst the group. The real individual is someone who has become "undivided" within themselves. The only way to become undivided within ourselves turns out to be to suffer clearly whatever divisions we might have. In other words, the only ones able to become whole are those willing to become truly divided. We must become conscious of the ways in which we are at odds within ourselves before we can clearly see ways to become whole. When we are able to suffer the divisions, we find ourselves next to the living spirit and core imagination that tries to live through us. When in the state of wholeness, which in this world is always temporary, we become agents of change able to bring some wholeness to the village of life.

Becoming a whole person has always been a challenging and difficult task; in the modern world, it can seem impossible. In times of fragmentation it becomes hard to hold any imagination of the wholeness of things. In mass cultures, people are much more likely to be seen as just a small part of a larger demographic. Amidst all the mass marketing and mass communications, mass weaponry and mass problems, it is easy to feel like half, or even less than half, of a person. In the statistical worldview, quantity overrules quality and simple head counts far outweigh any sense of individual value. The idea of a genuine individual with a meaningful life becomes submerged amidst the flood of facts and figures that group everyone by age, gender, income, and demographic trends.

It becomes easier every day to feel lost in the river of distractions and in the waves of meaningless trends. The individuality so highly touted in modern societies actually depends upon finding a meaningful connection to the spirit that brought us to life to begin with. Unless we connect consciously with inner genius, we remain divided within, always on the verge of becoming torn apart or split off. Meanwhile, the human soul knows that that there is more to life than simple survival or the accumulation of material goods. This is especially true during youth, when something strongly felt but as yet unseen tries to surface from within us. Only at that deep inner level can we find the uniqueness within us that allows us to become a whole person and a genuine individual.

Our deepest longings and the question of who we are intended to be cuts us in half, dividing us within ourselves. At critical stages and significant moments in the course of life, we sink with the weight of our own questions; we drown in our own psyche in order to reach a subtle ground that secretly sustains our every breath. In that sense, all separations, splits, and conflicts are evidence of a unity we long to find, both individually and collectively.

Our longings tell us that there is another half, a better half, a fuller life somewhere. We enter life full of longing; we are born to it, born of it. Each life is wrapped around longings set inside dreams, wound into the fabric of our souls. We die for a lack of knowing how big our longing truly is, and we die from allowing our true longings to be diminished by the banality of life and the ways in which we continue to abandon ourselves. The problem is not that we long for something; the problem is that so much of our genuine longing for life can become lost in the fog of memories or the haze of confusion and speed of changes that now characterize the human village.

CHAPTER 15

LOST IN THE FOG

Those who lose dreaming are lost.

- Australian Aboriginal

In this highly condensed version of the life of the human soul, the half-boy manages to leave the village that can only see the wounded part of him. However, instead of finding some relief, he winds up all alone on the dusty roads. Instead of finding a refuge, he enters the desolation of another wasteland and becomes even more conscious of the ways in which he is separate from other people. If we want to reach the river of life, we must cross the wasteland again and again. In seeking wholeness, we must look deeper into all that divides us and creates conflicts in the common world.

Although people often wish to know how a story ends, the key to understanding stories can often be found in the middle of it. The middle of the story of the half-boy involves a great conflict as the opposite elements of his life try to come together. It also includes a great descent into the underlying conflicts of life itself. In order to become whole, even for just a moment, we must touch the basic division in life itself. There can be no healing without touching the basic split in life. There is an education of the soul that only begins when we feel that all is lost, when we hit bottom and must learn what carries us when we can no longer carry ourselves.

The creative response to the wasteland in the world outside begins with facing and healing the inner split in one's own life by finding the wholeness within and learning to follow one's own genius nature. Of course, that is easier said than done. Notice that the opposite sides of the half-boy cannot see eye to eye. Like the village that cannot see him clearly, the half-boy has but one eye through which to see the world. Even when he tries to see things clearly, he can only see one side of a situation. Even when we come close to something that could offer some sense of completion, we can only criticize aspects of it or simply fight with it. The condition of halfness includes the state of being unable to see or connect to what we most desire, especially when we are close to it.

Wholeness may seem possible when the two halves of something approach each other; but in the wasteland, two halves don't necessarily make a whole. We fight with what we desire; we reject precisely what we need. Instinct goes against instinct, thought against thought, desire against desire. On our own, we cannot accept that which we most desire even when we encounter it. The battle becomes a stalemate and the struggle reaches a stuck-point. Sometimes becoming completely stuck is a requirement for learning how to let go.

Wholeness turns out to be a mythical condition, and in myth it is the third thing that makes the charm. A third thing is required to connect two things that have become truly separated. Wholeness is not simply a matter of adding one thing to another; it is a third thing altogether. In the depths of the soul, something older and deeper than all that can divide the human mind and human heart must be found in order for the split to be healed. Magic lies in the third thing that moves the whole thing and changes everything. A third way of seeing is required, a third eye if you will, another focus, a focus on the "otherness" that waits beyond the literal and the psychological.

When working with young people, I often stop the story at the place where the conflicting halves have raised a storm of fury and both halves have slipped into the fog and disappeared completely into the river. For a moment the half-boy seemed close to becoming whole; then everything became overheated and conflicted and it all fell apart and life became even more stuck. The half-boy disappears into his inner conflicts and confusions, while the outside world continues to run the way it does every day.

Something important and dangerous has happened; something that can be life defining and life destroying has occurred; yet no one may be aware of it.

When I ask a group of contemporary girls and boys what the turbulent river represents to them, they answer with little hesitation: drugs and alcohol that make you high only to bring you down even harder; violence and aggression that hurts others, but also tears you apart inside; rape and sexual abuse that has become rampant, though few seem to notice; racism and bigotry that cut off a person's life before it can even begin; the rise of hatred and all the "haters" who try to turn people against each other.

The litany goes on when considering the river of life that runs through the story as they also name the ravages visited upon nature, the pollutions that foul the air in which they must grow, and the poisoning of the atmosphere with all the denial that surrounds the problems of global warming and climate change. No matter if they grow up in impoverished communities or in privileged circumstances, they know that the ice caps are melting, that the waters are rising, and that the storms of life grow greater all the time.

By now, most young people know friends who are lost in depression, stuck in some habit, or caught up in violence. They name abuses that are visited upon defenseless children, but also the damage done by indifference and, increasingly, the dissociation engendered by technology. At an early age, young people learn the language and patterns of addiction as they have grown up in a world awash with addictive substances and obsessive habits.

I am not trying to simply speak for youth; rather, I am retelling what I have increasingly heard from youth. You may think that opening up all the strains and struggles that now trouble the world would be depressing to young people. On the contrary, I have found that they relish the opportunity to name the issues and tell the painful stories of how they feel torn and pulled apart by all the fracturing and fragmenting that characterize modern life. One result of mass communications is that all the tragedies of the world as well as all the calamities in nature are delivered to everyone instantly. It is the same thing to live in tragic times as to be in a tragic place. And, indeed, these are tragic times, in which both nature and culture become ravaged by the storms of change and the growing presence of chaos.

Youth cannot help but absorb the confusions and ailments of the society in which they grow. At this time, they tend to absorb and reflect massive cultural anxiety along with the storms of uncertainty and winds of despair that affect the climate of the whole world. Modern young people know what it means to be lost, even to be forsaken, in a world that runs faster and faster, chasing some idealized future but never arriving at any place of wholeness. In the modern world, the river of life is in tremendous flux, the waves of upheaval come from all directions, and people can readily become lost in the fog or disappear amidst the flood of changes.

Repeatedly, I have found that young people of all backgrounds identify with feelings of being unwelcome, undervalued, and uninvited, just like the half-boy. They understand the metaphor of dragging oneself along like a half person and relate intimately to being in or near the troubled waters repeatedly. For them, the tale of the half-boy caught amidst a great conflict and lost in a river of turmoil turns out to be reassuring because it offers metaphors for the conditions that they experience and face almost every day.

RED FOG, WHITE FOG

Under the banner of Voices of Youth, we held many retreats where young people from all walks of life could come together to share with and learn from each other. The tale of the half-boy often turned out to be a way to bring everyone to the vital edge where all the conflicts of contemporary life could meet. The place in the story where the battle of the two halves raised enough dust and fog to obscure the light of day became a place for young people to fully express themselves. One of the metaphors that made sense to everyone was the idea of becoming lost in the fog of life.

The fog comes between them and other people, between them and other ideas, between them and other possibilities. The easiest form of fog to identify is the red fog, which manifests as anger and rage and leads to violence and destruction. Young males can be attracted to and inclined toward anger and violence, especially in societies where there is no meaningful mentoring. Levels of anger and frustration throughout modern cultures help to create a fog of violence that can engulf youth at an early age.

Those caught in the red fog can often be easier to reach because their intensity makes them present in a palpable way. Their volatility makes them strangely available to change if you can meet them where they are and not be consumed by the fires of aggression they feel. However, those caught in the clouds of white fog, which manifests as depression and alienation, are often harder to reach than those who are burning; they can hide behind a wall of cold denial or be strangely elusive, either caught in a maze or lost in a daze. It may be hard to put your finger on who they really are and what they might truly be feeling.

The deep feelings are more elusive and at first seem less explosive. It's as if something wants to come out and become known, but it keeps getting lost in clouds of alienation and depression. Sometimes, the real story remains hidden behind a fog so heavy and dense that it feels like a wall. This state can often be found amongst suburban white kids and others who grow up in more affluent parts of the culture. The seeming safety and comfort of materialism can harbor a profound sense of alienation held back behind a haze of depression. They seem lost in a fog that makes them unable to move forward in life. Or else they move along, but it is a hazy journey on pathways that don't lead to individuation.

Voices of Youth retreats would bring together young folks from diverse backgrounds, thus bringing both fogs into the room, like the two sides of the half-boy. Typically, kids from the hood, those shrouded in the red fog, would speak up more readily, while we would have to find ways to bring the others out of the white fog. However, young people can always be surprising; once, the first person to speak about the place in the story where the two halves conflict was a young guy who came from an upper-class neighborhood. He spoke of growing up with caring parents and receiving a good education in private schools.

However, he painfully declared that he found himself to be split just like the half-boy. He was quite clear that in his case the split was horizontal. He could achieve good grades and offer an appearance that satisfied teachers and parents; yet he felt only half alive. Specifically, he found himself to be numb from the waist down. He felt as if a fog obscured the lower part of his body, leaving him emotionally, sexually, and sensually adrift, only partially present to himself and others. He felt that he was asleep in life because half of him had not yet awakened.

That admission caused another youth to talk of growing up in the smog and fog of suburbia, where he became confused and distracted by having so much "stuff." Surrounded by affluence, he had accumulated the finest distractions that money could buy. He had been given "everything a kid could want," but felt completely empty inside. He felt sheltered and protected; but also isolated and trapped. By the time he turned sixteen, he feared that he was slipping into a white fog of material abundance and a state of spiritual emptiness.

In seeking to fill the void inside, he began using all kinds of drugs only to begin fearing that he would disappear altogether. As the feeling of numbness seemed to spread, he felt he had to do something just to get out of his room. One day, out of pure desperation, he staged a garage sale and kept it going until he sold everything he had, even his bed. All he kept in his once cluttered room were some books, a lamp, and a sleeping bag. He decided to paint his room entirely white, including the floor, then he camped out right in the middle of his white fog.

It was kind of a homeopathic attempt to find something real by making the unreality of his life symbolic. He had realized that drugs were an attempt to break out of the white fog, but in the end they just added to the numbness. He came to see numbness as the other half of himself and as the enemy of his life. He felt that he had to face the fog and make the metaphor literal in order to find a way out of the numbing haze of excess, materialism, and a purposeless existence. Eventually, he left the room and began searching for something he could feel was missing from his affluent half-life, even if he could not yet name what it might be.

The white fog tends to be made of dreams deferred and mostly forgotten, about disappointments that seem to cancel all hope or substitutions, and distractions that start to subtract essence from one's life.

A listless confusion develops as feelings and passions diminish and are replaced by a numbness that becomes habitual, familiar, and dully persistent.

The white fog can be subtle as it creeps into someone's life, beginning with a little depression of spirit that grows into a distance from everyone and everything. Soon it can "white out" distinctions between things, making "whatever" seem like an answer to most questions. It dulls the senses, diminishes the mind, and obscures real emotions, leaving in their place an empty feeling, a vague loss, and a lack of direction. Life becomes a pattern of turning away, tuning out, and escaping to nowhere. A great pain exists, held behind a wall of white fog, until one day when it takes a deeper turn into suicidal fantasies or even erupts with cold-blooded homicidal intent.

The red fog describes the kind of intense conflicts and violence that characterize life on the streets and in the neighborhoods and barrios, where the battle between life and death can often be close by and can suddenly pull you down hard. The red fog erupts; it explodes and can envelop anyone who happens to be in the vicinity. Street kids and gang-involved youth recognize the intense struggles in their lives in the red fog of violence, drugs, and destruction. On the mean streets of poverty and neglect, it becomes easy for kids at a young age to get caught in life and death situations. It seems as if life is cheap and the likelihood of getting out of the rough life is not high. Those who feel rejected from mainstream culture not only burn with rage and outrage, they can also seek to go out in a blaze.

Young folks from the rough side of life understand the intensity of conflict. Sometimes they would champion the hardness they live with and manifest a red-line vitality truly opposite the demeanor of kids caught in the white fog. They would speak of having several dead friends by the age of sixteen and state that they didn't fear death as they appeared to accept that death at a young age would also be their fate. As the conversation at the edge deepened, the darker side of life on the mean streets began to surface.

After listening to some stories from the other side of life within the white fog, a young guy from the hood said: "OK, you want to hear what our lives are like; how things go down in the streets of the ghetto? You want to see how things look to us? OK." He told of having to deal with the possibility of being shot each time he left the house; of having to make sense of random bullets that could find their way right into your own house. He said with unmasked shock: "Even on the way to school in the morning, my friend was smoked by a rival gang. It happened real close and it could have been you. I mean it could have been me. You have to deal with that. That's in your life every day. If you do get to school, you face all kinds of dangers; you have to watch out all the time. You don't know where trouble will come from. You have to be ready to defend yourself and your friends."

"Listen to this," another kid began, "people disappear... just disappear. Friends and relatives get arrested and you don't know what happened to them. People die in front of you," said a fifteen-year-old, speaking of his brother killed in a drive-by shooting. "Out of nowhere a bullet found him; that's it; he's dead. How do you figure that into your day? How do you factor that into your schooling?" They were beginning to unburden themselves of a weight they carried in their daily lives. In dropping the poses and attitudes necessary to survive on the streets, they also unloaded stories of constant threat and the seemingly endless fog of violence.

Often the one speaking would tell the tragic story of the friend who was sitting nearby, remaining a mute witness to his own life story. He would nod his head to confirm what was being told, but not speak a word of it himself. You could see how the burdens were shared between them and how some of the weight was so heavy that it had to be carried by a friend.

Once the stories started to come out, they could become a chorus of rage and pain that slowly morphed into sorrow and fear. Eventually, tears of anguish poured forth as well.

"OK, OK... listen to this." A young guy wanted to tell why it was hopeless for him and for the rest of them. At ten years old, he had been given a gun and told to use it if he had trouble with anyone. He was pulled into the gang that ran the local projects where he grew up. At first, he was employed as a lookout and runner, passing messages between dealers and drug addicts. Later, it became running drugs and the gun became a tool of the trade, just a part of the job.

Now, he had turned eighteen and said this was the first time he had felt safe in over a decade. "I never talked about this before," he said, suddenly overcome with tears. After he pulled himself together, he had a question for everyone: "Whose fault is it, the ten-year-old who was given the gun and told to shoot, or the culture that gave the gun to the kid?"

He wasn't looking for an argument or trying to justify anything he had done. He had torn that question out of the torment of his heart, and it hung heavy in the air. It was a genuine question, everyone had to accept that. More than that, you could see two people in him, both of whom were asking for something. One was eighteen now and able to formulate the nature of the problem; the other was only ten-years-old, standing there like a puzzled child asking why a gun was being put into his hand and why such a weight was being put into his life. The two halves of him stood in the same question, which he was asking himself as much as he was asking us.

No one answered as the cutting question tore open the young life before us. We found ourselves in a silence as thick as a confessional. A space of tragedy had opened and we were all in it with him. As the silence grew, a weight that grows every day in the culture fell on everyone in the room. Like many others who live in torn circumstances, he was both child and man, both an armed threat and a threatened boy. Completely revealed in his own pain and anguish, he was eight and eighteen and eighty as time collapsed before the tragedy in his voice.

We continued to sit in silence, in mute compassion, in simple sympathy that transcended both age and all our differences. Eventually, he broke the silence himself by asking for forgiveness; not simply from us, but also of himself and of the ghosts of parents and others that we could not see but somehow could feel nearby.

No one moved. He went on. He said that the recent days in the camp were the best days of his life, and he meant it. Good food every day and no one trying to come through his door at night. No sirens. No gunfire nearby. He could see the stars clearly, for the first time.

And, his friend was here too. Through his tears, he said that he needed to get to his real reason for speaking to begin with. He made a plea that we help his friend survive the streets and return to school and reach college. He said his own life was over; that's why he was talking about it. His life was lost. He was so deep into the violence and dealing drugs, he would never get out. But, his friend was sitting in the group and was near to finishing high school; he could make it out and live for both of them.

He turned directly to his friend, telling him how smart he was and how hard he had worked at school. But he warned him that "the life" was trying to claim him too as he began to weep again. As this other side of him came out, you could see where his love was. In his elemental, tragic sense of life, he said he would die right now so that his friend could live. Now, the friend began to weep and argued through tears that they both had to make it. But, it wasn't convincing.

Everyone knew that for either of them to make it, a lot of things would have to change.

You could see them sinking before your eyes, like drowning kids, holding on to each other and pushing each other away. They shared a dream of surviving and escaping, but the weight of their lives was pulling them under and the dream was less and less able to hold them up. Now, one was saying that he would take all the weight so that the other could survive and follow his dream.

The dream could be lived by only one. But, anyone watching could see two souls becoming lost in the fog and drowning in the midst of the flood of their lives. It was tragic, there was no other way to see it; it was a living tragedy unfolding before us. Everyone present was touched by the heavy hand of fate that pressed the two of them together and held them as the waters of tragedy gathered about them.

In the almost eerie silence, another boy was weeping in quiet convulsions. He had arrived at the door of the event all alone, even though he was clearly too young to be on his own. He wasn't registered for the retreat and he offered little by way of explanation. Someone had brought him there because he had become so silent and withdrawn, and those who loved him only knew that he was quietly departing from life. We accepted him because he had the look of someone who had nowhere to go. He must have been eleven or twelve and small for his age at that—way too small for the invisible things he had to face.

He was barely able to speak up; but there was something he had to say. Slowly, he began to speak of fear, ever present fear, bone gripping fear. He had seen his cousin shot down for no reason. There was no explanation for it and no way to escape it, and he was still shaking in total fear. He had idolized his older cousin and could not comprehend what had befallen both of them. He was almost frozen in fear and he was being crushed by it. He could barely go out of the house because sudden dread would overtake him and sudden dangers were waiting for him. He wanted to just stay in the camp. He looked at us hopefully, as if we could keep him and hold him there. As if we could make it all go away.

Now, the room became a sea where people were drowning in sorrow or just hanging on, hoping it would end and that there wouldn't be another heartbreaking story told. As the stories piled up, a weight accumulated that pushed open all the hearts in the room. Part of the tragedy in that room was that the distribution of human suffering has become radically out of balance. As the young ones spoke, they were not just unloading emotionally, they were releasing a weight that burdened their hearts and made them old before their time. Tragedy has weight, has psychic substance that falls with the gravity of pain and seeks the ground of human souls to hold it.

When adults refuse to acknowledge their mistakes and tragedies or fail to accept their share of the burden, the weight falls too heavily on the hearts and minds of young people. It robs them of their youth and it can crush their spirit and leave them desperately isolated inside. The defenses of young people tend to be weak even if their posturing looks ominous and strong. Once caught in the fog it is hard to conceive another way of life. Along with the numbness there is a dulling of the mind and a loss of imagination.

Young people can become seriously alienated from most people and identify only with those who feel as they do. The fogs work like a spell or a possession in which the spirit of a person is trapped. All they see is colored by a haze of violence or depression. Within both the red and white fogs, the person becomes isolated and alienated from the full range of feelings and emotions. There is a narrowing of imagination that can lead to obsessive ideas and a process of literalizing aspects of both life and death.

Whether the culture pays attention or not, the psyches of young people are engaged with the archetypal pattern of birth, death, and rebirth. If the psyche of a young person becomes stuck in a fog, they can over identify with the aspects of their lives that need to be cast off and think that they must die altogether. The need for a thorough dissolution can become a fixation on death without the awareness of rebirth, the other half of the archetypal dynamic of change.

A BLACK FOG

As is the case with many aspects of life, there is a third element, a third kind of fog. Besides the red fog of violence and the white fog of depression, there is a black fog of despair that can lead to suicide. This fog can become an outgrowth from either the red fog or the white fog. Under the black fog, a person can see suicide as the only way out of the anguish of a half-life that seems to have no possible redemption. All manner of seemingly inexplicable acts erupts from the numbing effects of the red fog of rage or the white fog of depression and alienation. The black fog can lead to suicide or to mind-numbing tragedies such as school shootings and mass killings.

One of the devastating results of suicide is the possibility that it can become contagious, especially amongst younger folks. The painful process of discussing suicide with those closest to the fallen one repeatedly involved the statement that the deceased friend "felt empty inside." Life felt pointless, empty of meaning and lacking in value. Yet, the friends could name the unique and endearing qualities in their mates that were now lost from life. When asked about their own lives, too often, the close friends of suicidal youth acknowledged that they too felt empty; both devoid of inherent purpose and lacking in internal worth.

Repeatedly, I have found myself emphatically telling young people that it is not simply that they must make something of themselves, but that they already are something in themselves. Many are completely surprised by this, as if they are hearing it for the first time. Yet, it could quickly become clear that under all the pain and alienation, there remained the glimmer of an idea, the seed of something that might be rejected but could not be erased or completely destroyed, either by the ignorance of common culture or even by one's own self condemnation. It might be mostly ignored, and might even be used for the wrong purpose, but most could still recognize and value some elements of genius, at least in their close friends.

Meanwhile, the lack of elders in the culture and the loss of meaningful rituals of healing cause unhealed wounds and unfinished tragedies to fall on unwitting youth. Youth tend to act out the psychological condition of the culture in which they must grow and try to become themselves. Youth can be a barometer of the underlying emotional and psychological conditions of the culture around them. Currently, the levels of nihilism and extremism found in economics and politics, as well as in the extremism of religion and ideologies, have put all children and young people at greater risk of being lost in the fogs of violence and numbness that lead to both individual and collective tragedies.

CATHARSIS

If the older people don't accept some of the weight from the tragedies of life, no one should be surprised when the young act out or break down under the ignored burdens of the past. Some of the weight had been falling for a long time, down from the past; falling from generations that could not or did not unburden themselves enough. The residue of unknown tragedies falls upon young people and speechless burdens drop into their hearts before they can understand or defend themselves. The voice of tragedy needs to be expressed so that a cathartic moment becomes possible and the release of the burdens of the heart and the soul can occur.

The old Greek word katharsis includes the sense of a "bodily purging" and deep cleansing that can free the soul from the burdens of shame and guilt and outrage at the tragedies that inevitably befall us. Washing clean the agonies of the soul can precipitate forgiveness of the human condition as it purges the psyche of self-loathing. The ancient Greeks understood that when they made theater the center of community. Tribal people knew it when they put ritual and myth at the center of their world. The weight of tragedy does not simply fall to the floor or disappear into thin air, even after it has been expressed. Some of the weight goes beyond words and falls into the hearts of whoever will listen. Too often, no one is there to listen or take up some of the weight of unlived dreams and unacknowledged genius, leaving those most affected by tragedy isolated and alone.

Modern people often believe that avoiding trauma and trouble will make life more pleasant and easy to bear. Yet, the weight that burdens the soul does not move until it has been engaged and acknowledged and has been given a voice. Whether the danger takes the form of becoming lost in the reckless violence and destruction of the red fog or of disappearing into the annihilation of the white fog, it becomes clear that modern youth are increasingly lost and universally at risk. They are at risk of not finding themselves amidst all the conflicts and mass confusion; they are at risk of not knowing that something essential hidden within them can help them feel whole. The culture that tells young people they "can be anything they want to be" has created a subculture of young people who feel increasingly empty and unable to feel valuable and meaningful within themselves.

The touch of wholeness must be found, and it can only be found in encounters with the "other half " of life. That is, with the missing, denied, avoided, and feared aspects of oneself. The story of the half-boy indicates how important this self-discovery is by having the missing part be equal to half of our whole self. It also reminds us that genuine community depends upon the awakening of genius in young people. The village of humanity must be recreated again and again. Each generation arrives with a new dream trying to be brought into a world that needs continuous renewal. Without a meaningful community, it becomes very difficult for individuals to grow into themselves and become able to give the gifts that they came to life to give. Without awakened individuals, a community becomes self-limiting and lacks genuine inspiration and that can leave both the young and the old lost in the wasting fogs of unlived lives.

CHAPTER 16

HOLY WATER

We are more closely connected to the invisible than to the visible.

– Novalis

It is the nature of genius to be born into the world along with its human host; yet to become conscious of our inner genius requires that we experience a second birth. A second labor is also needed to bring our inner nature to light and our god-given gifts to the world. In order to become a genuine individual, a second birth is required; for genius is born—not made—and we must be born again for it to become conscious and fully known to us.

The first birth in life involves "biological imperatives" that include the continuance of the species as well as the growth of the family. By contrast, the second birth is a birth out of the family and into the unique story trying to unfold from within one's soul. This second nativity involves a revelation of qualities and characteristics that are indigenous to the individual regardless of family patterns, social status, or cultural conditions. What is familiar, familial, and taken for granted must dissolve in order for a new view of the world to emerge. We must go blind in order to gain a fresh vision and grasp a worldview the seeds of which only crack open through genuine struggle and suffering. The second birth involves the uncovering and discovering of the genius nature of the individual soul. This second birth takes place as an inner event; a psychological birth intended to awaken us to the original agreement of our souls.

Often, it takes an emergency, a tragedy, or what feels like a life and death circumstance to create the conditions needed for the second birth to occur. Something drastic may be required to generate a forced labor that allows the uniqueness of the soul to emerge from the depths of our being to the level of our conscious life. Emergency and emerge both arise from the same Latin root, emergere, meaning "to rise up, to bring forth, to bring to light." A psychological or spiritual emergency may be needed to bring forth the genius self that entered the world with us when we were first born. The issues of awakening and renewal cannot be solved at the level of the ego; for that is where the problems have solidified and the emergency has formed.

The notion of emerging incudes a sense of rising in a watery medium by virtue of an intrinsic buoyancy. The human soul has always been connected to water; as such, it tends to be resilient and buoyant. Yet, we may have to hit rock bottom or be at an existential impasse before the buoyancy of the soul can be found and the imagination and energy trying to arise within us can be released. Often, we must feel that there is no way to move before we can find again that which deeply moves our souls. Sometimes, we must fall apart in order to re-collect essential parts of ourselves that we could not manage to hold onto during the abandonments experienced early in life.

A NECESSARY DESCENT

It may feel distinctly otherwise, but the struggles of life are not intended to destroy us, but to induce a descent to the origins of life in order to bring to the surface the originality hidden within each of us. We become worn down, burned out, broken in half again and again after marching through the wasteland of life. We become lost in the flux of the world, forgetting that we set out looking for a way to become whole. We fall out of coherence, become half of what we might be, and must drag ourselves to the river to be washed clean, to be baptized and born again. For, at an instinctive level, the human psyche seeks forms of dissolution and renewal, again and again. Seeking renewal and rebirth is instinctive and natural to humans; after all, that is how we first began life in this world.

At critical moments in the course of life, we sink with the weight of our own disappointments, descend in the grip of our inner conflicts, and drown in the depths of our own psyche. We fall through the planks of reason, down through the splits in ourselves and through the cracks in our view of the world. The weight and burdens of life sinks us, pulling us down until we begin to seek a solution at a deeper level. The struggle of two halves—of the two instincts, desires, or emotions—reaches a point where the whole thing has to be seen differently. The entire viewpoint of the ego must shift or collapse or dissolve.

All meaningful change requires a genuine surrender. Yet, to surrender does not simply mean to give up; more to give up one's usual self and allow something other to enter and redeem the lesser sense of self. In surrendering, we fall to the bottom of our arguments and seek to touch the origin of our lives again. Only then can we see as we were meant to see, from the depth of the psyche where the genius resides, where the seeds of wisdom and purpose were planted before we were born. We fall in order to find what has secretly carried us all along and would now become consciously known.

In genuine surrender, we arrive at a silent place, a still point within the turmoil of life, the place of baptism and renewal. Baptism is one of the oldest rituals of humanity, one that involves an immersion in the waters of life in order to revive the vitality of one's being. Baptism requires a symbolic return to the watery womb of the world, a return to primordial origins in order to briefly dissolve the fixations of the personality and renew one's spirit for life. Such an immersion requires a surrender that can feel like death. In a sense, part of us does die as we let go of our current form of "halfness" in order to feel whole. Baptism repeats the archetypal pattern of birth, death, and rebirth as a "little death" is needed for a greater rejuvenation and resurgence to occur.

Water can simply be seen as the element that makes up seventy percent of the world we live in and seventy percent of our own body. Yet, water can also be the primal sea before time began, the mythic flood that submerges the world in order to renew it, the healing water of life that can reconcile all opposing things. Water dissolves and it resolves; it also absolves and renews.

Water is the transformative substance that was there at the beginning of the world and there at the beginning of the labors that gave birth to each of us.

Water symbolizes the primal material: the ultimate source of life for humans as well as for the world. Water exists at the beginning of creation and returns in the great floods that symbolize the end of each cosmic cycle. The mythic imagery of water is connected with our earliest bodily experiences and sensations of being soothed and lulled, nourished, refreshed, and cleansed. Yet, water also holds our first terrors of suffocation and blind panic. Immersion in water is a return to pre-existence, similar to what occurs at death and in the throes of transformation. Immersion is also what occurs when primal emotions flood our consciousness and the ego, or the little self, temporarily dissolves in order for the deeper, greater self within us to become better known.

Like devotees entering the Ganges, we must enter something old and greater than ourselves: god's water; the birth waters of the Great Mother; the waters of reconciliation; the waters that dissolve hardness of the heart and allow life to flow freely again.

Originally, baptism was not a one-time event connected to a religious doctrine or system of belief. Holy water might be used to bless the forehead of the newborn soul; but a full immersion in the watery womb of a river, lake, or salty sea was an instinctive ritual known throughout the world. Something within us knows the beauty and meaning of devotees entering the Ganges River to pray, or of native people immersing in the ocean to be renewed. The word baptize comes from roots that mean "to dip, to immerse." The little word dip, which sounds like water dripping, comes from "deep," so that even a little dip in the ocean can feel quite renewing.

Any meaningful descent can be felt by the soul as an attempt to renew oneself by touching the origins of life again. The ego fears that it will die or disappear in the waters of the deep unconscious. But the soul knows that any descent in life can become a potential baptism that will return us to the full potential at the origin of our lives—back there at the beginning; down there near the source, where the underlying unity of life waits to be found and be touched again. The holiness of holy water derives from the wholeness of creation that continuously arises from the eternal sea of life.

Ancient people all over the world used to go down to the waters whenever life became too much of a burden, each time a great loss needed to be washed away, or when a conflict needed to be resolved by everyone entering the waters of reconciliation. In some traditions, the whole village would enter the baptismal waters at least once a year. The end of the year was symbolically connected to the end of the world, and the collective surrender and deep immersion helped start everything anew. In the deep stillness where our first breath once formed, life can return in an initiation by the invisible that buoys us back to life, imbued with the breath of wholeness and ready to start things over again.

Something ancient in us bends us toward the origins of the whole thing. We either drown in the splits and confusions of our lives, or we surrender to something greater than ourselves. The water of our deepest troubles is also the water of our own solution. In surrender, we descend down to the bottom of it and back to the beginning of it; down into what is divided in order to get back to the wholeness before the split. Healing, health, wealth, wholeness: all hail from the same roots. To heal is to make whole again; wholeness is what all healing seeks and what alone can truly unify our spirit.

The second birth through which we become fully born is something that we need to experience over and over again. What continually requires healing is the original split in life, thus healing requires that the original split be touched. Mythologically, each split goes back to the division of night and day, light and dark. Thus, any wound, any split, leads back to the break in the world that was the beginning of time. Pursued far enough—followed deeply enough—the personal tends towards and bends to the mythic. In mythical terms, any division implies the original separation, any wound becomes the original split; any longing, loss, or descent returns to the original split in the world itself. No healing without the touch of something timeless; no renewal without the initiating touch of the eternal.

THE FOUNTAIN OF YOUTH

We no longer have rituals that convince the soul, but our psyches seek dissolution and rebirth anyway, though often through the abuse of substances. People will experiment with all kinds of life-altering substances in order to feel something substantial in themselves. We try to fill the huge hole, felt as the absence of the deeper self or our missing other half, with any substance that might momentarily seem fulfilling. The various types of substance abuse attempt to replace the kind of transubstantiation that the psyche truly longs to experience. Secretly we seek an overall solution, a return to paradise in order to immerse in the waters of renewal.

We need rejuvenation at critical points in our lives. We need some taste of paradise, a visit to nirvana, a vacation in some wondrous place, preferably with a Fountain of Youth. The word holiday comes from "holy day," and the idea of vacation comes from the need to vacate our usual ways of being and doing in order to renew and rejuvenate ourselves by feeling whole again. Weary and drained of spirit by the daily rounds of life and the daily grind, we need a "solution" that alters us completely; something that renews our soul and reconnects us with the Soul of the World.

Old stories tell of Ponce de Leon and many other explorers sailing all the seas of the world in the hopes of finding the fountain of eternal youth. Yet, tales of sacred, restorative waters existed long before the conquistadors. Alexander the Great sought a healing "river of paradise" centuries ago. Similar legends and myths appear throughout the world. Often, the mythical fountain of youth would be connected to a river of gold. To this day, people search for one of these streams or the other; either the waters that claim to cure old age and illness or the veins of gold that promise to cure whatever ails you.

The facts of the matter are clear: no actual rejuvenating fountain has ever been found. In that sense and at that literal level, the Fountain of Youth is "just a myth." At the same time, the sense that a person might find a magical source of vitality and renewal continues to intrigue many people. The newest forms of the fountain of youth are found in the form of supplements and pills, magic formulas, and creams that make one feel or look much younger than their biological years. Strangely, the field of practical science has become the new area that promises relief from the pains of aging along with the promise of living longer and longer.

Biologists now search for a "longevity gene" that can reverse cell degeneration associated with aging. They're not just offering a sip from the fountain; they are intending to turn back the clock at the molecular level. The longing for rejuvenation is so deep and alluring that even the "hard sciences" begin to join the search for the legendary fountain that can make us youthful again.

The Fountain of Youth presents an archetypal image that sits deep in the memory pools of the human soul. It keeps springing up in all kinds of places because it is a mythical spring, an eternal image that remains part of the inheritance of the human soul. In ancient Greece, each fountain was believed to have its own spirit or genius. Some were visited for medicinal purposes, others to purge the effects of sin or a criminal act. Certain fountains possessed oracular powers and were linked with famous oracles like Delphi, others were seen as mirrors that could reveal the future. Ancient people made long pilgrimages to such holy waters and modern people continue the practice in journeys to Lourdes in France, the Ganges River in India, and the holy wells of Ireland to name but a few.

PATH TO THE CENTER

Touching these waters is like going back to the womb and the origins of life, as the holy rivers, streams, and wells were considered to arise in the otherworld and flow from the eternal source of life into this world. The intuition of it makes sense at the level where people long for the divine connection; but it is helpful to know that all bodies of water can be as the holy water and that everyone must have access to the healing center of life. The holy exertion required for a pilgrimage, like the struggles of the half-boy, are intended to drag us to the depths of the soul and the center of our being. Only in surrendering completely can the object of the pilgrimage be reached, for the object of every pilgrimage is the center of the pilgrim.

People set off to a famous shrine and seek a holy center and the point seems to be to arrive at that distant destination and somehow be renewed and confirmed by the experience. Yet, on a pilgrimage, the moment of awakening can happen anywhere along the path. The real aim of a pilgrimage is the center of the soul with its inner connection to the watery womb of existence. Any renewal that happens must happen within the seeker, and it only happens when the center of the self becomes awakened by the intensity of the effort made combined with the grace of the unseen.

The wonder of this world is that there are so many holy places in it and sacred paths on it. When the time comes for descent, many places in nature can offer the elements of life that help us reach a subsequent renewal. All of life is a pilgrimage aimed at the center of our origins, in the depths of our souls, and any genuine path will lead us there. The greatest pilgrimage involves becoming oneself and sustaining an awakened self within us. Inside that awakening, any step in life can become a pilgrimage. "Each step is a whole journey" is a true statement if the one taking the step is truly awake and not sleepwalking. Any step that leads to the center of the self is a full journey; anything that awakens us is a call from the divine.

This world may increasingly be a broken place and the spread of conflicts across the globe may make travel increasingly dangerous. Yet, the sacred can be found again, as it used to be found so often by our ancestors, in the nearby haunts of nature where the spirit of life waits for our attention. All of life is sacred in some way, yet the sacred in life can often become revealed where nature and human culture meet.

Part of the charm of old folk myths is that they locate everyone in the village of life and they discover the wonders of life in the nearby elements of nature. The half-boy enters his great conflict and surrenders to the river that happens to be nearby. The holiness of the occasion is made from the longing for wholeness he carries and the capacity for healing found in the basic waters of life. Then time stops, the holy water becomes present, and we see as we were meant to see—from the depth of the psyche where the genius resides in the soul and waits to fully awaken.

Then, we are in the Ganges of the mind, in the still waters of the soul, near the fountain of knowledge and the eternal promise of youth. Not a water that can return us to a simple state of youthful physicality; more a subtle and enduring water that can return us to the vitality and purpose that our life carries even if we have forgotten it for years. The Fountain of Youth exists inside the soul, at the place where our souls were touched by something sacred and we became whole for a while.

We seek the Fountain of Youth because youth was when we first tasted the water of life from the eternal fountain that resides in the soul. The point is not simply to prolong life or relive the golden days of youth; the real point is to find again the inner gold of our genius nature. The genius within us is the root of something eternal and therefore ever capable of being renewed. Not in the sense that the body never grows old, but in the idea that the soul and heart remain young as the dream of life and the inner gold becomes more real, more palpable and more able to be given away.

Each person enters the world gifted in some way and aimed at something that can provide moments of wholeness. Each person has at least one experience of awakening to the genius set within their soul; that is the genuine "promise of youth," as well as the root of longing for a Fountain of Youth. Although the recollection of that promise often becomes a nostalgia for the memories of youth, the true longing of the soul is for a rejuvenation from within and a regeneration of the inherent purpose set within our lives.

ALCHEMY OF THE DEPTHS

Having been driven to the depths by the inevitable conflicts of life, a timeless image is found again and the potential of the soul can renew. An answer occurs to us, a baptismal moment in the river of the mind, a change in the subtle earth of the heart. We find a union that is more accurately a reunion with the spirit that bore us to life to begin with. No one sees it; it happens in the depths of psyche's river and in the fecund mud of the soul. We don't even see it ourselves, because we are it as we become more of what we came to life to be.

In that moment, we ascend again, as a person rises up from the baptismal waters. Carried by the buoyancy of the soul, we rise with a wholeness we cannot fully know, awakened by an answer we may never fully enunciate. Life boils up in us; we boil back up into life. In a hidden moment we reenter our life as it reenters us. Already beginning to forget where we have been; stumbling towards the new village, which is the old village seen anew, the old world seen with the eye of the heart refreshed by the waters of eternity and energized by the ground of being.

No one sees the inner alchemy that occurs in the depths. We may see the results of renewal, the effects of wholeness; yet, the moment of being transformed remains a mystery. The moment of unity, renewed continuity, and inner coherence remains an open secret in human life. In the unseen depths of the soul, that which is hidden changes the visible, the conflict becomes a dance, and the spirit of life arises anew from the healing of the original split and the awakening of the genius that hides in the original wound. The genius in each person can be seen as the source of both the imagination and vitality through which we can continually restore, renew, and re-invent our lives. The roots of genius reside in the unseen realm where this world and the otherworld connect, where the human and the divine secretly meet.

There are times when we must glimpse something of the other side of life and touch our unique connection to the divine or else become stuck or drown in the common eddies and backwaters of life. Yet, there is a price to pay for entering the waters of change and touching the deep sense of self within us. In the waters of rebirth, we must lose sight of most everything else in order to find a fresh vision of the world. We must give up the one-eyed view of the ego and whatever is familiar or familial and taken for granted in order for a new view of the world to emerge. Feeling whole means breaking out of the bubble of the "little self," slipping out of the narcissistic shell and shedding the half-life of the isolated, self-involved, modern "I." We must go blind to what we know or think we know in order to gain a fresh vision and a deeper way of being present in the world.

THE PROBLEM OF WHOLENESS

At the point in the story where the half-boy rises from the depths of the river, there also arises the problem of wholeness and the issues of re-entry. In traditional terms, the half-boy made whole has entered a sacred condition; he is momentarily whole and therefore holy. He is disoriented in this world because he is reoriented to the otherworld of genius and imagination and the capacity to create and transform life. Having crossed the wasteland and survived an initiatory experience, he is ready to give the gifts he originally brought to life. However, the rest of the world has gone on, as it does on any day, and that usually means operating along the lines of the half-village.

Wholeness puts us in touch with the whole divine thing and that can be wildly disorienting and deeply troubling if no one is there to welcome, confirm, and bless the awakening that has occurred. Just as the vulnerability at birth needed to be held and comforted, the wholeness of the second birth needs to be seen and known. If the half-boy, temporarily made whole, cannot find a way to deliver his gifts, he may become lost again. The newfound wholeness of the half-boy seeks to be known, accepted, and blessed. At the beginning of the story the incompleteness of the half-boy presented a problem; now his wholeness presents another problem to the human village. Any attempt at genuine human community will encounter the problem of wholeness.

For the half-boy imbued with a sense of wholeness, the whole world has changed. Yet, he doesn't know his new place in the new world and can't even tell what state he is in. One of the hardest things in life turns out to be trusting oneself even after a profound experience of the deeper self. The story from thousands of years ago points out that a touch of wholeness can be disorienting at any time. In the modern world, where fragmentation and dissociation have become more common, the condition of wholeness can be entirely overwhelming and leave us betwixt and between one world and the other. The first problem is to not have a true experience of being whole; while the second problem is to feel whole and have no one to share it with or have it confirmed by.

In the first village of life, people learn how to survive but not how to live fully. Thus, the half-village is the place where people see with the single eye of self-interest and act with the habits of self-involvement. The half-village denies the presence of universal pain and suffering in order to get on with the basic activities of life. Typically, the half-village will ignore the wounds of life until they become insufferable. Beyond that, the half-village will often reward and even sanctify the kind of self-involvement that drives the frequent misuse of power and the extremes of greed.

In the half-village, people reduce everything to polarities—oppositions in which everyone is expected to pick a side. All that can be seen are the opposing halves of life: left or right, right or wrong, up or down, good or bad, white or black, male or female, old or young. The very idea of wholeness presents a problem, as most people cannot even acknowledge the common state of divisiveness and opposition. Thus, there is always the danger that the half-village will blame the wounded for revealing the presence of the wound. Not only that, but the more that people deny their genuine longings and persistent wounds, the more they will reject those who have found some sense of healing and wholeness.

The half-village has difficulty seeing the wholeness of anything, for wholeness can only be seen with genuine vision. Wholeness requires an act of imagination that includes the entire mind and the whole heart. In times and in places of intensifying conflict and fragmentation, it becomes increasingly difficult to hold an imagination of the unity and wholeness that secretly underlies the world.

In the modern world the need for experiences of feeling whole grows greater and greater, while the problem of wholeness grows larger as fewer people recognize the need for healing and the longing to become whole becomes lost in the distractions and delusions of mainstream activities.

CHAPTER 17

DANCING TO BE WHOLE AGAIN

*We must make ourselves capable of longing and make the world
open to the divine again.*

In the old mythic way of viewing the world, the center of things was
also the beginning place, so that finding the center could allow everything
to begin again. Each time it seems like the whole world is coming to an end,
we might be closer to it all beginning again, if we can only find the center
that has been lost. For, the center can go missing but cannot become lost
altogether. When in touch with the mythical center, everything becomes
possible again and the wonder and beauty of the world begins to return. A
renewed sense of the potential of life can arise and new solutions to age-old
problems can emerge.

When the problems of life become huge and overwhelming, when the
tasks seem impossible and the conflicts become intractable, when the whole
thing seems hopeless and people feel helpless, then the time has come to
seek for the missing center again. The surprise of it is that when the center
no longer holds, it must be sought where most are reluctant to go: in the
margins of life and at the very edges of creation. People must be willing to
admit that the problems have become overwhelming, that the usual policies
fail, that the usual beliefs and common practices no longer work.

If we then become willing to go to the edge and seek in the margins
of our lives, we each might find there a clue—a thread of meaning or
beauty that otherwise would remain unknown. If those willing to enter the

darkness and face the unknown within themselves would simply gather whatever thread of meaning they might find and begin to follow it, new ideas and relevant symbols would be found and old oppressions could be relieved. If those holding the threads of imagination and meaning would carry them from the edge and draw them toward the center, then things could begin all over again.

The center could be made anew if all the threads of individual genius were woven together. No one would have to heroically save everyone, or even pretend to do so. There would be no single idea or system, no theory or doctrine that needs to be believed or followed. Rather, each would follow their own thread of life and learn how and where to weave it to the living community of souls. Then the world could become again what it has always been and is meant to be: a place of awe, beauty, and wonder; a living ground of renewal and revelation, the manifest place of creation ever ongoing.

As above, so below, goes the old saying intended to remind everyone that we are threaded to the unseen center and held in life by invisible cords of genius, feeling, and imagination. There is a seam along which the two worlds are secretly stitched and sewn together so that the eternal realm remains threaded and tied to the limited world of space and time. As the conscious agents of both worlds, we suffer the burdens of time, the limits of place, and the weight of tragedies; yet, we also remain connected to the timeless threads and renewing energies of the eternal.

We each may be tiny, frail, and insignificant in the great scheme of things, yet we are each woven to the center of the whole thing. As with the image of the labyrinth, the thread of life goes to the middle and back, each person having a lifeline directly to the source of life. The infinite thread within can also be imaged as the continuous breath of life that gives us a pulse and a rhythm, secretly connecting each living soul to the center of the living, breathing cosmos.

The unique inner thread that ties us to the pulse of life is the clew of genius that gives us a meaning and a purpose and endows us with gifts intended to be given. When enough people awaken to their natural sense of purpose, the threads of life can be rewoven and the center of life can become known again. This cannot be proven by simple analysis or grasped by reason alone. Yet, we know it intuitively when we feel like we are hanging by a thread and wishing and praying that something or someone might pull us to a better place.

The center that we seek is also the otherworld, the source of inspiration and the vertical imagination that the horizontal world lacks but sorely needs. For, the world becomes flat again whenever the horizontal view and literal perspective obscures or excludes our spiritual inheritance of a diverse and unending capacity for mythic imagination. Myth connects us to a greater dimension of existence by virtue of vertical imagination, which includes the heights as well as the depths of life. By virtue of the power of imagination, the human soul can reach the heights of awareness and inspiration; by virtue of its capacity to truly feel, the soul can plumb the depths of compassion and understanding.

The inner gradient tries to pull us through all the obstacles and puzzling events of life while keeping us threaded to the hidden center underlying the whole thing. At times we can "get it together," while at other times we simply "fall apart." Typically, we only become conscious of the inner gradient and metaphysical ground of our being when we become altered either by the wonder of life or by the palpable trauma of living on this earth.

Lacking a sense of mythic imagination, a person is left without a clue as to what their inner life is all about. Without realizing that there is a gradient thread that connects each of us to the center, we must become lost in the maze of existence. The further we drift from the inner gradient of the soul, the more things seem to fall apart, the less life seems to make sense.

When we lose the genius thread of our own soul, we must enter the dark again and seek the hidden light. The spark we discover in our own depths is intended to be given back to life as a manifestation of both the individual soul and the Soul of the World. This act of giving back is the test of the return and an act of creation, it is the instinctive and intuitive way we can each help renew the fabric of life and contribute our threads of genius to the healing of the world. Threads of genius and purpose are present in everyone, but may only become visible when we attempt something truly creative. That which is genius in each person remains secretly connected to the origins of existence, as an aspect of creation it can only find fulfillment when it has been given back to life.

THE BRIDGE OF THE ELDER

When the half-boy first left the village, he crossed a threshold and a major turning point in life occurred. There was no one there to witness his departure or to wish him well; he had to set off on his own. The counterpart to that turning point occurs when he returns in a state of disorientation caused by his descent to the depths and the transformation that made him whole. He finds himself stumbling between the waters of renewal and the village he thought he had left behind. At this point he has something important to give, but it is as if he has been born again and cannot find his way on his own. He needs a witness to confirm what he has found in himself and learned of life. He needs someone who can recognize what he has been through and guide him through the threshold of return.

The half-boy has become whole, yet someone else is needed to bring things to completion. Another division appears and another union becomes necessary. The half-boy is in touch with his natural gifts and genius qualities, but that is not enough. He must deliver the gifts of wholeness and genuine presence to the community that remains stuck in the half-village of life. Someone has to help reorient the one who is in a whole and holy state. Right near the end the old story, a key character appears on the stage.

What happens is another meeting at the edge, similar to what occurred when young Telemachus encountered Mentor on the shore of the troubled realm in the Odyssey—a meeting of youth and mentor at a critical moment when the young person felt torn apart personally and broken by the conditions of culture. That was the tale of a prince of the realm; this is the story of anyone, of everyone who suffers the agonies of abandonment and the longing to be whole and have something to contribute to life. This is a meeting of youth and elder on the other side of the river, on the healing side of the struggle to become oneself.

The half-boy made whole winds up back at the place where he began, back at the half-village that could not recognize his inner worth and might fail to do so again. He has the touch of wholeness that they need, yet they may fail to see the transformation he has undergone. Young Telemachus was rebuked after he entered the court under the inspiration of Athena and gave his passionate speech. Yet, he was at the beginning of the adventure and only needed to find his voice and gather his energy for a departure. In this case, the young seeker is on the return journey, needing a welcome and a reception for what he has become and what he has to offer.

While mentoring naturally involves the youth of a community, it also extends to reimagining meaningful roles for elders. Mentoring can be seen as a bridge which invites youth more fully into life; but it is also a proving ground where "olders" practice becoming genuine elders. The return of youth is also the return of the elder.

In this case, the elder was not waiting at the edge of the village by accident. The elder appears as a wise person sitting at the threshold between the ground where people struggle to find themselves and the village where people keep forgetting what it is all about. In traditional terms, an elder has a foot in each world and knows how the two sides can be brought together again. Knowing that things must become clearly split before they can become truly whole, the elders wait for the very troubles most people would avoid. They keep one foot in village life and one foot on the ground of the sacred, where suffering and healing make the way.

An elder is someone who has extracted wisdom from the struggles of their own life. Elders know something of the relationship between trouble and solutions, between a 'little death' and an increase of life. Elders "know the ropes" and, more importantly, learn to protect the fine and subtle threads that connect people to the eternal things of the world. The elder appears as a living bridge between the half-village and the wholeness of life that is always nearby and waiting to be found. The elder knows that while in touch with the eternal, the newly awakened youth can bring a touch of wholeness to life and therefore acts as ritual leader, introducing the opportunity of wholeness into the village.

Elders recognize the halfness of common society and know something of what can make things whole and holy again. The wisdom of the elders comes from knowing the wounds of life well enough to value the moments of wholeness in themselves and in others. The elders know that wholeness is a mysterious gift and that those who experience it need protection as well as guidance. Despite being in touch with the otherworld, an elder maintains contact with the village of daily life. At the cultural level, the elder acts as a bridge between youth and society; at a mythic level, the elder becomes a guide between halfness and wholeness. One foot remains in the issues of the day, while the other remains in contact with the unseen world. As the old proverb puts it: "A village without elders is like a tree without roots."

AT RISK TOGETHER

In modern cultures, both youth and elders are at risk of being invisible and meaningless. Both are diminished by the insistence on material productivity and the reduction of life to short-term goals. Youth and elder have become questionable conditions on either side of the mainstream of adult life. Youth remind us of our deep uncertainties, strange quests, and unanswered questions. Older folks remind us of our human frailty and the inevitable, mysterious approach of death. Both youth and elders disturb the current aims of collective life and threaten the goals of a society focused only on short term aims and measurable achievements.

Elders are supposed to be in touch with what is meaningful, enduring and authentic in life. They may forget someone's name, but should not forget that each has a purpose and a meaning. They may suffer short-term memory loss, but only to recall the things of eternity. Aging involves an opportunity for the concentration of attention on essential things. Failing eyesight dims the outer world and its passing glories, but this is not a complete loss when balanced by an increase of inner vision. An elder uses old eyes to see what those with fresh eyes typically overlook. In losing sight of outward things, the vision of elders tends toward things internal and things eternal. Many things fade, but certain things clarify. An old proverb states that: "What the elders see while sitting others can't see while standing on their toes."

Meanwhile, youth and elders inhabit opposite extremes of the road of life. Youth are at the beginning of the road, while elders can see the end approaching. Being at the extremes, each is beyond the pale and more open to becoming a potential vessel of imagination and creativity. Old and young are opposites that secretly identify with each other because they contain the same secret. Both are secretly attuned to the timeless and can help redeem the time that everyone else can't seem to find. Something ancient in each connects the young and the old, who represent another symbol of the two halves of human life. Within the contradictions there exists a secret identification, a union of opposites that connects to the underlying unity of life. Youth and elders each carry a part of an essential and timeless gift that becomes more visible when the parts are joined.

The underlying dynamic of mentoring involves the archetypal pairing of the eternal youth of the soul and the inner sage, or wise old person. The basic idea is that we each have within us an eternal youth that carries the dream of our lives and an inner sage that has seeds of wisdom waiting to crack open. The youthful side of the archetype contributes the sense of ideal beauty and transcendent truth. If repressed or rejected, the inner spirit of youth remains "juvenile" and becomes increasingly self-serving. This pattern can be seen in those who grow older but fail to become any wiser for it. Instead of opening up and recognizing the wonder of life, they simply become more full of themselves and more self-involved. An old idea suggests that wisdom combines insight with experience and genuine vision with maturity. If maturity expands vision, it leads to wisdom; if not, maturity becomes a time of degeneration.

The elder side of the archetypal pairing would ripen experience into wisdom by means of reflection and facing up to the core issues in one's life. If this inner ripening does not develop, people can turn cynical and become bitter. Where bitterness resides, wisdom cannot dwell. Rather than becoming a genuine elder, those who remain bitter just get older and become more rejecting of life rather than embracing it more fully and enhancing it for others.

The search for the dream of life begins in youth and is the defining condition of youth, but it also keeps a youthful spirit present at any age. The presence of wisdom is the defining condition of the elder, yet the seeds of wisdom are sown in the soul from the beginning and can bear fruit even at a young age. When seen through the lens of the youth-elder complex, it becomes clear how the young can at times be wise old souls; and also how an elder can remain youthful in certain ways. There is an inner sage in youth and an eternal youth in elders. When both elements become connected in a person, the result is enduring creativity and a growing generosity of spirit. The courage needed for living life fully depends on the dreams of youth and the vision of elders. Both are essential for finding and extending the human spirit for life. Each young person is a poet of sorts, trying to sort out the poetics of their inner life and its relation to the great world around it. Each elder is a philosopher of sorts, trying to sort out the meanings and gleanings of a life as well as the necessary implications of the presence of death.

Meanwhile, the only ones more idealistic than youth are the elders. The difference is that elders know that the ideals may not be realized or may only be attained for a fleeting moment. In fact, that is what makes ideals so ideal. The elders seek to awaken the genuine ideals of humanity in order that the deepest meanings of life and the beauty of the world do not become completely lost or forgotten. An ideal has the right idea in it; it is exemplary of something necessary to life, like love or beauty, like courage in support of the truth, or compassion that protects nature or those who are most vulnerable. Ideals are hard to reach and harder to hold onto. Thus, an ideal is a light to follow, an idea that can open up a path of seeking and learning and growing. Our ideals lead us to experiences of both hope and despair, yet can also lead beyond those extremes to places of deeper acceptance and greater understanding.

No amount of social security will convert the olders into elders, in the same way that no amount of information can change common knowledge into wisdom. Some risk has to be taken for life growth to continue and transformation to occur. Meanwhile, all youth are at greater risk when their elders try not to be at risk at all. Youth experience a vague sense that life must be meaningless as they observe people living longer and longer, but not becoming any wiser for it. Until the olders risk living more of their own lives, youth will continue to be severely at risk. Youth need to see others taking meaningful risks and surviving those risks. Then the issue is not simply risking one's life as much as risking being fully alive in the midst of the life one has been given.

DANCE OF THE GREAT LONGING

Seen in reverse, the struggle of the half-boy to find wholeness was necessary for the village to be renewed. The revelation of the innate genius and core vision and delivery of it to the community is the essence of the rite of passage. The return of the youth becomes the occasion for the community to commune again; the generation gap is bridged as youth and elder, young and old, dance together. The dance is a celebration of life that includes a second birth into the village. The elder acts the role of midwife as the second birth redeems all the trouble that began at the birth of the half-boy and at the same time symbolically redeems all the torn and divided conditions of the world. The two halves of the youth come together, the two halves of adult life join together, and the wholeness of the village soon follows. On another level, as the two halves become joined the sacred sense of life returns to the otherwise mundane village.

The half-boy had to surrender to the inner spirit of life in the baptism that occurred in the depths of the river. Upon his return he must surrender again to the dance that brings the spirit of renewal back to the village. Dancing is a symbol for being fully present in life, being part of the vital flow, being a channel of and expression for the immediate and universal rhythms of existence. The stars of the Milky Way dance along their spiral course through the long cosmic night while atoms secretly dance inside the cells of our bodies, even as we sleep. Our dancing imitates the swirling of the heavens, animates the imagination, and reconnects humans to the animal realm.

A feeling of wholeness makes people dance and people dance in order to feel whole. It works both ways; for genuine dance is a complete act of imagination that connects the pulse of the dancer with the rhythms of eternity. A true dancer surrenders to the dance, loses their "little self," dances it away; disappearing into the dance, becoming the dance. For, who can separate the dancer from the dance? Dance pulls the dancer through time and out of time to find again the touch of the eternal. Half-heartedness ruins a dance; so does too much self-interest. A genuine dance uses all our halves in order to integrate them, and invites the hidden unity in everyone to be present.

The omissions and abuses of the half-village are temporarily redeemed in a moment that becomes momentous. Another kairos moment arrives as time stands still, as the old become young again and the young feel the blessings of life. In such a moment, everything can be forgiven. A touch of redemption releases everyone from the limits of life and from the wounds of time. At that moment, the middle of the village becomes the center of the cosmos. For a while, everyone dances at the center of the world. All are joined by a secret thread, touching a hidden strata and subtle ground that no one can control or fully describe, yet through which the inexhaustible energies of the cosmos pour into human life and revive human community.

It is the village within the village, the unity within all the oppositions, the natural village that connects human nature to all of nature. The second village is the original village in which everyone can find a place and each can express the originality of their soul. The second village is what people mean when they refer to community, the community of souls and of the spirit. Communitas was the old Latin word for a deep sense of soulful presence that draws everyone together, despite the usual differences, and generates genuine moments of community.

There is a recurring need to be young again; not to be juvenile, but to be revitalized and restored to life and feel part of the continuous renewal and ongoing creation of the whole world. The ancient Bushmen of Africa said that was the true essence of the dance; especially the dance of the great hunger and the great longing. There were other dances, some enacted before and after hunting, or before planting and during the harvesting of crops. Those were considered the dances of the little hunger because they expressed more of a need than a deep longing. The dances of the little hunger conveyed the basic desire for food and nourishment in the ongoing struggle for physical survival and the need for storing something for the hard times. Even the dances to express gratitude for the gift of life or for the birth of a child did not reach to the ground of the great hunger and longing that reconnected people to the movements of the stars.

The dance of the great longing was different; it opened another level of the human soul that had little to do with physical survival, yet it was there, part and parcel of the human heart from the very beginning. It had little to do with receiving the fruits of the earth or the rewards of a success. It had everything to do with gathering the subtle energies within us and all the feelings of desire. It initiated again the deepest longings that moved all of life—the hunters and the planters, the tough-minded and the tender-hearted, the animals too, as well as the living, breathing forest. The dance of great longing aimed all the way to the stars that, after all, must have their longings; why else would they keep turning in their orbits and spiraling through the cosmic ocean of night?

The dance of the great longing aimed at the parts of a person and the elements of life that could not be fully satisfied. For, in their great imagination, ancient people intuited a longing that penetrated all of life; that burned within the star in man, but also fueled the stars in the heavens as well. This second level of hunger and desire was connected to the stars and thereby to the origins of life and the deep sense of longing that turns the whole, endless dance and drama of existence.

A LITTLE REDEMPTION

Modern life has fallen so heavily under the spell of reason and the rule of literalism that it misses the living center, continually losing the threads that secretly tie us to the stars of our origins and the redeeming heart of the world. Lacking any idea of the secret unity of the world and a felt sense for the source of great imagination leaves people unable to imagine ways out of the increasing problems of life. Literalism is a kind of madness that reduces a person's imagination and limits their vision to things that appear to be solid fact. Yet, even while danger and destruction grow, the balancing symbols develop within us. Where the danger grows, there also the saving grace and power of renewal must grow. If accepted, the new imagination connects with vital instincts, placing both vision and energy at the disposal of conscious awareness in service of the human community.

The point includes redeeming human genius as an innovative agent for restoring the world to balance and to beauty. Meanwhile, redemption itself must be redeemed from simply being something that happens when life is over and you go to the world beyond. Little acts of redemption happen when we live our lives more genuinely. When we live the life we came to live, we can redeem ourselves from wasting our lives and, in doing so, can help redeem the world—without having to be heroic or messianic. We do it by finding our footing on a genius path and learning to give the gifts we came to life to give. In that way, we join the great dance and contribute some wholeness to a world that increasingly seems to be torn with conflicts and hatred and appears to be unraveling at the seams.

When great troubles abound, whether on the world stage or at a critical stage of a person's life, what we need is a touch of the mythic, a hint of the eternal, and a feel for the thread that secretly holds us together. This can be a helpful image to hold when listening to troubling news reports of the litany of threatening issues plaguing both the world of nature and the realm of culture. It can also be a useful story to tell to young people who have their whole lives before them as they enter a world that seems to be unwelcoming and unredeemable.

At a time when human society faces impossible tasks in every area of culture as well as in most aspects of nature, we may be able to redeem genius as an inherent aspect of soulfulness that connects us to both nature and purpose. As the world seems increasingly threatened by extremism, terrorism, and fanaticism, as nature suffers the storms of climate change as well as the ravages of exploitation, there is a desperate need for the inventiveness, creativity, and resiliency that are the natural and essential elements of human genius.

The thread that ties us to the center is the hidden cord of the heart, it is the thread of genius that can connect the mind with the heart, that allows the mind to feel and reveals the thought set within the heart. It is both subtle and determined; it can be elusive, yet it is also fixed within us. Our inborn genius is our innate and indelible connection to the otherworld of great imagination, original thought, and endless renewal. The otherworld is a completely different place, yet it is always near at hand. It points to a transcendent aspect of life that makes human transformation possible. Part of the open secret of the secret center is that each person can discover it for themselves because it is also hidden inside them.

As the endless story of the world enters another cosmological turning point and the fabric of life loosens, the veil between this world and the otherworld thins and becomes more transparent. As some things seem to become impossible, other things become more possible at the same time. As time seems about to run out on everyone, the sense of the eternal tries to slip back into our awareness. For, the wonder of creation is not about what happened a long time ago. The true wonder of creation is that it continues to create and that each of us has been invited to participate. And, the way to participate most fully and most creatively in life on earth is to find the unique thread of our genius and begin weaving it into life despite and because of all the troubles in the world.

INDEX

Abandoned, 30, 33–36
  children, 27
Achilles' heel, 63
Acorn Theory, 89–90
Aging, 233
  Fountain of Youth, 221–222
  eagle, 109
Alchemy
  of the depths, 224–225
Altar, 148–149, 153–157
Angel
  as messenger, 72, 74
  Gabriel, 74
  genius as, 6, 47, 178
  guardian, 7, 72–73, 182
  Lailah, 76–81
  meaning of, 72
  of conception, 70, 75–76, 78
Angel of the Lip, 77–80
Ariadne, 17–19, 113
Athena
  goddess of wisdom, 116, 127, 127–128,
    130, 137, 138
At-risk
  rich kids, 141
  young people, 24–25, 33, 139, 215
Atropos, one of the Three Fates, 18
Authentic, 45–49, 105, 114, 120, 135,
    191
Author
  and authenticity, 114
Authority, 46, 52, 55, 114–116, 119,
    150–152
  inner, 135–136, 152
Baptism, 218–220, 224
Big Bang, 161
Blank slate, 86–87, 91–94
Blueprint
  of the soul, 94
Calling, 4–5, 46, 86, 93, 95–96, 111,
    180–181
  and genius, 93–96, 180–181

and true education, 111
Candle, 75, 80
  on birthday cake, 80
Candles, 80
Charisma
  meaning of, 166
Chicken
  and eaglet story, 97–98, 107–108, 110
  pecking order, 102
Child prodigies, 180
Clew, 17–20
Clotho, one of the Three Fates, 18
Clue, 15, 17–20
  to inner nature, 89
Concealed mission, 91, 93
Daimon
  and happiness, 179
  meaning of, 179
Death, 29–33, 35, 118, 140, 159, 218
  birth, death, and rebirth, 114, 213
  denial of, 115, 123
  in initiation, 114
  little death, leads to rebirth, 123, 218
  need for conversations about, 121–122
  of world, 41
  red fog, 208
  spiritual, 179
  youth suicide, 115–122, 213
Desert, 141, 145, 152–156
  camp, 141, 145, 147, 149, 152
Destiny, 19, 43, 86, 92, 94, 96–97, 97,
    163–166, 198
  and genius, 4, 11, 198
  and stars, 163, 166
Dharma, 5, 48
Dire straits
  strait is the way, 50, 67
Dream, 215
  a culture needs to bless, 196
Dream of life, 97, 187, 224
Dreams, 4, 13, 132, 143–144
  and imagination, 101

ABOUT MOSAIC

Mosaic Multicultural Foundation is a 501(c)3 nonprofit organization that has initiated innovative projects and unifying events that support and educate at-risk youth, refugees, combat veterans, and communities in need. Mosaic creates community through events involving artists, activists, community builders, healers, and spiritual teachers working in inspired ways to develop cross-cultural alliances, mentoring relationships, and forms of community healing.

Mosaic seeks to inspire awareness through community activities and creative ceremonies that reconnect people to meaningful traditions and the sacred ecology of place, while offering opportunities for personal growth, spiritual awakening, and leadership development. Mosaic publishes and produces the work of renowned storyteller and mythologist Michael Meade through an extensive collection of books, audio, essays and podcasts, as well as producing a full calendar of national and international community events.

Mosaic's projects include mentoring youth and awakening the wisdom of elders, finding common ground between those in opposition, shaping community events that unite people of various cultural and spiritual backgrounds, and encouraging greater understanding between people with diverse and divergent backgrounds and experiences. We address contemporary issues by combining traditional ideas and practices with fresh insights to reveal where new cultural forms can be conceived and developed.

GreenFire Press and **Mosaic Audio** are imprints of Mosaic Multicultural Foundation that serve to foster cultural literacy, mythic education, and multicultural community development. Proceeds from sales of books and recordings directly benefit Mosaic's work.

For more information or to order additional titles contact Mosaic:
P.O. Box 847, Vashon, WA 98070
(206) 935-3665
www.mosaicvoices.org ~ info@mosaicvoices.org

Books by Michael Meade

Awakening the Soul: A Deep Response to a Troubled World

The Genius Myth

Fate and Destiny: The Two Agreements of Life

The World Behind the World: Living at the Ends of Time

The Water of Life: Initiation and the Tempering of the Soul

Why the World Doesn't End

Mosaic Audio Recordings by Michael Meade

A Song is a Road

Alchemy of Fire: Libido and the Divine Spark

Branches of Mentoring

The Ends of Time, the Roots of Eternity

Entering Mythic Territory: Healing and the Bestowing Self

The Eye of the Pupil, the Heart of the Disciple

Fate and Destiny: The Two Agreements in Life

Finding Genius in Your Life

The Great Dance: Finding One's Way in Troubled Times

Holding the Thread of Life: A Human Response to the Unraveling of the World

Inner Wisdom: The Eternal Youth and the Wise Old Sage

The Light Inside Dark Times

Initiation and the Soul: The Sacred and the Profane

Poetics of Peace: Peace and the Salt of the Earth

Poetics of Peace: Vital Voices in Troubled Times, with Alice Walker, Luis Rodriguez, Jack Kornfield, Orland Bishop

The Soul of Change

Podcasts by Michael Meade

Living Myth, a free weekly podcast

Living Myth Premium, a membership-based podcast

Books edited by Michael Meade

Crossroads: The Quest For Contemporary Rites of Passage,
    edited by Louise Carus Mahdi, Nancy Geyer Christopher, and Michael Meade

The Rag and Bone Shop of the Heart: A Poetry Anthology,
    edited by Robert Bly, James Hillman, and Michael Meade

All books, audio and podcasts are available at mosaicvoices.org

GreenFire Press
An Imprint of Mosaic Multicultural Foundation

*All purchases support Mosaic's Genius-Based Mentoring,
Community Healing Events and Living Myth Project.*

P.O. Box 847, Vashon, WA 98070
(206) 935-3665
www.mosaicvoices.org ~ info@mosaicvoices.org